EVERYDAY THINGS IN AMERICAN LIFE

1776-1876

By

William Chauncy Langdon

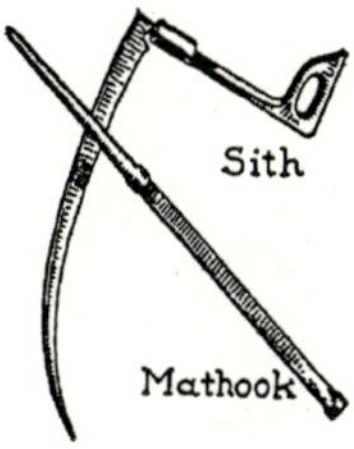

NEW YORK
CHARLES SCRIBNER'S SONS

(See reverse for description)

I–12.60[V]
Printed in the United States of America

Preface

EVERYDAY things took on greater interest and greater importance as American life passed on from the first period, 1607–1776, to the second period, 1776–1876. The first, the Colonial period, was essentially a period of settlement. Life centered in very large measure in the home and in the ordinary things daily used in the equipment and maintenance of the home—the houses, whether architecturally simple or elaborate, furniture, cooking utensils, pewter and silver, glass, farming implements.

This second volume is concerned with American life in the hundred years between the Declaration of Independence in 1776 and its national celebration at Philadelphia in 1876. During this period American life centered more and more in transportation under the enabling power of steam. The everyday things of this period were boats of various kinds, from flat-bottomed rowboats to steamships for water travel, the conveyances of roads and of railroads for land travel, and the appliances rendered possible by steam for use in mining, agriculture, invention, manufacture, and communication. Further, the Constitution, embodying the instinctive spirit of cooperation and unity, exerted from beginning to end an almost magical effect. The community element steadily grew in the national emphasis. The everyday things were not merely things in daily use, but also things that were in general use. The nation was growing across the continent and was striking its roots deep from the Atlantic to the Pacific.

My grateful appreciation goes to the many friends who have given me valuable assistance in the writing of this book. Especially I should like to mention Charles Penrose and other fellow members of the Newcomen Society both in England and America; Henry Butler Allen and members of the staff of the Franklin Institute, Philadelphia; the New York Public Library; the New York State Library, Albany, through its interlibrary system; and the Bronxville (New York) Public Library. Grateful credit also goes to S. Elizabeth DeVoy, Art Editor of Scribners, who has had the chief responsibility for the illustrations in this volume.

W. C. L.

Contents

CONTENTS

CONTENTS

Illustrations

DRAWINGS IN THE TEXT

ILLUSTRATIONS

ILLUSTRATIONS

ILLUSTRATIONS

ILLUSTRATIONS

PHOTOGRAPHS

ILLUSTRATIONS

ILLUSTRATIONS

EVERYDAY THINGS IN AMERICAN LIFE 1776-1876

CHAPTER I

The Eastern River Craft

IN THE many river-mouths and the estuaries and bays that the sea had dug out along the Atlantic coast, all of them natural harbors, finished or in process of making, there was for the people living within smell of salt air and sight of salt water one simple means of communication, the small boat. For twenty-five years after the outbreak of the Revolution these conditions remained measurably the same as for the twenty-five years before. It will be remembered that in April, 1789, fourteen years after that date, when George Washington came from Mount Vernon to New York to be inaugurated as the first President of the United States, he was rowed in a barge from Elizabethtown Point to the Battery. And indeed the many large steam ferryboats that still give regular service to Long Island, Staten Island, and New Jersey—have they not a right to claim membership by direct descent, despite appearances, in the ancient and very honorable small-boat class!

The small boats found operating on these inland waters, whether in the colonial days as far back as 1750 or farther, and as far into the new period as 1800 and farther, were all alike in one thing. They had all of them one peculiarity in common. They were different from one another, suited to the particular local conditions of that river, estuary, or bay, and to the needs of its commerce. The seagoing ships, crossing the Atlantic or sailing regardless of shore line through the open sea north or south to Canada or to the West Indies, were of another genus, one which did not take the trouble to recognize these local affairs as vessels at all. Nonetheless they rendered a service that was essential to the welfare and prosperity of the larger, more imposing craft. It is ill-advised to underestimate these small boats. Though simple in construction, they were adequate to their tasks and accurately adapted to the conditions in which their work had to be done. Environment is fortunately, second to personal character, the dominant factor in life. So difficulties create new means of achievement with an exquisite accuracy. As various as the water conditions of each of those bays, rivers, or estuaries were the small boats used on them. Little enough is known of them specifically. In those days a boat was not without honor except in its own waters. Further, with some reason, it was generally supposed there was little to know about these small boats. But so vital an element in this river commerce was the carrier that the importance of the carrier itself can hardly be exaggerated.

Flat-bottomed boats prevailed on all the rivers from Maine to Georgia, and later beyond the mountains, and also around the peninsula of Florida on all the rivers flowing directly or ultimately into the Gulf of Mexico. But there was considerable, almost infinite, variety among them. Most of the boatmen built their own small boats. Every boatman was theoretically and practically free to build his boat to suit himself, subject only to the will and caprice of his river, and the nature of the cargo he was to bring downstream to port. But, these requirements fulfilled, what was left for the play of the boatman's own caprice!

Maine was before 1820 a district of the Commonwealth of Massachusetts. Early conditions prevailed until then, and long after. Up the swift rivers the woodsmen cut the tall pine. The forest conditions of Maine grew stems over 100 feet in height and 35 inches in diameter at the base, with clean straight trunks up to the high crown—perfect for the masts of ships, while the shorter trunks were excellent for the frames of houses. Wood had long been getting scarce in England, so the pine of Maine had real export value. Its quality promised good prices and years of sale in both the foreign and the American markets.

Up the trunk climbed a single woodman with his axe and topped the tree—cut off the crown. It was work for cool nerves and iron muscles. As the crown snapped off and fell to the ground, the woodman clung to the inverted pendulum of his trunk until it stopped, and then came down. Then another man, the rigger, went up and adjusted the rigging, so that when the tree was cut down, at the base, it should not crash to its damage. Then two men went to work with a bandsaw, much like the cross-cut saw with which many of us are familiar, and so cut that when the tree fell it should lie in the direction most advantageous for sliding into the river. Down the river the logs were floated, with all the danger of log jams, until the river was of such a size that it was possible to gather the logs into rafts for sending them down the lower courses and through the harbors and bays to the seaports. Thus were combined cargo and carrier into one convertible product. The raft was distinctly a flat-bottomed piece of marine architecture. After its short life as a "boat" it was broken up again, and again became simply logs in the lumber market.

Massachusetts was not an agricultural region. Her rocky shores and stony fields, even when persistently cleared and the stones economically lined up as stone walls, had never spoiled the inhabitants with overlarge crops. Those who preferred more of a farm life moved to Connecticut, to Long Island, to New Jersey, the Mohawk Valley and the West. The colonial name pointed out where its great crop was to be found, in Massachusetts Bay. For Massachusetts there was fish. Out onto the water the men went and came back with great hauls of cod and mackerel. At first, for the offshore fishing, shallops were used, open boats with ample space for the catch and propelled by several pairs of oars, or by mast and sail, or by both. But they were within comparatively short sailing distance of the Newfoundland Banks and that opportunity had long been used by habit and as of right. When the fishermen went out into deep water the larger sloop was used. Arrived near the Banks, the men put off in dories, an open-ocean variety of river boat—flat-bottomed rowboats, pointed bow and stern, and with steep sides, well adapted to riding the high seas. From these they cast their lines and in these they brought their fish home to the mother sloop, guided through the fog by the thutter of the horn blown for the purpose by their comrades. To these Massachusetts fishermen the Gulf Stream was the largest of their rivers, and the dory was "their boat."

The similar nature of the Maine and New Hampshire rivers developed a special kind of boat for the river commerce of that region. The Merrimac in Massachusetts also belonged to that region by nature though not by right of statehood. This boat was the gundalow, variously spelled: gunlow, gondela, gundalow, gundaloa, and gundeloe, but generaly pronounced in two syllables, gunlow. The name originally came from the old Italian gondola, but through a forgotten history that entirely shook it free from any Venetian reminiscence. In the Revolutionary War there were correctly spelled and correctly pronounced gondolas in the river forces of the Colonists. But they were not correctly built on the old Italian model. Rather they were very independently built into quite a different kind of craft, as was entirely appropriate.

The gundalows were sailing scows. They were sloops rigged with a bowsprit. Most of them, except in the earlier days, had a centerboard, or a leeboard; some had two leeboards. Many of the larger gundalows had a house forward or aft and were steered with a tiller or with a wheel turning the rudder by means of wheel-ropes. In some the mast was in a tabernacle, so it could be dropped to pass under bridges. The gundalows were indeed a development, a progressing type of river boat. The name has often been applied to a kind of service on the rivers rather than to a definite type of boat form, and at different periods would progressively vary in structure and somewhat in appearance. That service went back to the chief cargo of lumber, and continued, as industries multiplied, to the carrying of all the commodities of river commerce.

Beaver skins were during the colonial days the most valuable yield of the Hudson-Mohawk River system, and they continued after the assumption of Statehood to be one of the most valuable. Furs were important to New York for international export, not for domestic sale. A beaver hat, for example, was *de rigeur* in London rather than in New York and Albany. So the New York fur trade itself suffered when English fur companies sought to divert the Indian traffic to Montreal, and still more when silk and silk plush took the place of beaver in the making of hats for London men of fashion. Wild animals have a keen sense for danger and retire before it. So they did from the forests of central New York. But that region was fine farming land and soon wheat and flour were increasingly added to the lumber and furs of the river commerce coming down to New York. Beaver and barrels of flour have honored place on the shield of New York City, and New York is still one of the great fur markets of the world.

As the strength of a chain is that of its weakest link, so

the depth of a river is that of its shallowest reach—or certainly it was in the days of which we are speaking, the first twenty-five or thirty years of the Republic. The Hudson-Mohawk had many shallows. As the Hudson was really an estuary, and practically a narrow sound rather than a river, all of these shallows were above Albany, in the Mohawk. So flat-bottomed boats, keelboats, and even a large sort of

For New-York,

The Sloop ROVER,
Abm. Bird, master,
A regular trader, and a good substantial vessel. She will be dispatched with all possible expedition. For freight or passage apply on board, at Smith's wharf, or to ISAIAH MANKIN,
Who offers for sale at very reduced prices, to close sales,
320 quintals Codfish, in good order, and
2000 Sugar Moulds.
may 24 d

From the "Enquirer," Richmond, Virginia, February 16, 1810
Coastwise shipping notices

canoe, until about 1825, brought the beaver skins and the other up-state produce down to Albany for transshipment to New York and the final markets.

The keelboat of the Mohawk was a large flat-bottomed boat, built of stout plank, that had a heavy timber, about 4 by 4 inches in size running down the middle of the whole length of the bottom. This took the shock in case the boat ran upon a rock or other obstruction in the stream. In length the keelboat might be anywhere from 40 to 75 feet, and was from 7 to 9 feet wide. It usually had a mast, so it could raise a sail when the wind was favorable. When it was not, the watermen relied on great oars called sweeps on either side, and on poles. Along the sides there were running boards for the men to walk on when poling the boat against the current. Such a keelboat cost about $2.50 or $3.00 a foot of its length. Varied somewhat in form and in size to meet the special conditions of river and of cargo, the keelboat was practically the same on all the navigable rivers in the country, not only in the East, but later, when migration got over the divide into the Ohio-Mississippi Basin, also in the West. The different varieties of keelboats were often called after the river for which each was built and on which it was used, as, for instance, Mohawk boats, and Susquehanna boats. The Durham boat was the large sort of canoe that has been spoken of. It was in shape very much like an Indian bark canoe, and was about 60 feet long. It was named after Robert Durham, who first built them for use on the Delaware River.

The navigable rivers of Virginia and Maryland were tributary to the Chesapeake Bay. In the early days water communication naturally organized itself in double units on either side of a watercourse rather than according to political states. The larger rivers, such as the Potomac, the York, and the James, bred plantations along their shores rather than towns and village settlements. They raised an almost universal product in tobacco This crop was mostly packed in casks and hogsheads and rolled down to the wharves of the larger plantations, where the ships docked to receive it in export. The Virginia rivers were estuaries, like the Hudson, on a smaller scale. It might well seem there would be no distinctive river shipping, for flat-bottomed boats or for any other kind. But there was in the inland waters of Virginia and Maryland a good river commerce and also the social custom of plantation life. These together kept the shores of Chesapeake Bay happily peopled with small craft. Every planter had his light-draught sailboat, with which he and his family conducted their social life, visiting their relatives, friends and neighbors. They also conducted therewith a considerable river commerce. These small boats had a long and interesting history behind their building.

The canoe—or to give the boat its full official title, the Chesapeake Bay log canoe—came down in direct line, builder and boatman to builder and boatman, from the Indians. At first blush it might be thought it must have been at best a crude sort of craft. This was by no means true. An instinctive skill was necessary to its well making. An improved finish was attained with the passing generations, but this was in part due to better tools, as iron replaced stone implements and clamshells. In historical and numerical order the canoe was made of from one to five logs. Thomas Hariot in his *Briefe and True Report of the Newfound Land of Virginia,* 1588, gives a concise account of the way the Indians made their canoes when the Englishmen first arrived:

These [the canoes] they make of one tree, by burning and

scratching away the coles with stones and shells till they have made it in forme of a Trough.

Somewhat later Captain John Smith saw some Indians at work on a canoe and his account of what he saw is similar to Hariot's.

They used large trees for their canoes. Captain John Smith said that some were "fortie or fiftie foot in length and some will bear 40 men, but the most ordinary are smaller." George Percy wrote of seeing a specific canoe that was "five and fortie feet long by the Rule." The beam naturally depended on the diameter of the tree, usually about one-eighth to one-seventh of the length. Captain Smith said that "some are an elne [about 3 feet 9 inches] deepe." This gives an idea of the diameter of the trees they used. Such was the ancient heritage of the Chesapeake Bay log canoe!

A boat 40 feet long and 5 feet wide could transport a goodly cargo. When the white men adopted the native kind of navigation, so well adapted to their river commerce in waters which were in considerable part rather shallow, they had a kind of light shipping which was just what they wanted and needed. For their tobacco crops they lashed two canoes together side by side and rolled eight or nine hogsheads of tobacco on their gunwales. Simply and appropriately these were called "tobacco canoes."

When the Englishmen and their American successors took to using three logs and even five logs to a canoe, the business of boat building became forthwith a branch of the art of wood carving. From the first selecting of the trees, the fit of the logs into the curves of the boat was planned and carried out. This is made clear in a little book, *Chesapeake Bay Log Canoes,* by M. V. Brewington of The Mariners' Museum at Newport News, Virginia. For those who have caught this fever there is little hope of recovery in this book. There will be no desire for recovery on the part of the fever-stricken.

A few log canoes are still built. They are prime racing boats, carrying a high and large sail area. One advantage they have over the framed boats is that if after a race the racing owner thinks he can improve the lines of his boat and have a better chance in the next race, he can take out his jackknife or other sharp tool and whittle away a shade off his keel log, or off the garboard logs, or off the wing logs, and benefit by his courage and practical wisdom, if such it proves to have been. According to the common trend of language in provincial regions, as the period advanced, the canoe came to be called a conner, so spelled and so pronounced. Indeed these hand-carved boats are frequently so known in tidal Virginia and on the Eastern Shore of Maryland to the present day.

South Carolina has had three great staple crops. Indigo lent color to the early days; the Revolution put an end to its importance. Then rice spread over a much greater area, covering with profit much of the swamp lands along the coast. Finally cotton swept those crops out of its way and appropriated all the southern country for itself.

The river conditions of South Carolina differed from Virginia as they affected the marketing of the inland produce. The coast of South Carolina was in recent geological history raised from below sea level as a broad sandflat. On this the rivers have been depositing fertile silt. But these stretches of fine land are frequently subject to inundation, either by freshets from the rivers or by high tides from the sea. Comparatively easy drainage and irrigation adapted this coastal land to the cultivation of rice to an exceptional degree. Rice required rich soil, steady warm temperature, and abundance of fresh water. The work could be done well by Negro labor. Rice plantations grew up along all the lower courses of the rivers wherever the marketing of the rice was practicable.

The same geological dictation, however, limited the points of marketing to those harbors where dry land suitable for a seaport and all its business occurred on the edge of deep water. This necessity made Charleston and Savannah the two chief seaports and business centers of that part of the coast. The commercial disadvantage of the other rivers is instanced by the Santee River, which lacked harbor facilities at its mouth and even emptied into the sea through a swampy delta with a shallow bar across its mouth. For all the purposes of the rice plantations flat-bottomed boats were adequate, with adaptations, but the Santee boats were obliged to meet both the conditions of shallow water in the rivers and the more serious conditions of the ocean in much of the fifty-mile voyage to Charleston. Wide as are the general differences of the work and trading of the rice fields of South Carolina from those of the other rivers to the north, the flat-bottomed boat still prevailed. One of these differences was that the rice crop was carried upstream by the flatboats instead of down. Mrs. Elizabeth Watris Pringle, in an account of her personal experiences in managing a rice plantation, has given a vivid picture of the flatboats used in the harvesting.

> This is the gayest week of the year. Thursday the field was cut down by the hands with small reap hooks, the long golden heads being carefully laid on the tall stubble to dry until the next day, when it was tied into sheaves, which the negroes do very skillfully with a wisp of the rice itself. Saturday it was stacked in small cocks to dry through Sunday, and today it is being loaded into flats, having had every advantage of weather.
>
> If only no rain or wind comes until it is unloaded at Cherokee, fifteen miles up the river! I have sent for a tug to tow the two flats up on the flood-tide this evening—just now it is dead low water, and the flats are aground, which always scares me; for if by chance they get on a log or any inequality, they get badly strained and often leak and ruin the rice. Flats are one of the heavy expenses of a rice plantation—large flat-bottomed boats from twenty to eighty feet long and from ten to twelve feet wide, propelled in the most primitive way by poles and steered by one huge oar at the stern. They can be loaded up very high if the rice is properly stowed.

Rice is still a hand-tended industry, as it was one hundred and fifty years ago. Mrs. Pringle's account is a true picture of the work in the rice fields as it always has been, despite the fact that she lived recently enough to have a tug come and tow the flats up the river instead of having her Negroes slowly pole them up. South Carolina has kept her profitable hold on rice, and its culture still remains practically the same, despite the coming and going of cotton as a predominant crop, despite the passing of slavery, and despite depressions and other changes in the rice market.

The haughty attitude of the river mouths toward the boats bearing the wealth of the plantations, whatever that wealth consisted of, whether rice or cotton, made it certain that the boats had to be closely adaptable to local conditions and even to the specific work required under the particular circumstances. The most common name for the flat-bottomed boats of this region was pettiauger. But the qualifications for this peculiar name were not definite. They were propelled by sails or by oars or by poles, as the exigencies of wind, tide, weather, and the unexpected might require. Some were dug out, which suggests kinship to the early Indian canoe; some were frame-built. Some were round-bottomed, comparatively; some were keeled. The common denominator for the pettiaugers seems to have been a general reliability in boats of the name to meet any fresh-water or salt-water emergency that river, swamp or sea might put up to them.

Individual requirements also showed in another matter. There was on every plantation tributary to these South Carolina rivers, across whose mouths sand bars were apt to cause the deposit of sand and silt in the rivers themselves, one able Negro who was master of the boats. He must know in detail all the changing channels of the river, the shoals, the snags and other obstructions that might cause damage or delay to the cargoes. He must also be a real master of the other Negroes. In South Carolina he was called the patroon. To the New Yorker this title suggests aristocratic associa-

From "The Great South," by Edward King, 1875

A cotton-steamer at the height of its prestige

tions with a Dutch ancestry. This Southern master of the boats held a very responsible position. On him the planter relied for the safety of his crop; on him as on a sea-captain his fellow Negroes often had to depend for the safety of their lives. He had authority in trust, and he exercised it for the benefit of his master and of all. And he no doubt did it handsomely. A Negro patroon in action was, without question, an imposing sight!

Before 1812 three quarters of the cotton raised in the United States was raised in South Carolina and Georgia. Cotton was made possible as a great crop by Eli Whitney and his cotton gin in 1793. Charleston and Savannah, as with rice, were the chief cotton ports, and cotton speedily became very profitable. Flatboats steered by singing darkies floated the bales of cotton down the Ashley-Cooper, the Savannah, and other rivers to the seaports. The flatboats on which the cotton bales were brought down the rivers were of a special variety to adapt them the better to their purpose. As cotton was not heavy, these light-draught boats, by having high sides, could carry large cargoes and keep the cotton perfectly dry without capsizing. They were commonly called cotton boxes. On arrival at the port they were broken up and sold for lumber. Up-river freight went on poleboats. These had keels to help keep them straight in the current, and their bows and sterns were pointed or at least rounded to reduce the resistance to the water. They made about ten miles a day.

There was another kind of boat, flat-bottomed of course, which is of curious interest, though it did not come into much use. It was called a teamboat. Between 1818 and 1827 one was used as a ferry across the Ashley River at Charleston. On a platform over the main deck, a number of horses hitched to a beam were driven in a circle. Through gearings the power was transmitted from the pivot of the beam to paddle wheels. There is record of such a boat, propelled by 8 mules with a crew of 5 men, carrying 350 bales of cotton

250 miles in 15 days at a cost of $116.25. Every kind of power was tried probably, at least once, but the day had not yet come for the old ways to yield to a new power. So cotton was still floated with the current down the rivers by Negroes singing and steering the boat clear of snags and sandbanks to its market.

So Negroes steered cotton-laden flatboats down the Coosa-Alabama River, and down the Tombigbee, the Chattahoochee, and the Pearl rivers. But cotton exhausted its soil. Even as the demand for cotton was increasing, the cotton fields were spreading over into Alabama and Mississippi. The new fields were exceeding the old fields in yield. It seemed not unlikely that the cotton sovereignty would pass from Charleston and Savannah to the Gulf ports of Mobile and New Orleans. If so, would the Atlantic ports be able to send back to the up country the return that was necessary to keep the supremacy of Charleston and Savannah in the cotton market? It was a serious, a critical commercial question.

Such were the means by which the river commerce was carried on in some of the regions through which America was extending westward. They carried also an important message, the assurance that upstream and to the west opportunity was to be found, more important than all their cargoes, of whatever kind and value. Rafts, gundalows, dories, keelboats, log canoes, cotton boxes—all of them flatboats of one kind or another, they were everyday affairs, in their common appearance, and in their common use. As gradually they disappear, unnoted and unsung, almost undistinguished, may they keep the grateful tribute of history, the fact that later civilization has been built upon their work!

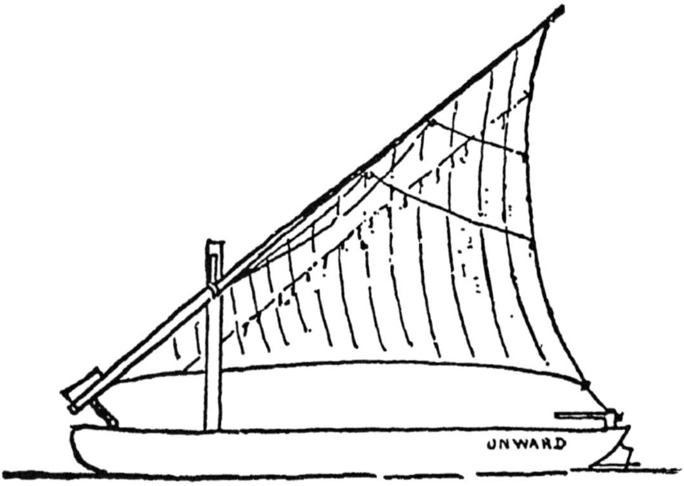

From "History of New Hampshire," by John N. McClintock, 1889

Piscataqua gundalow

CHAPTER II

Early Roads and Turnpikes

UP ALONG the various inland waters, most of which were getting to be called rivers, settlements multiplied and became depots for the local commerce. Every settlement had its waterfront, from which and to which its travel proceeded, and which in colonial days at least dominated its life. On the land side every settlement faced the back country with roads or streets, all of which went "out of town," whether or not they soon petered out into mere horsepaths through the woods leading to the next settlement or leading nowhere.

As the settlements went farther and farther up the rivers, it became more and more a disadvantage when people on one river wanted to communicate or do business with people on another river. By the previously convenient water route they had to go around three sides of the intervening land. It was so much shorter to go across by land, though it was very much more difficult, sometimes forbiddingly so. But the urge to undergo the difficulties steadily, persistently increased. The result was horse trails through the forests, and then land roads from one settlement to another, and sometimes thence to a third settlement, and so, following that strange growing instinct to go farther and farther on through the forests and over the mountains (so much stronger than it had ever been in colonial times) to "through land roads." These through land routes were naturally located by the established settlements, villages or towns, whatever dignity of designation they could claim. And thus it was that the through land roads usually followed the water routes of the rivers. Water travel upstream, especially in the rivers with strong currents, was too slow and too uncertain of conditions, owing to floods and droughts, for the purposes of through travel. Resort to land travel was inevitable, despite all its difficulties and "impossibilities."

There were land roads in the East before the establishment of the new nation but they were local affairs.[1] The first roads were mere horsepaths, and not necessarily good ones at that. The traveller was certain to find primitive conditions in full rigor and variety a little farther on. It is almost absurd for us to use the same word for what was called a road in the first twenty-five years of the United States, and for what anywhere in the United States we call a road now. As late as 1835 Chief Justice John Marshall suffered "severe contusions" while returning in a stagecoach from Washington to Richmond on a road that lay all the way through tidewater Virginia and did not go up into the mountains at all.

The building of roads almost followed a progressive

[1]See *Everyday Things in American Life,* Volume I, Chapter XVIII.

formula. The eastern slopes of all the Appalachian Mountain ranges and foothills were forest-covered. Piercing the forests was the first task of the roadbuilders. The future road was usually first "underbrushed through"; the bushes and saplings were cut down and burned. This made it possible for a horseman to get through. The large trees and the lay of the ground, with its streams and cliffs, made the trail a winding one. Then the road was widened by further "underbrushing" on either side, and it was somewhat straightened by cutting down some or all but the largest trees. This was a great improvement, but there still remained the stumps of the trees. And the roots of the larger trees still claimed the right of eminent domain anywhere underground, to the frequent breaking of horses' legs. Also every low place held the rain water in practically permanent swamps and marshes, as the sun could not get through the heavy foliage to dry them up before the next rain came.

These swamps and marshes gave natural occasion to one of the most common of the early roads, the corduroy road. Wood was plentiful. Trees of fairly straight stem and of six to eight inches diameter were cut down, their branches trimmed, and the trunks laid in the road crosswise. The surface of the road, so like corduroy, the stout-ribbed cotton cloth in common use at the time, suggested its name.[2]

[2]The name originally came from France. The Cordon du Roy was the lace band or ribbon by which the royal orders were suspended. Possibly in the simpler form of corde du roi the name crossed the Channel into England and somehow became transformed into the aristocratic name for a democratic fabric of ribbed linen and cotton

To even up the surface of the road soil was shovelled in between the logs and on top of them. This was good as long as the soil lasted, but the next rain usually washed it off and left the road bare to stand the test of use on its wooden merits. It was not an easy task for the local man to make a good corduroy road, even if a benevolent State did credit him as working off his taxes. He got little praise or thanks from the people who came out of the East. Few of them wanted to settle in his neighborhood. They lingered only long enough to complain about his road, and went on, still swearing, to the West. If they knew how to make a better road, let them do it! But at that time, and in the miscellaneous swamps and marshes of the forest, no one did know how to make a better road. Certainly thousands and thousands availed themselves of the corduroy roads whenever they could to make their way on to the Ohio Valley and the limitless promise of the great West.

One traveller wrote about the corduroy road with feeling. He was not a pioneer seeking a home. He was an Englishman who came over in 1842 to see for himself what America was like. It was Charles Dickens. He experienced a corduroy on his way to Toledo and Sandusky.

> It was well for us that we were in this humour (disposed to enjoy even the roughest journey), for the road we went over that day was certainly enough to have shaken any tempers. At one

with an imitation velvet surface. Across the Atlantic the phrase became familiar as the designation of a cheap (by virtue of the cotton) and durable (by virtue of the linen) fabric for the clothes of hard-working pioneers, plain ordinary corduroy.

time we were all flung together in a heap at the bottom of the coach, and at another we were crushing our heads against the roof. Now one side was deep in the mire, and we were holding on to the other. Now the coach was lying on the tails of the two wheelers; and now it was rearing up in the air, in a frantic state, with all four horses standing on the top of an insurmountable eminence, looking back at it, as though they would say, Unharness us. It can't be done. The drivers on these roads certainly get over the ground in a manner which is quite miraculous, they so twist and turn the team about in forcing a passage, corkscrew fashion, through the bogs and swamps. . . .

A great portion of the way was over what is called a corduroy road, which is made by throwing trunks of trees into a marsh and leaving them to settle there. The very slightest of the jolts with which the ponderous carriage fell from log to log was enough, it seemed, to have dislocated all the bones in the human body. It would be impossible to experience a similar set of sensations in any other circumstances. . . . Never, never once that day was the coach in any position, attitude, or kind of motion to which we [Englishmen] are accustomed in coaches. Never did it make the smallest approach to one's experience of the proceedings of any sort of vehicle that goes on wheels.[3]

This may not be a literal description of Mr. Dickens's experiences that day; on the other hand it may. Certainly this is how Mr. Dickens felt about a corduroy road.

Another traveller, Henry Tudor, wrote as feelingly in his *Narrative of a Tour in North America,* published in 1834:

I think the unhappy wight who has once traveled over them [corduroy roads] would never be inclined to wear a garment made of the stuff whence the name is borrowed, however fashion-

[3]*American Notes,* Chap. XIV.

able it might become, from the ungrateful association that would always be connected with it.

The dates of these two testimonies indicate that the corduroy era was at the respective periods well along. Corduroying was no longer a new idea. What it had to contribute to language and to civilization it had given.

The plank road was another of the early roads. It may logically be described at this point, though out of chronological order. Like the corduroy it was a wooden road. The corduroy used rough timber, merely axe-trimmed of its branches. The plank road used milled timber. It could not be built under as primitive conditions as the corduroy, nor was it built, anywhere, at as early a date. It came into popularity after the hard-surfaced turnpike was well known because it could be built much more inexpensively than the turnpike. Plank roads were usually built in fairly well settled regions, within a reasonable distance of towns. The first plank road in the United States was built in 1845 between Syracuse, New York, and Oneida Lake, a distance of about fourteen miles. It was built under the direction of an engineer, George Geddes, who had gone to Toronto to see the plank roads there. Geddes' plank roads were so successful that within the next five years 182 private companies were chartered in the State of New York with roads totalling 2019 miles. For about twelve years they were very popular.

The plank road itself was usually about eight feet wide, laid on only half of the road, the right hand side going toward the town, so that the farmers would have the benefit of the planking when going with their heavier loads to market. The other half of the road was left as a plain dirt road. The planks were laid crosswise, like the logs of the corduroy roads of unhappy memory, upon joists of heavy timber that ran lengthwise along the road and were embedded in packed earth to prevent decay from soaking in standing water. These joists were four by four inches square or heavier, and the planks laid across them also were at least four inches thick. No nails or spikes were used in them; the weight of the heavy planks kept them firmly in place. The sides of the plank road were left uneven on purpose, to prevent the forming of ruts, and to help heavily laden wagons that had got off the road to get on again. A plank road could be doubled by laying another road eight feet wide on the other side, but the traffic seldom justified this; the plank road itself was usually a one-way affair. The planks further were laid on a slight slope from the center to the side so that the rain water would drain off without settling on the planks. Double the weight of loads could be hauled over these roads, enough of itself to ensure their success. As said, they were much less expensive to build than good hard-surfaced roads, only about $1800 a mile. By 1857 New York had chartered 352 plank-road companies. But the life of a plank road proved to be hardly more than five years. The wear on the planks from the calks on the horses' shoes and from the wheels, and the inevitable gradual decay of the wood from the rain made dangerous holes in the roadway. The panic of 1857 discouraged most of these local companies from repairing their roads. More and more they removed the planking from them and the plank roads passed from popularity and from general use almost as rapidly as they had attained it.

The right road construction for American land travel was found many years before the plank road entered upon its short but popular career. It was the turnpike. The name, as will be seen, came from the gate erected at intervals on the roads on which tolls were charged for use by travellers, in order to help defray the cost of maintenance. The first important road built on this principle of construction was the Lancaster Turnpike in Pennsylvania. It was sixty-two miles long and ran from Philadelphia to Lancaster, the largest town in the farming district of the State. In 1792 a private company was organized and chartered, and the capital raised by subscription from 600 stockholders. David Rittenhouse of Philadelphia, the astronomer, made the preliminary surveys. The land was secured, the trees felled, and the right of way cleared in the approved fashion. With intent to make a specially fine piece of work of it, great boulders were dragged and rolled over the roadbed while more earth was strewn over it. The result looked well. But heavy rains came and the result was disheartening: holes, great stones, deep ruts. Horses stumbled, floundered and broke their legs. In this crisis appeared an Englishman who had seen hard-surfaced roads in his own country. He offered to accept a contract to make a durable highway of the failure.

The company agreed to the proposition and the Lancaster Turnpike was reconstructed on the principles previously advocated by the Scotch McAdam. From this success the art of road-building in America steadily advanced.

It has been said that an earlier turnpike was built in Virginia, in 1785–86, from Alexandria to the southern end of the Shenandoah Valley, and that Thomas Jefferson pronounced it a success. It may be. It does not appear, however, that this Alexandria-Shenandoah Turnpike resulted in any special extension of good road-building, as was the case with the Philadelphia-Lancaster Turnpike. Within a few years a considerable number of turnpike companies were chartered and roads were built in other sections, particularly in the southern part of New England and in New York.

The first turnpike company to be incorporated in New York was the Albany and Schenectady Turnpike, in 1797. The inland produce came down the Mohawk to Schenectady in Durham boats and in Schenectady keelboats, and was carried across to Albany on wagons. This saved many miles in transit, and the falls and rapids in the rivers between the two towns made the hauling by land unavoidable. The distance by land was only fourteen miles, but the soil was sandy, the going difficult, and the traffic very heavy. Few people lived on this fourteen-mile stretch of road, and they did not see a great mission for them in keeping the awful road in good condition for the benefit of a through traffic that did not affect them at all. At this important point in the commercial route, practically a bottleneck, the situation was almost impossible. Then word came about the Lancaster Pike. The suggestion was promptly investigated and adopted, and a charter was secured. Construction was begun in 1802 and completed in 1805 at a cost of about $10,000 a mile. The turnpike was a great success. It solved the problem of the Mohawk River commerce.

The Mohawk Turnpike and Bridge Company, chartered in 1800, carried the hard-surfaced road on from Schenectady to Utica. The Seneca Turnpike Company, also chartered in 1800, carried it on from Utica to Canandaigua over the old Genesee Road, which had done heroic service in its time and no less had required heroism every day on the part of the traveller, be he passenger or hauler of freight. After the War of 1812 the Ontario and Genesee Company carried the road on from Canandaigua to Lake Erie. Earlier the Rensselaer and Columbia Turnpike constructed a hard-surfaced road eastward from Albany to Lebanon Springs, New York, just west of Pittsfield, Massachusetts, to meet the migration and the traffic coming from Springfield and other parts of New England. This gave New York by 1807, between Lebanon Springs and Canandaigua, 234 miles of hard-surfaced road on its main route to the West.

This meant to the settler along the road, to the boy and girl growing up and doing chores on the roadside farms, new experiences: familiarity with more kinds of people whom they saw every day; with the greater variety of clothes they wore, more breeds of animals, more kinds of furniture (so much of it home-made) that they were taking with them to the West, more even of the tales and yarns they told while they were feeding their animals or bedding

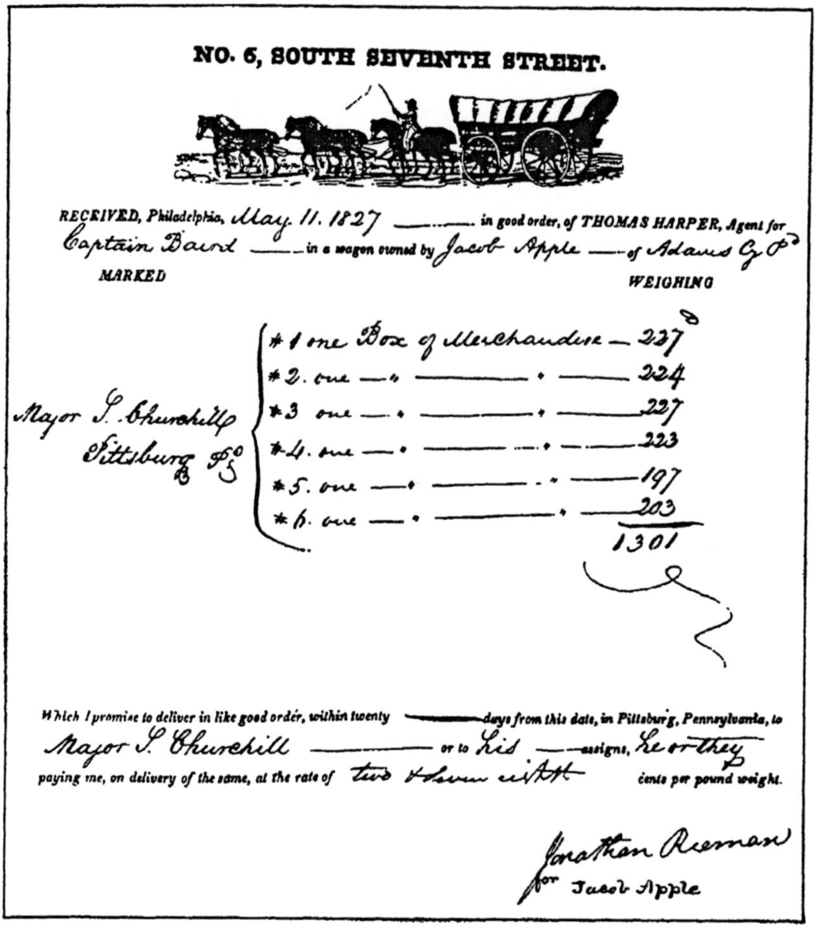

NO. 6, SOUTH SEVENTH STREET.

RECEIVED, Philadelphia, May 11. 1827 —— in good order, of THOMAS HARPER, Agent for Captain Baird —— in a wagon owned by Jacob Apple —— of Adams Cy P.

MARKED — WEIGHING

Major S. Churchill
Pittsburg Pa

#1	one Box of Merchandise	237
#2.	one "	224
#3	one "	227
#4.	one "	223
#5.	one "	197
#6.	one "	203
		1301

Which I promise to deliver in like good order, within twenty —— days from this date, in Pittsburg, Pennsylvania, to Major S. Churchill —— or to his —— assigns, he or they paying me, on delivery of the same, at the rate of two & seven eighth cents per pound weight.

Jonathan Rieman
for Jacob Apple

A receipt for wagon transportation from Philadelphia to Pittsburgh

From "The Development of Transportation Systems in the United States," by J. L. Ringwalt, 1888. Courtesy of the New York Historical Society

them down for the night. The horizon was expanding right there on the farm. Therewith came new ideas, and sometimes new settlers, new neighbors, making the local color of their own life richer and more varied. Now and then one or two of their own neighborhood families drifted into the stream and went on looking for new homes in the fabled Farther West, nonetheless leaving alluring dreams behind them. The gain to commerce was extraordinary. Wagons covered with canvas and drawn by four to eight horses were soon seen streaming along the turnpike highway. The sight became common. Some wagons carried freight straight through from Albany to Buffalo. So the chain of connecting short turnpikes reached across the State and from local units built up a through highway.

Turnpikes were also built going into other parts of the State. They formed a veritable network. All converged on Albany, the head of navigation on the Hudson River. The Northern Turnpike went through Cambridge and Salem to Granville on the way to Castleton and Middlebury, Vermont, important towns already in those days. The Albany and Greene Turnpike, down the west side of the Hudson, to Catskill, and the Farmers' Turnpike, down the east bank, to the town of Hudson, formed backbones for local roads going off into the country. When it became evident that the saving of time in travel was to be one result of the turnpikes, the Highland Turnpike continued the Farmers' down the east side of the river to Highbridge on Manhattan Island. The Farmers' and the Highland together came to be called the New York and Albany Post Road.

The part of New York State that drains into the headwaters of the Delaware and the Susquehanna rivers, reaching as far west as the present location of Elmira, had been separated from the Hudson-Mohawk population by wilderness, and seemed almost to be considered as practically a part of Pennsylvania. The reclamation of this region by New York was now begun by means of the Susquehanna and other turnpikes. Around the headwaters of the Delaware, however, the wilderness at this time was more than a matter of forests. The men in that region were lumbermen, and a freshet in the local streams to float their logs down to market suited their interests better and won their enthusiasm more quickly than the proposal to build a "neversink" turnpike through their country.

These turnpikes were built in general accordance with the principles of John Loudon McAdam (1756–1836), the Scotch engineer. These principles he briefly asserted in the following passage:

> The roads can never be rendered perfectly secure, until the following principles be fully understood, admitted, and acted upon: namely that it is the native soil which really supports the weight of traffic: that while it is preserved in a dry state, it will carry any weight without sinking, and that it does in fact carry the road and the carriages also; that this native soil must previously be made quite dry, and a covering impenetrable to rain, must then be placed over it to preserve it in that dry state; that the thickness of a road should only be regulated by the quantity of material necessary to form such impervious covering, and never by any reference to its own power of carrying weight.[4]

The way these roads were built under McAdam's per-

[4] J. L. McAdam: Remarks on the Present System of Road Making, quoted by Kirby and Laurson.

sonal direction in England has been told graphically by one who had seen the work in process:

> M'Adam's plan consists in breaking into small pieces the stones which are employed in constructing and repairing the roads. This operation is performed by women and children, who sit down and break the stones with small hammers. No fragment of stone measuring more than an inch longitudinally, or weighing more than six ounces is laid down on the road. For ensuring the observance of this rule, the people who break the stones are furnished with sieves made of iron with circular holes, similar to those used by shot manufacturers for ascertaining the calibre of bullets. Every piece of stone that will not pass through this sieve is laid aside. Besides this instrument, Mr. M'Adam furnishes all the overseers of the work with a balance and a weight for weighing two or three of the largest fragments of each heap of broken stones, to ascertain that none exceed the specified weight.[5]

From this account it will be evident that macadamizing has remained essentially the same to the present day; and also that the much-abused machine age has simplified the process to the advantage of the public, especially of the women and children who used to wield the small hammers. Most of the turnpikes, and the better ones, were built in this way and it could correctly be said that they were macadam roads, but there were also many that were simply earth-surfaced with the crown shaped for drainage.

In most cases the turnpikes were built by private companies chartered by the State through which they passed. State boundaries were pretty real things; interstate local

[5] F. P. C. Dupin: The Commercial Power of Great Britain, quoted by Kirby and Laurson.

traffic had not yet started in to ignore and thus practically to obliterate them. The charter secured, the road was laid out by a surveyor and built by private capital raised by the

From "Picturesque America," edited by William Cullen Bryant, 1874

A tollhouse on the Newburg turnpike

stockholders of the company. To provide for the reimbursement of the stockholders and for the maintenance of the road the charter usually allowed the company to charge for the use of the road and to erect every ten miles a barrier across the road, a gate or turnpike, which was opened or turned aside when the toll had been paid. The great advantage of this was that the users of the road paid for its maintenance.

This authority to charge tolls brought to the road its familiar name, the turnpike, soon appropriated in its original and shorter form of the pike. The pike was originally the weapon of a foot soldier in European armies. In America it was the customary weapon of the guards of the Colonial Governors. It consisted of a long wooden staff with a pointed steel head. In military service it was superseded by the bayonet, which originated in a short flat dagger. At the entrances of forts and other official entrances soldiers barred the way by crossing their pikes in front of parties seeking entrance until satisfactory explanation had been given of the right to pass. The pike was adapted for use in the government-authorized barring of the road until the toll had been paid by placing a pike or a wooden bar (the steel head was not necessary) on a turnstile or a gate. It was called a turnpike from the device for ensuring the collection of the tolls, and by natural abbreviation the road itself soon appropriated the original designation and became known familiarly as the pike.

The tariff of tolls was worked out in considerable detail and was posted at every toll gate. In New York the charge for each ten miles was 12½ cents for every wagon with two horses or oxen and 3 cents for each additional horse or ox

BOSTON,

Plymouth & Sandwich

MAIL STAGE,

CONTINUES TO RUN AS FOLLOWS:

LEAVES Boston every Tuesday, Thursday, and Saturday mornings at 5 o'clock, breakfast at Leonard's, Scituate; dine at Bradford's, Plymouth; and arrive in Sandwich the same evening. Leaves Sandwich every Monday, Wednesday and Friday mornings; breakfast at Bradford's, Plymouth; dine at Leonard's, Scituate, and arrive in Boston the same evening.

Passing through Dorchester, Quincy, Wyemouth, Hingham, Scituate, Hanover, Pembroke, Duxbury, Kingston, Plymouth to Sandwich. *Fare,* from Boston to Scituate, 1 doll. 25 cts. From Boston to Plymouth, 2 dolls. 50 cts. From Boston to Sandwich, 3 dolls. 63 cts.

From the New York Public Library

En route to the Cape in 1810

used in drawing the wagon; 25 cents for every coach, coachee, phaeton, curricle or other pleasure carriage with two horses; 12½ cents for every one-horse pleasure carriage, (pleasure vehicles ran into money); 4 cents for every horse and rider; 20 cents a score for horses, cattle or mules, and 6 cents a score for sheep or hogs. There were many other items and financial distinctions. Freight wagons whose wheels were 6 inches broad or more received a reduced price as they did not cut into the roadbed so much. Stagecoach companies using the road regularly also usually had a reduction, at times as much as one half. Stagecoach companies also paid their toll charges every three months, so that their stages might not be stopped on their way but sweep straight on through the tollgate with swaying grandeur.

The local interest was also recognized by certain sensible exemptions. Any one who lived within a mile of a tollgate was exempt from paying tolls at that gate at any time. Any one going to or returning from a church or religious meeting, the polls on election day, the court if on jury or witness service, or training on muster day passed through the gate free. Any one going to the gristmill or the blacksmith shop, or returning therefrom, passed free; and any one going for a physician or a midwife not only did not have to pay toll but no doubt had the gate swung open wide when the gatekeeper saw him coming. The tollkeeper was a good neighbor, and knew everybody who lived and everything that happened within five miles of the gate in either direction.

The turnpikes proved themselves to be practical, popular among those who had occasion to use them, and much more durable than any other kind of road known in America. Of course the longer they were the better! When the entire length of a turnpike was in one State, everything—the raising of the capital, the construction, the repair and extension if needed or desired—all could be done under the authority of the one charter granted to the company by their State. That was a very practical advantage. When a turnpike went from one State on into another State, other questions, many of them legal questions, arose, imperatively demanding consideration.

Courtesy of "The New York Evening Post"

Stage coaches on Broadway in 1800. When *The New York Evening Post* was founded, New York City extended only one mile north from Battery Park

CHAPTER III

The Directing Power

THE early river commerce of the advancing pioneers was naturally restricted to the one watercourse up which they had come and near which they settled. The commerce operated between the head of navigation and the sea. The newer land traffic cutting across from one waterway to another, while it might greatly increase the opportunities for trading, came into existence only as the result of a terrible struggle. The prospect of a rewarding future ahead for the settlers was by no means encouraging. Even survival was questionable. What overcame these hopeless conditions was the persistence of the people who were settling the new territories and who were relentlessly pressing on from the seacoast regions toward the west, beyond the mountains, and ever on and on. This spirit began to show itself even in the colonial days, when in many instances the people of one colony were of very different nation, religion, type or class from those of the next colony: English Puritans in Massachusetts Bay; Dutchmen in Nieuw Netherland; Quakers, South Germans, and Scotch-Irish in Pennsylvania; Catholics in Maryland; Church of

England aristocrats in Virginia. The time was, actually, when New Netherland and Massachusetts Bay did not want to be united by a travelable road. It was not very long since New York and East Jersey, though both English Colonies, were threatening to go to war with each other over the import duties at Manhattan on truck-garden produce; while Connecticut laid an embargo on New York because of the duties on firewood. There was no unity among them except such as physical conditions of the country forced upon them. What, originally, had they in common? Little or nothing except the isolation imposed upon them all alike by the ocean-wide and stormy sea.

Up the rivers toward the mountains, the settlements progressed. Down these rivers the settlers sent their surplus goods to the larger towns and cities on the coast to be sold. This was the small boat river commerce. No man who produced only what he and his family needed to eat could grow affluent. He had to be a trader too. No settlement that produced only what it consumed itself would prosper. The settlers naturally produced and sent down to the coast towns only what they could profitably sell there. In turn the merchants on the coast could sell to the settlers up-river only what they needed. The farther inland the settlements went the more it cost to transport the goods to market on the coast and to effect the return. Therefore the greater must be the quantity of their surplus products and the more positively must they be in demand; the more vigorous and successful must these frontier communities be.

Neither settlers nor merchants could afford to be content with the customers on one river, the single water highway between them. They must get access to other settlers on other rivers, and to merchants at the mouth of other rivers. Somehow they must pierce the forests, and get shorter direct land routes for their commerce. A promised land of prosperity ahead was to both settler and seaport merchant not merely a hope; it was a necessity. This bred a nascent spirit of accommodation and unity among the various peoples of the various Colonies. So was the balance of trade asserted on the sound business principle that both parties to the bargaining must gain desired advantage or the bargaining would cease. This early river traffic started the expansion of America to the west, started the simplification of America into an ultimate unity, and no less established the prosperity of America on the coast.

In the colonial separation of the Colonies from one another there was a physical circumstance that suggested a common destiny. Along their eastern front extended a series of waters which were enclosed from the storms of the Atlantic by long, low coastal islands. These islands were made and were still being made by the rivers that poured down from the Appalachian Highlands into the ocean, depositing their silt when the force of the river currents abated. Some of these rivers emptied into the sea through estuaries they had themselves washed out in prehistoric ages. Long Island was one of these islands; the Hudson was one of these estuaries. These rivers, with the sounds, presented to the Colonies very attractive opportunities for intercolonial commerce. Long Island Sound and the Hudson River offered sheltered access for trading to East Jersey, New York, Connecticut, and Rhode Island. Chesapeake Bay assured Virginia and Maryland that their commerce with each other was their own affair; and Albemarle Sound and Pamlico Sound naturally suggested that North and South Carolina might easily be added to the Chesapeake commercial group.

It required no originality to see that the extension of these inland waterways and their connection with one another by canals was not at all impracticable. The rivers had done much. The Colonists might themselves well do a little. Cape Cod had always threatened with storms and shipwreck any who dared to sail around it on the outside course from Massachusetts Bay to Long Island Sound. As early as 1623 Captain Myles Standish proposed to dig a canal joining two streams by which it would be possible for their shallops to cross the isthmus of Cape Cod and meet the Dutch for trading at the head of Buzzards Bay. During the Revolutionary War Washington considered the feasibility of such a Cape Cod Canal for its military value in his strategy against the powerful English navy.

In the south, a route for a canal through the Great Dismal Swamp, to afford a waterway from Hampton Roads to Albemarle Sound was surveyed by Washington and Fielding Lewis in 1763.[1] A canal was built there in 1828 and

[1]This would save the dangerous voyage out through the Capes and around Hatteras.

was long the main line of commercial transportation for the products of North Carolina to the Virginia markets and seaports.

In the middle region, the Chesapeake and Delaware Canal was so obvious an idea that it hardly needed to be suggested, though nothing definite was done about it until 1799. So too, in 1804, serious consideration was given the idea of a canal across New Jersey. The forty miles of construction rendered it impossible at the time, but it was finally realized, connecting the Delaware River at Bordentown with the Raritan River at New Brunswick and so through the Arthur Kill at Perth Amboy with New York Bay, the Hudson River, and Long Island Sound.

All these early canals were small affairs compared with some of the later canals. They were merely supplementary elements, connecting links in the river commerce system of the North Atlantic slope. But they were significant. The desire and need of people up one of the "rivers" to get into practical communication with people in other regions was increasing. This determined spirit, instinctive and it may be unconscious at first, resulted in such improvements as these canals to the waterways. They were the only commercial highways of the time. The same spirit produced and developed the land roads into commercial land routes, and had its own insistent way in many other phases of life.

The greatest need of people is more people, different people, not merely more of the same kind. When circumstances in the latter half of the eighteenth century compelled the people of the American Colonies to get together, even though they were very different from one another, it greatly stimulated the creative American spirit. Striking instances were seen when in the Revolution the people of democratic New England accepted George Washington of aristocratic Virginia as their general to lead its local war; when the people of the north and of the south alike accepted Robert Morris of Pennsylvania as their Superintendent of Finance to manage the endless complex problems of ways and means, of cash, credit and indebtedness; when the Carolina riflemen tramped through the forests under Daniel Morgan to fight at Bunker Hill and on Long Island. Nor was this American spirit confined to Americans. It was exemplified in the Scotchman, John Paul Jones, the French Marquis de La Fayette, the Germans, Kalb and Steuben, the Poles, Kosciuszko and Pulaski. The climax of the achievements of this spirit came in the swift creation of a successful legal system to embody a way of living for all Americans, combining ample variety with effective unity, only thirteen years after the first Continental Congress for tentative cooperation in 1774, and only six years after the unsuccessful Articles of Confederation in 1781. This was the triumphant Constitution of the United States, of 1787. It reacted upon all American life and speedily became the greatest force in the future of the American people. The central personality in the creation of the American Constitution was George Washington. He, gathering devoted followers around him, with them gave life to the

Constitution and power to all the activities resulting from its acceptance and operation.

Consider the dates of these early canals. It is a striking fact that before the adoption of the Constitution there was nothing done to construct any one of them; and that after the adoption something was done and was carried through on all of them. Their importance was recognized during the Constitutional Convention. John Jay pointed this out in *The Federalist* (No. II) in referring to the territory of the proposed Union:

> A succession of navigable waters forms a kind of chain round its borders, as if to bind it together; while the most noble rivers in the world, running at convenient distances, present them with highways for the easy communication of friendly aids, and the mutual transportation and exchange of their various commodities.

For at least fifty-nine years we have thought of the United States as in shape a broad band straight across the continent of North America. In 1787, when the Constitution began its work, it might be thought of as a reversed E with many arms or river-arrows pointing inland to the west, the direction of hopes and possibilities.

With the Constitution there came rapidly a great change in the attitude of the people of the American States. The change was not merely one of political form or of executive control. Every American had been primarily and as by nature of some one Colony or State. He was a Massachusetts Yankee, a New Yorker, a Pennsylvania Quaker or Dutchman, a Virginian. Now suddenly he was primarily an

American and only incidentally a Yankee, a New Yorker, a Pennsylvanian, a Virginian. At once he began to get used to the idea, to get used to it as a fact, and to consider what specifically the fact meant, whether his feeling about it was enthusiastic or distrustful. Under the Constitution all alike were to consider public questions as the questions of all and decide them for all. The union was not the imposition of any group, even of a majority. It was the deep, instinctive desire of all, whether or not they believed it practicable or even possible. This was what made the Constitution the powerful instrument it was.

How the Constitution worked through and by means of its political machinery is evinced in the following concise statement of a general situation in 1810 by Peter B. Porter, a Congressman from New York, before the United States House of Representatives. He was speaking not merely in behalf of his own constituents but as the champion of all the people beyond in the Ohio regions.

The great evil, and it is a serious one indeed, under which the inhabitants of the western country labor, arises from the want of a market. Such is the present difficulty and expense of transporting their produce to an Atlantic port that little benefit is realized from that quarter. The single circumstance of want of a market is already beginning to produce the most disastrous effects, not only on the industry, but on the morals of the inhabitants. Such is the fertility of their lands that one-half of their time spent in labor is sufficient to produce every article, which their farms are capable of yielding, in sufficient quantities for their own consumption, and there is nothing to incite them to produce more.

It was no bare Constitution, no mere legal document, that could rejuvenate those impoverished pioneers for whom Congressman Porter appealed. It was a Constitution that immediately began to result in practical means for American life. Americans forthwith began to invent and to make new things to solve their problems in a larger way. The United States Patent Office was established in April, 1790, and the first United States patents were issued that summer. Without the Constitution the American people could hardly have got started in this creative encouragement and protection of their industry. Without the Constitution no subsequent improvement in the everyday things of American life can be understood.

The ways and means of doing things usually focus in money. The herculean struggles of Robert Morris as Superintendent of Finance under the Articles of Confederation to get the people of the disparate American States to conduct their public business in an honest and sensible way contributed essentially to prepare for the Constitution. A letter he sent to the States in September, 1783, called for reports on their population and natural resources under four general heads—geographical, moral, political, and commercial.[2]

Geographical:

1. The general area of the country;
2. The mountains, rivers, and superficial features;

[2]See Ellis Paxson Oberholtzer: *Robert Morris, Patriot and Financier*, The Macmillan Company, 1903.

3. The soil and the natural advantages of the land for agriculture, mining, and other pursuits.

Moral:

1. The size of the population;
2. Mode of life and occupation of the people;
3. The state of husbandry;
4. Development of the arts, particularly the useful arts;
5. Character of the building;
6. Improvement of the land and the number, character, and location of mills and factories.

Political:

1. The constitutions;
2. The magistracy;
3. The system of interior police;
4. The revenue system;
5. The state of public and private credit.

Commercial:

1. Produce;
2. Roads and navigation;
3. Imports and exports;
4. The value of lands;
5. The value of money.

In this census-like set of reports Robert Morris hoped to secure the comprehensive information that would be needed for a united national life. As usual, however, he was unable to get the sincere cooperation from the States properly to carry out his inquiry. Nonetheless, Robert Morris's great work, of which this inquiry was only a single item, very materially helped to pave the way for the Constitution and the America it brought into being. Under the Constitution the first census was taken in 1790. It was not comparable to

Morris's plan of seven years before. It covered little more than the number, sex, and color of the population, but it made an effective and actual beginning.

No more than in the matters of the census and the Patent Office did the Constitution in other matters spring at once into instantaneous success. But the change in the attitude of the American people toward public affairs was radical, and comparatively it was rapid. It was not merely that they took more interest in public affairs, as by addition. They now began to consider the point of view of others as never before. Their point of view was multiplied. At the start the multiplier was 13, and the multiplication steadily increased as the settlements advanced along the Ohio, the Mississippi, and the Missouri rivers, prospering as they went, and opening new territories to American pioneers in the West.

This is strikingly indicated in the name of the country. We of the twentieth century do not hesitate to speak of it in the singular number, saying the United States *is*. It has become so. But in 1787 it was an extraordinary name for a nation, and the plural verb was always used as a matter of simple grammar. The name proved to be itself a thrilling challenge. The United States of America was not the name of a finished nation. It was the name of an ideal, of a possibility for the nineteenth century to work out. In every activity and detail of life since 1787 the Constitution has been working out into practical results. America lives and breathes in the Constitution. No event in the history of the country, however great, no detail of its everyday life, however small, can be truly understood if there be not seen therein the Constitution working out the destiny of the new united American people.

From a drawing by Stanley M. Arthurs for "Scribner's Magazine"

At the junction of a stage and steamboat route

CHAPTER IV

Covered Bridges

AS HAS been seen, travel was for the settlers at first a matter of water travel. They got into their boats and went where they wanted to go. They were not attracted to going far back from the water into the tangled underbrush and sapling growth that filled the space between the giant trees of the forests. But as settlements increased and cut their way into these jungles, and as roads reached out through the endless forests, more and more the question arose of crossing the streams, of crossing water. Land travel was beginning to assert itself, to rival and to take precedence over water travel.

As crossing the streams became more than a concern of the neighbors, as what we would call real travel developed, with people wanting to cross, who were quite frequently strangers and had no boat of their own, ferries were established across the larger streams. The traveller paid his fee and went on his way, content and sometimes rejoicing, to make his way through another stretch of forest.

The smaller streams, 20, 30 or probably at most 50 feet wide, used to be crossed on foot or on horseback at fords.

When the neighborhood coming and going and the stranger travel became rather impatient with detours and fords, the immediate problem was sufficiently solved by felling a few tall trees and laying them across from one bank to the other, with maybe short lengths crosswise. For surface this was no worse than the corduroy roads of pioneer memory,

Crossing at a ford

From "The Development of Transportation Systems in the United States," by J. L. Ringwalt, 1888. Courtesy of the New York Historical Society

in fact it was very similar. This was indeed fine—except when some inconsiderate flood came along, lifted the simple bridges off their moorings, and took them downstream, where they were not needed nor wanted. The resulting inconvenience was however a temporary matter. The settler living near by would lay a rough-hewn plank across the stream for pedestrians until the bridge could be replaced. There are not a few instances when horsemen have gone across these single plank bridges quite safely simply by trusting their horses.[1]

When, however, travellers became increasingly impatient with ferriage across the wider streams and clamored for bridges (which was entirely justified by the increased land travel), a new problem arose. The bridges demanded

Crossing by ferry before the advent of the bridge

From "The Development of Transportation Systems in the United States," by J. L. Ringwalt, 1888. Courtesy of the New York Historical Society

would have to be longer than the length of the tallest avail-

[1]There is an instance in the writer's family in Alabama in 1842. Going home horseback from a visit at the plantation of friends on a dark stormy night, this boy of eleven crossed unknowingly a flooded stream on such a single plank. He heard the stream roaring beneath him and wondered if the bridge would hold. Returning the next day for some effects he had left behind, he was surprised to find the bridge gone and only a single plank across the still raging stream. A man who lived near by told him the bridge had gone out and he himself had placed the plank across for pedestrians in the early evening. The boy's intelligent sure-footed horse had carried him safely across on the plank during the dark night, and did again by daylight the next morning.

able trees. The simple single-span bridge of the lesser streams was not practicable. There was found, however, a way of extending the usefulness of the single-span bridge. It was simple enough: multiply by two, build a pier in the middle of the stream and then build two bridges, one continuing the other, each within the length of available timber. Later of course the same mathematical principle was carried further: multiply by three, build two piers; by four, and so on. One difficulty was that it was not always easy in those days to build a pier in the middle of a large stream. The development of the covered bridge used the pier idea too, as many of them to this day bear witness, but there was something brought into the solution of the wide stream problem that the pier could not bring.

Some have asked why they did not build stone bridges, with which all were familiar in Europe. Stone was not available. The soil of the Atlantic coast, where the growth of the Colonies was producing towns and cities and land travel, and where the larger streams were sweeping toward the sea, was deposited by these streams in recent geological times, burying the rock strata deep and fostering the growth of forests. The stone industry further was comparatively slow in developing with its quarrying, dressing, transporting, and handling. Timber was the available material, and timber it was the American pioneers used. To timber they turned to solve their building problems of all kinds.

Land travel was increasing. Also it should be noted that the approach and the realization of national unity between the Colonies that with 1776 had become States, emphasized the practical importance, indeed the necessity, of developing interstate travel. The question of how to make a bridge reach across a wide stream, across all streams, had really become a question of national importance on account of what its solution could contribute. The details of the beginnings are lost: when and where the first attempts were made, where and when the first failures were met and forgotten. It seems plausible to believe they were not far in date from 1776, when we think of Morgan's green-clad riflemen coming up through the Carolinas and Virginia and Pennsylvania to meet Washington before Boston; and when we think of the pioneers under George Rogers Clark, for lack of a land road, making a waist-deep footpath of the Wabash River in their attack on Vincennes. Whatever and wherever the beginnings, the problem was solved, and the solution soon developed into the sturdy, reliable masterpiece of timber construction, the covered bridge.

The credit for discovering the principle that solved the problem of reaching across the wider rivers, of creating the covered bridge, has been given by competent engineering judges[2] to Theodore Burr, an American, who in 1798 used the principle in building a bridge. That principle was previously discovered and used by an Italian, Andrea Palladio,[3]

[2]See Frank O. Dufour and C. Paul Schantz: *Bridge Engineering,* pages 2–8.

[3]See *Everyday Things in American Life,* Volume I, pages 127–28, and 135.

in 1570. It was then, it seems, forgotten, and strictly speaking, rediscovered by Theodore Burr, more than two hundred and twenty-five years later. There was no connection at all, so far as is known, between Palladio and Burr. Burr has full right to his credit, so far as America is concerned. The principle was the "king-post truss." Supposing that the longest available timbers be used for the diagonals slanting from

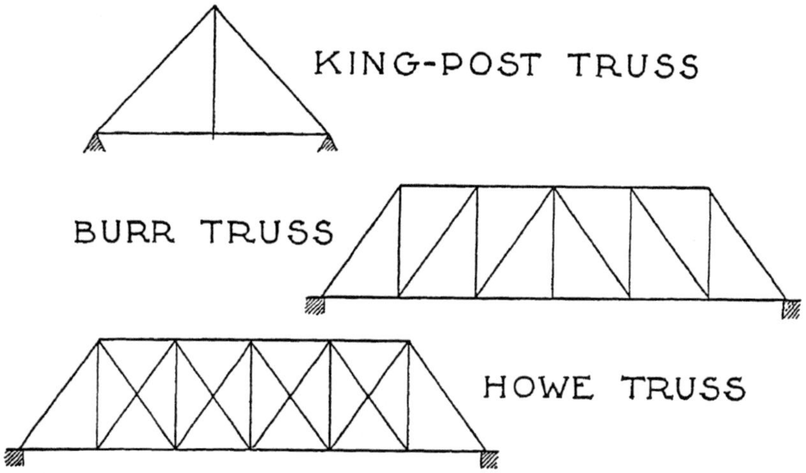

From drawings by E. G. Lutz

Principles of the King-Post, Burr and Howe truss

the ground-base to the top of the king post, it will readily be seen that the two bases of the right triangles together will be longer and will reach farther than either diagonal, *i.e.,* than any available timber. A series of parallel trusses on the sides of the bridge, joined and braced by the floor beams below and the rafters above, made a strong bridge structure. However many times multiplied, the single-span bridge was in principle just a plank laid across the stream. When this is recognized it will be seen how great a contribution Theodore Burr made to bridge construction with the king-post truss and the Burr truss which in 1798 he developed from it by overlapping trusses at half the length of the triangular bases. Others during the next fifty years developed the truss into formulæ still stronger and more extensible, so that a timber bridge, especially with the use of piers, could be built quite as long as required or desired. Travel was greatly facilitated.[4]

There were timber bridges across considerable streams before 1798. It has been said that it is quite probable that in 1780 General Washington crossed the upper Housatonic River on the old covered bridge at Cornwall, Connecticut. But we do not know whether or not it was at that time a covered bridge. Again, in 1785, it is recorded, Colonel Enoch Hale built a two-span bridge resting on a pier in the middle of the Connecticut River at Bellows Falls, Vermont. This was not covered, though it was built of the finest white oak and pine, free from sap, *i.e.,* well seasoned, had a plank flooring and hand rail, and further "terminated in a handsome toll gate which was painted a pleasing color." In 1799 this bridge was replaced, after fourteen years' service, by the old Tucker Toll Bridge, which unquestionably was a covered bridge and lasted until 1931. There was, no doubt, an early period of active experiment and steady development

[4]For travelling conditions before the times of the timber truss bridge, see *Everyday Things in American Life,* Volume I, pages 241–51.

before Theodore Burr and 1798. The covered bridge was not a sudden blooming forth of genius into an initial perfection. But at present it seems that probability is the best we can assert of the achievements of that early period.

One thing seems certain in that early period, and later. There were a goodly number of practical men working on the problem. The solution had almost to be re-solved at every bridge location. It had to be adapted to the local conditions—the width of the stream, the nature of the banks, the height and kind of available timber, and other considerations—adapted so much that it amounted to a re-solving of the problem. This called for originality, as well as ability and experience in the handling of timber.

Many of the covered bridges were toll bridges. This was natural and fair. To bridge a wide stream was not an ordinary matter. The general vote of a town meeting would often not feel justified in appropriating money for such an uncertain venture. On the other hand, some individual would often be willing to risk his money, lumber, and ingenuity in the problem, looking into what had been done elsewhere and deciding how to work it out in the present circumstances. In the event of his success, was it not fair, right and proper for him to have a way to recoup his expense and to make an advantageous profit? Further, the system of tolls was quite familiar on the turnpikes. A bridge was a piece of road over a stream. Accordingly, the toll-gate became the usual and accepted way of "building a bridge." Later, naturally again, the tolls caused plenty of trouble and brought up incidentally some curious questions,[5] all of which were satisfactorily disposed of by abolishing the toll-gates and making the bridges, like the roads, free to the public.

Regarding the cover itself, the roof of these bridges, there has been much said, but most of it untenable. The pattern of the truss diagonals allowed abundant ingress for wind and rain, but hardly enough for sunshine to dry the bridges

[5]In the spring of 1913 there was a flood in the Connecticut River. The present writer was going to Meriden, New Hampshire. When I got off the train at Windsor, Vermont, expecting to take the mail-stage across the covered toll bridge I learned from the station agent that the flood was lapping the flooring of the bridge and no vehicle was allowed to cross. The mail carrier had had to leave his stage up on the top of the hill on the New Hampshire side. When he turned up, I accosted the old man and arranged to go along with him. I picked up my heavy suitcase with sincere sorrow for myself as I looked up at the heights on the other side, and with genuine concern for the little old mail-carrier stagedriver with the big sacks on his back. I feared he could never make it, would break down under their weight climbing the hill. (But he did not, oh no!) So we walked down to the bridge and footed it across. At the other end, where the toll-gate was, the keeper posed a real question: Was I on the stage or not? I was with the stagedriver and so was a passenger and entitled to go across the bridge free. But I was not actually on the stage, though through no fault of my own. I was walking. I did not deny it. (And carrying a suitcase full of books—which was not deemed revelant, except by me.) As a pedestrian I ought to pay 3¢. The fair-minded toll keeper in the judicial capacity imposed on him by the emergency declared it was a matter of principle, not of the 3¢. He decided after some three-sided discussion that I was a passenger, that my walking was not of my own choice and volition, (it was not), but compelled by the flood, which was an act of God (Poor God!). So I kept my 3¢ and we went on, the mail carrier swiftly leading, to scale the heights before us. It would be very interesting to know what the United State Supreme Court would give as its final decision on this delicate legal question (it was an interstate question, and so could come before it), but I fear I shall never know.

out afterward. In many bridges a vertical side boarding was added, but, it is believed, not in the earlier bridges. Incidentally the side boarding made it very dark inside in the evening and at night. As to keeping the snow out, most if not all towns in the north regularly voted money

From "Picturesque America," edited by William Cullen Bryant, 1874

Old bridge on the Wissahickon near Philadelphia

to pay men "to snow the bridges," so that sleighs and sledges could get through.

A better conjecture would be that to those bridge builders it would have seemed distinctly lacking in sense not to put a roof on a timber bridge, if the bridge was to be of any length. They built out of experience and judgment. Probably some one of them in the early period considered that if truss construction made the sides of the bridge stronger, transverse truss construction would also make the top bracing stronger. He tried it. It did make it stronger. Others followed. It became the natural thing to do, just as it was in putting a strong roof on a house. Finally, with all that skeleton up there over the bridge, they naturally put on shingles. "Treating bridges as if they were houses, putting roofs on them? Why?" "Why not?" would likely have been their answer. Such structure of the roofs, whether on house or bridge, was an element of strength. Strength was what they wanted, the more the better. And they got it.

Among those other bridge builders who contributed to the development of the covered bridge was William Howe (1803–1852), an uncle of Elias Howe (1819–1867) of the sewing machine. In 1838 he built his first bridge at Warren, Massachusetts. An excellent authority[6] says of William Howe that during the last ten years of his life or more he "was busily engaged in constructing both bridges and roofs of his design." In 1842 he designed and built a roof for the depot of the Boston & Worcester Railroad in Boston using his own patented truss in the structure. Bridge-building and roof-building were closely similar, if not the same. Howe also was the first to use iron partly in the construction of his bridges. The change to iron from timber was an improvement in material, and of course a great improvement, allowing for greater developments in bridge building, but it was not a radical change in construction, as is shown in the use by Howe of iron with timber for the vertical elements in his Warren bridge.

We of the present are more familiar with the king-post

[6]C. W. Mitman of the Smithsonian Institution, in the *Dictionary of American Biography*.

From a drawing by Lucia Howe

The bridge near Center Conway, New Hampshire. This shows later development in the timber arches and in the overhanging entrance

truss and its descendants by modification and improvement than we realize. Trusses are used in most gable roofs, where we do not see them because of the ceilings of the stories beneath. But in many churches, especially in those of Gothic design, in which the structure of the roof is easily visible, one can see the king-post truss in manifold repetition above the heads of the congregation. Also, in many of the railroad and other iron bridges—not in the stone arch bridges, nor in the suspension or cement bridges—one will quickly recognize the Burr trusses, the Howe trusses, or other types, with persistent regularity, quite the same, though of iron or steel, as those of wood in the covered bridges.

Those covered bridges were strong structures, and not the less when the truss bridges were multiplied by use of the mid-stream piers. In acknowledging this as a general truth, it should still be remembered that many of them were home-made, local-built, while some of the bridge builders—like Theodore Burr (1771?–1822), Ithiel Town (1784–1844), William Howe (1803–1852), Nathan Cushing (1793–1872), Nicholas M. Powers (1817–1897), and Squire Whipple (1804–1888)—built more than a few; every one of them so gained considerable experience, before the calculation of stresses was introduced by Whipple. They became indeed experts in the art. Wood, even the most thoroughly seasoned timber, was not as strong nor as durable as iron and steel, of course, but instances may be cited in proof of the strength of these structures.

Along the top of the covered bridge over the Connecticut River at Greenfield, Massachusetts, the Boston & Maine Railroad laid a track on the beams of the top braces, using the structure as a deck-bridge, and for some years ran the trains of a branch line, surely a notable test for the strength of the structure. Again, in 1883, a flood brought a log jam down the Grand River in Michigan which piled up 39 feet high with a length of 7 miles. Three railroad bridges were swept away, but the Pearl Street covered bridge in Grand Rapids held. It was somewhat damaged but was never at any time out of use. A covered bridge of considerable length across the Winooski River at Waterbury, Vermont, was floated off its abutments and went down the river. It knocked a five-span railroad bridge off its piers as it went, and finally came to rest, not seriously damaged, in a field a mile or more below its original location.* The reliable old covered bridge across the Lamoille River at Cambridge, Vermont, as recently as 1927 gave evidence of its sound construction. The great flood of that year lifted the whole bridge off its abutments and carried it intact some forty feet downstream, where it was caught and held by some tall trees. When the flood subsided, the bridge settled down across the river and was there used as a detour until the necessary repairs had been made to the abutments at the original location. Then it was moved back, put in place, and has ever since been carrying traffic across the river as if nothing had happened. It was the everyday good workmanship that built that bridge. The name of the builder is not positively known. It is simply said that it seems to be like the bridges of Nathan Cushing.

No wonder the feelings of those who had personal knowledge of those old bridges expressed themselves in poems like the following! The last stanza, to be sure, may seem a little boastful when we consider the great advances of the

[7]Clara E. Wagemann, *Covered Bridges of New England,* page 149.

iron, steel and cement bridges since the covered bridges passed the height of their career in or about 1859, but then—it was not one of those bridges that wrote the poem!

AN OLD NEW ENGLAND COVERED BRIDGE

I know an old New England covered bridge
That spans a silvered, splashing mountain stream,
A bridge whose every sturdy bolt and beam
Was made secure by men who loved their work.

A masterpiece of grace and strength they built;
And into it the village pride they put,
Insuring that all travel, horse and foot,
Might cross in safety to the farther shore.

Its tunneled length down through the aging years
The ruthless hand of progress has repelled;
And though ofttimes the flood its doom has spelled,
Still stands the rugged bridge of yesterday.

Its sagging, shingled roof that leaks the rain,
Its weather-beaten walls and rumbling floor
Hold tales romantic of those days of yore,
When youth was brave and maids were passing fair.

With instruments precise at their command,
And all the knowledge science may reveal,
No modern engineer, with stone and steel,
Can build an old New England covered bridge!

ADELBERT M. JAKEMAN

From a drawing by R. Emmett Owen for "Scribner's Magazine"

The old covered bridge at Campton, New Hampshire. The overhanging entrance with simpler arch and the absence of timber arches indicate the earlier type of bridge

CHAPTER V

The Cumberland-National Road

IN APRIL, 1802, Congress passed an Enabling Act authorizing the people of Ohio to hold a constitutional convention. Their representatives assembled in Chillicothe in November, 1802, and framed a constitution. In this they provided for a fund from public land sales for the building of roads. The people of Ohio wanted better means for transporting their produce over the mountains to market on the Atlantic coast. This meant, of necessity, a road. Such a road was one of the objectives to be secured with Statehood. The next spring, in 1803, part of this fund was appropriated for that purpose. But it was entirely too small an amount. Further, whatever route was chosen, it would pass through other States and the consent of these States must be secured. The Ohio people urged that the Federal Government build the road, claiming that for just such projects did the Federal Government exist. But many who were more concerned for the local independence of the States claimed on the contrary that the Federal Constitution did not give Congress the right nor the authority to build roads in the States. It was a legal question between the national and the local points of view. The final decision was not reached for seventeen years, until 1819, when Chief Justice

John Marshall laid down the doctrine of the implied powers of the Constitution.

The road received its name by description. The Act of Congress authorizing its construction did not give it the name of the Cumberland Road. It simply designated it as "a road from Cumberland in the State of Maryland." By 1805 the general route was decided upon, from Fort Cumberland on the Potomac River, to which point navigation was possible, from the east, along the line of General Brad-

Courtesy of the Public Roads Administration

dock's route across the southwest corner of Pennsylvania, to the Ohio River somewhere between Steubenville and Wheeling. In 1806 President Jefferson was authorized by Congress to appoint three commissioners to lay out the road. The States of Pennsylvania, Maryland and Virginia gave their consents that Congress should construct the road, though Pennsylvania gave its consent only after it had been agreed that the route should pass through the Pennsylvania towns of Washington, Brownsville, and Uniontown (where Albert Gallatin, the Secretary of the Treasury, lived). Kentucky joined with Virginia in securing the terminus of the road for Wheeling over the claim of Steubenville and Ohio. It was 1811 before the route was finally approved and the first contracts for building had been awarded. These contracts were most of them given to farmers who lived along the route. It must be said they did a fine piece of work, so that for some time the Cumberland Road was generally said to be the best in the United States. One of these farmers received tribute from a traveller who had seen his constructing in progress:

> Mordecai Cochran, with his immortal Irish brigade, a thousand strong, with their carts, wheelbarrows, picks, shovels, and blasting tools, graded the commons and climbed the mountain side, leaving behind them a roadway good enough for an emperor.

The building of the road was delayed by the War of 1812 for a couple of years, but thereafter contractor after contractor completed his assignment, and it was opened to the use of the public progressively farther and farther west. The road was completed and opened to the Ohio River in 1818. The roadway was four rods wide, with a raised wagon way in the middle and ditches on either side. The highest point, in the Allegheny Mountains, was 2325 feet above sea-level. Permanent stone bridges were built wherever streams were crossed; many of these are still in use. So soon did the road come into crowded use that it was not completed to the Ohio River before it began to need repair at the eastern end. Despite the hard stone surface, the wheels of the heavily loaded wagons wore deep ruts through the road-bed and seriously interfered with travel.

Construction on the Cumberland Road proper was hardly more than well begun before it was proposed to continue the road on through Ohio, Indiana, and Illinois to St. Louis. This raised legal questions again, including now the right of Congress to repair, and put the road into politics once more. The brilliant young Speaker of the House of Representatives, Henry Clay of Kentucky, led the West in this issue of internal improvements, and with the young John C. Calhoun of South Carolina among his supporters, passed a law through Congress providing for the repair and maintenance of the Cumberland Road. But President Madison, though realizing the importance of the legislation, considered the law unconstitutional and vetoed it, giving his reasons for so doing in a long message. Then President Monroe came into office. Though he agreed with President Madison on the constitutional question involved, he considered that the practical aspect ought to determine his action and he signed the bill.

In these confused circumstances the Cumberland Road played an important part in the development of the national spirit. It emphasized to the people of six or seven States, indeed of all the States, the practical value of their union in a nation and the importance of their joint action as such. Every immigrant going over the Cumberland Road with his household to the great plains of the Middle West; every driver of a wagon hauling produce to the Eastern markets knew the constitutional question involved and knew that it concerned them. They discussed it among themselves at the taverns where they stopped at night and in the yards where they changed their horses or bedded down their teams. They heard "statesmen," speeding by stagecoach along the Cumberland Road to the National capital or to some State capital, argue the pros and cons of the constitutionality of the question or of its common sense. It was literally a live question. Accidents were not infrequent, especially as these same repairs became more immediately needed, and high office in this democratic country received no exemption from them. One time, Henry Clay was on his way to Washington from Kentucky by the Cumberland Road, and the stagecoach upset near Uniontown, Pennsylvania. The "Idol of the West" was fortunately unhurt, either in person or in humor. As he was being dragged out of the coach, he remarked that the Clay of Kentucky had been mixed with the limestone of Pennsylvania.

At last there came the occasion which gave the United States Supreme Court, through its Chief Justice, John Marshall, the opportunity to lay this constitutional question to rest, and thereby to advance the national union another step toward its permanent form and practice. Under the American Constitution the courts cannot lay down any principle of law, however essential, except on occasion of an actual instance. Law in the United States is based on the experience of life, not on theory, however excellent. With the case of M'Culloch *vs.* Maryland there came before Chief Justice Marshall on March 6, 1819, the opportunity to discuss judicially the character of the Constitution itself and to define the implied powers of the Constitution. This decision applied specifically to the repairs on the Cumberland Road. In this opinion he said:

> Let the end be legitimate, let it be within the scope of the constitution, and all means which are appropriate, which are plainly adapted to that end, which are not prohibited, but consist with the letter and spirit of the constitution, are constitutional.

This declaration came at a most important moment. The American people were pouring over the Allegheny Mountains by way of the Cumberland Road to fill the interior of the continent. That entrance was coming into jeopardy. Just at this moment Chief Justice Marshall with all the authority of the United States Supreme Court established the legal fact that the Constitution was as flexible as it was unchangeable, as practical in emergency as it was ideal in theory. This legal doctrine of the implied powers permanently opened the gates to the West, permanently bound the East and West in one, and enabled the American people to realize their future.

It was in 1825 that an extension of the Cumberland Road by authority of Congress and under its direction was actually begun. It was the work of the West. This extension was the National Road proper. Soon the entire road, old and new, from Cumberland, Maryland, west, was familiarly known as the National Road. It was a great vision that impelled this undertaking. On January 31, 1824, Henry Clay declared its purpose in these words:

> The gentleman from Virginia sought to alarm us by the awful

emphasis by which he stated the total extent of post roads in the Union. "Eighty thousand miles of post road!" exclaims the gentleman; "and will you assert for general government's jurisdiction and erect turnpikes at such an immense distance?" Not today, nor tomorrow, but this government is to last, I trust forever; we may at least hope it will endure until the wave of population, cultivation, and intelligence shall have washed the Rocky Mountains and mingled with the Pacific. And may we not also hope that the day will arrive when the improvements and comforts to social life shall spread over the vast area of this continent? It is a peculiar delight to me to look forward to the proud and happy period, distant as it may be, when circulation and association between the Atlantic and Pacific and the Mexican Gulf shall be as free and perfect as they are at this moment in England or in any other country of the globe.

The National Road was to be 80 feet wide, as well built of stone as the Cumberland Road had been, and to be equipped with turngates and a system of tolls for maintenance. The route was to pass through the capitals of the new States of the Northwest Territory, and through Indianapolis, Terre Haute, and Vandalia toward St. Louis. It was never finished as a federal undertaking through to the Mississippi. Better means of travel and transportation came into use than the turnpikes. They were relegated to local traffic and the development of local community life. Meantime, the emigrants swarmed along the road to the west, and the trains of wagons with produce came back in seemingly endless procession to the east. Trade routes were being established for generations to come, and in the opinion and intention of the Atlantic seaboard at least, commerce was being safely diverted from New Orleans, in territory still considerably Spanish and French in habit and character, to Philadelphia and Baltimore, back over the mountains by land routes, at home.

In those early days it was a live procession that swept along this highway! Boys brought up along that greatest of roads never forgot the sight! Those wagons—Conestoga wagons—named like the horses that drew them from the valley of their origin in eastern Pennsylvania, were large, magnificent in their lines, and gorgeous in their color. Underbody blue, so blue the blazing summer sky was not bluer; the upper body red, bright red; and over all the white cloth or canvas covering the frame of wooden bows, making a roof for the women and the children as well as a strong wrapping for the load. Very adaptable this huge conveyance was, and strong, with its woods specially selected for every part, to stand whatever hard conditions the crossing of the mountains might impose. To get down an icy hill with safety the hind wheels were often locked with a chain of heavy rough links, and often also fitted with an iron or steel ice-cutter, which looked much like a small sled. The long deep bottom, with ends curving up at front and back so that none of the load should spill out when going up or down the hills, however steep, sometimes carried a load as heavy as "a hundred and twenty hundred pounds." When a river or deep stream was to be crossed, the wagonbed could just be taken off the wheels—and it was a boat. All the immigrant's possessions or the hauler's freight could be ferried over and reloaded onto the wheels again. But such a necessity lost much time. On the Cumberland Road stone culverts and stone bridges had been built, obviating most of this ferriage. Those wheels, ponderous affairs, with broad wrought-iron tires, went ahead of everything!

An average Conestoga wagon may well be described with dimensions such as these. The wagon bed was 19 feet along the top, 14 feet along the bottom, and along the bulwarks

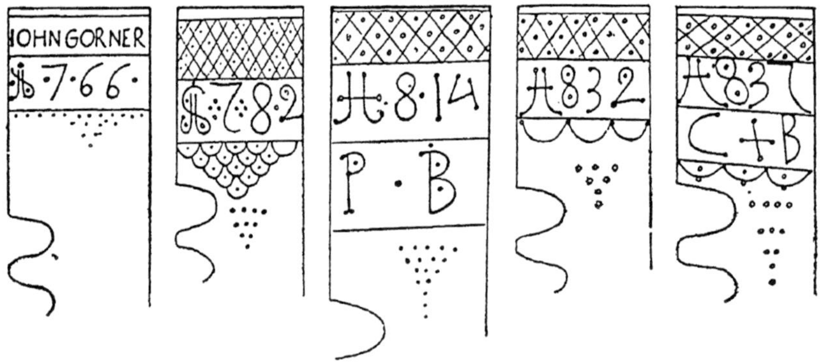

Wagon jack inscriptions, showing the date and initials or name of owner

From drawings by H. K. Landis from the originals in the Landis Valley Museum, Lancaster, Pa.

4 feet deep. The top of the front hoop of the 12 that held the covering was 11 feet from the ground; the top of the rear hoop was still higher. The white homespun covering closed in the two ends of the wagon as well as covered its length; it was 24 feet long. The rear wheels were 5 feet, 6 inches in diameter; the front wheels 3 feet, 10 inches. The capacity has been stated as high as 10 tons, but of course this depended on the nature of the load. These figures should be understood as average.

The Conestoga horses, a special breed, powerful creatures, standing 16 hands high, with strong legs, full manes, and short arched necks, weighed 1350 or 1400 pounds, and sometimes more. They were well adapted to their work, were not only capable of doing it, but of doing it with style. Two

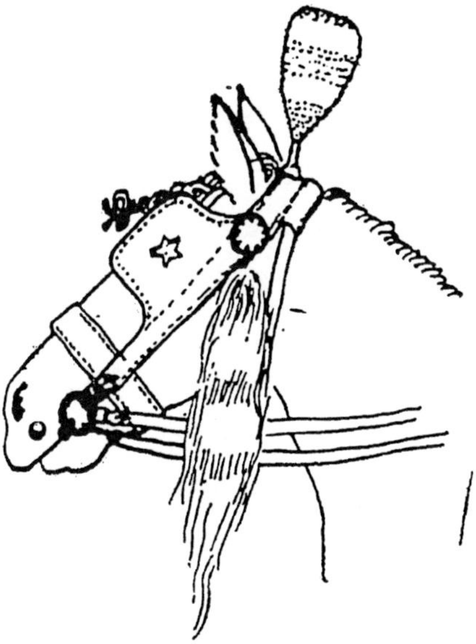

Fully equipped headgear of a high-mettled Conestoga horse

From a drawing by H. K. Landis, Landis Valley Museum

and two, regularly six horses in a team, drawing their great loads, they came along the turnpike, proudly conscious of their achievement. When the six horses were all hitched up and pulling, the whole team, from the nose of the lead pair to the rear of the Conestoga wagon stretched out to 60 feet!

The harness used on these teams was called a set of gears. It took a strong man to throw a set of gears across the back of a Conestoga horse. The back bands were 15 inches and the hip straps 10 inches wide, for instance, and they were heavy in proportion, and the housings covered the horse's shoulders down to the bottom of the hames. The traces were of iron chains with short thick links. They were decorated with gaudy red trimmings, and in cold weather half-covered with bearskins. With the barbaric music of the irregularly concerted jangle of many bells, they announced their approach from afar, for every horse bore his own finely toned cone-shaped bells fixed on wrought-iron arches over the tops of his hames, always four, usually five of them, on each horse—from 24 to 30 bells in all! Altogether they were something to see and hear!

The driver ordinarily rode on the left-hand wheel horse. He did not drive from a seat inside the wagon, or even under the hood. Probably the air would have been too close for him there. He had a saddle and rode on the nigh wheel horse. But, especially when he was making speed, which was most of the time, he rode on the lazy board. The lazy board was a sliding board of tough white oak that could be pulled out on the left-hand side of the Conestoga wagon. From the lazy board the driver could call to his horses, and also could operate the brake in sweeping down steep hills in the mountains. The derivation of the term is not known. It may have originated in gentle sarcasm and referred to the incessant activity that must have been continuously and instinctively carried on by the driver upon its small foot-space.

Among these "sea-captains" of the road there were two

distinct classes, those who carried passengers, and those who carried merchandise, the stage drivers and the wagoners. The earliest of all to appear were undoubtedly the emigrants, going west with their families and their goods to settle. After the roads made east and west trading regularly practicable the wagoners started. After back and forth travelling became frequent and habitual, the stage drivers appeared with their stagecoaches, making speed. The teamster was not the same as a wagoner, nor his equal—by no means! A teamster merely drove and cared for a team of horses. Later he was a driver engaged for short hauls, for "moving." A wagoner drove his horses, which he usually owned, and had full charge of and responsibility for the load he hauled. There were two types of wagoners, the regular and the sharpshooter. The regular was continuously on the road with his horses and wagon; hauling goods was his regular occupation. He drove about 15 miles a day quite steadily. The sharpshooter was in most instances a farmer who put his farm teams on the road when the rates for hauling were high and took them off when they went down. He drove about 20 miles a day on the average, and supplied unwelcome competition to the regular. There was feeling between the two, which showed itself sometimes in races on the pike, sometimes more personally.

The old wagoners seldom stabled their horses at night. They were unhitched and rested in the wagon yard of the taverns tied up to the long wagon tongue, three horses on each side, with the feed trough placed between them.

Weather made no diffierence. In bad weather, the horses were covered with blankets. Many of the wagoners had a big bulldog tied at the rear of the wagonbed that ran along under the wagon by day, pressing forward as if to help the horses, and served as very real protection to team and load at night. There was a common saying that a man could do as much as "a six-horse team with a cross dog under the wagon."

After feeding and caring for their horses, and installing the bulldog as guardian for the night, the wagoners went into the tavern for supper and a social time in the barroom. This included all the whisky they wanted at three cents a glass. Sometimes they had a dance on the barroom floor, with such girls as might be available, or without. Not a few of the innkeepers were excellent fiddlers, and dancing was a popular sport. The wagoners used no end of tobacco in every form, but regular cigars were too expensive. There was, however, in common use a long, roughly made cigar of cheap tobacco that gave forth voluminous clouds of dense, black, acrid smoke, and which sold at four for a cent. Only those with strong stomachs could indulge in them, but to them life without them was not life. Probably no one thought them too strong. The name of Conestoga cigars was naturally attached to them, borrowed from the wagons and the horses. The name at least still survives in the stogie, a challenge still to any one who claims equality as a real smoker with those of old, though they say the stogie's present-day successors are, compared with their rough and ready ancestors, but a gentle smoke. Then when they had smoked and talked and drunk and danced as much as they wanted, every wagoner unrolled his bed, which he carried with him, on the barroom floor, all in a circle with their feet to the fire, and slept soundly till dawn. In the morning the wagoner's bill, including supper and breakfast, and

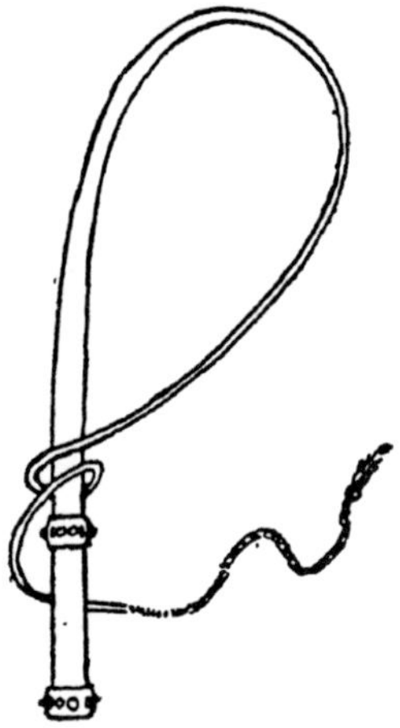

Wagoner's whip of leather

From a drawing by H. K. Landis, Landis Valley Museum

grain and hay for his six horses, never went over $1.75. And off they went, one by one, again, to the east with their flour or other produce; to the west with their salt or other supplies!

The stage driver was a superior being. Speed was of first importance with him. One of them said:

> Stage drivers as a class did not rank as high morally as wagoners, but despite this there were among them men of good sense, honest intentions and steady habits. . . . Stage driving was quite a lofty calling.

The stage driver lived and worked under greater nervous strain. He drove as a rule twenty miles a day over the mountains, to the wagoner's fifteen. To become in time a stage

From a drawing by Stanley M. Arthurs for "Scribner's Magazine"

The stage driver

driver was the height of many a young man's ambition growing up along the National Road; and a good many of them achieved it.

There was the same difference between the stagecoach and the Conestoga wagon that there was in later days between the passenger train with its high-speed locomotive and the freight train; or between the ocean steamship liner and the freighter. Speed was the important element in one, dependability in the other, type of transportation; and speed adds a thrilling element to a spectacle. The same man wrote out of a long life:

> To see it [a stagecoach] ascending a long hill, increasing speed when nearing the summit, then moving rapidly over the intervening level to the top of the next hill, and dashing down it, a driver like the stately Redding Bunting wielding the whip and handling the reins, revealed a scene that will never be forgotten.

The stagecoach had three seats on the inside with comfortable cushions and room for three passengers on each, and one outside sitting with the driver, ten in all. None rode on top on the National Road; it was too precarious. The stagecoaches did not yield to the Conestoga wagons in point of color and decoration. Each stagecoach had its name bravely painted on its sides, such as the General Harrison, the John Tyler, and the Industry. One had painted on its gilded sides the picture of a postboy with flying horse, blowing his horn and beneath in gilt letters the inscription:

> He comes, the herald of a noisy world,
> News from all nations lumbering at his back.

In prosperous times, it was not uncommon to see fifteen stagecoaches passing any point on the Road, one after another, almost in procession, in either direction—east and west together, thirty a day.

Naturally business organization reached the stagecoaches

with its stimulus and combined numbers of them into well-systematized companies. Lucius W. Stockton was the head of the naturally named National Road Stage Company. There was a People's Line. James Reeside put on a line which Stockton called the June Bug Line, claiming it would not survive the coming of the June bugs. But it did, so he

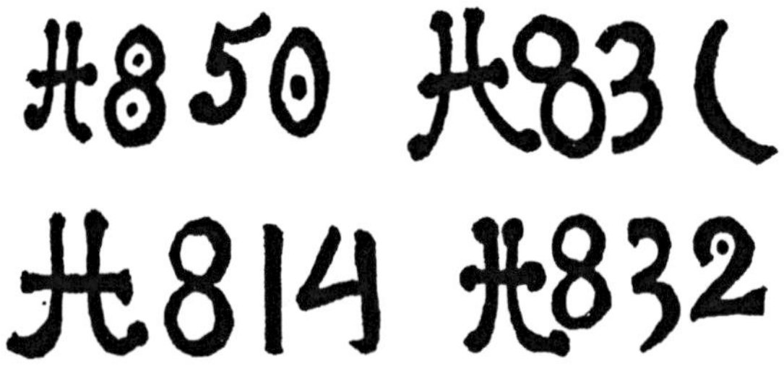

Courtesy Landis Valley Museum

Conestoga wagon dates in iron. It has been suggested that the odd form of the numeral one may stand for Jahr Herr Jesu

bought it out. There was a line of stagecoaches called the Good Intent Line, because they intended to stay; they did stay too, many years.

The mail coach was a special type of coach requiring the very greatest speed. It was built on a model supplied by the Post Office Department. Only three passengers were carried, in a special compartment on springs at the front end of the coach, just behind the driver. It was commonly called "the monkey box." The mail bags were carried in a long wooden box, resting without springs, on the axles. It was in use, however, not many years. The regular stagecoach took its place. The special inside construction of the mail coach proved to be not necessary, indeed the regular coach was more practical in the matter of accommodating the number of passengers to the quantity of mail to be carried.

Another memorable feature on the National Road was the postilion. He was a groom who with two horses ready harnessed waited the coming of a coach at the foot of the

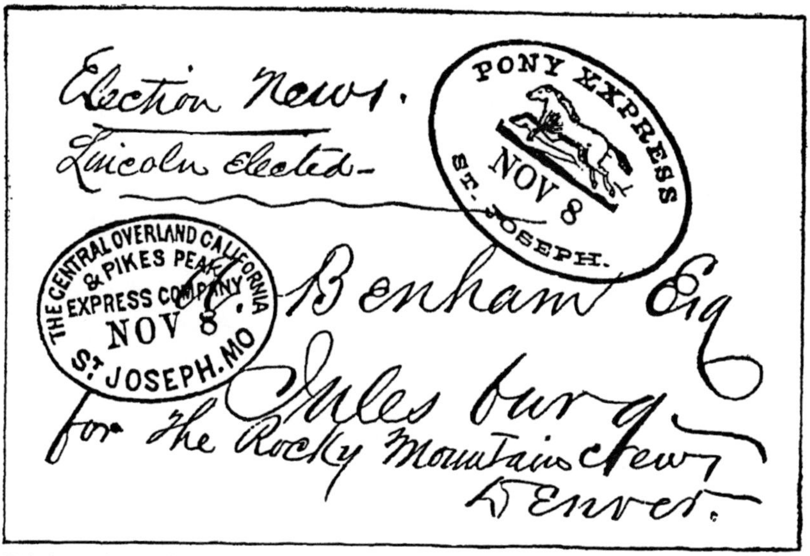

This letter is now in the Denver Museum

The first letter carried over the plains by the Pony Express, bearing the news of the election of Lincoln

longer, steeper hills in the mountains, who added his pair to the coach's four and helped the team up the hill. At the top he quickly detached his pair and returned to the bottom of the hill to wait for the next. There was a noted old postilion, a picturesque character, tall and thin, named Nathan Hutton, who built him a log house by the side of the National Road in a deep valley between two long hard hills about five miles east of Brownsville, Pennsylvania. He served stagecoaches going either west or east. A thoroughly reliable man himself, he believed implicitly in faithfulness in man and beast, and on occasion would exhort horse or man alike "to stand by his 'tarnal integrity."

The arrival of a stagecoach in any town was an exciting event. The horses were beautiful animals, lighter and more swift than the Conestogas, of fine breeds. They were cared for in stables, and every twelve miles or so a fresh relay was awaiting the coach. Driving at full speed up to the relay station, the driver stopped in the road, threw down his reins, and remained there in his seat. The grooms instantly detached the team, put in the fresh four horses, and tossed the reins up to the driver. Off he went at full speed again, night and day! Three styles of driving were generally recognized among the stagecoach drivers. They were: (1) the flat rein, which was the English style; (2) the top and bottom, which was distinctively Pennsylvanian; and (3) the side rein, or Eastern style, which was the one adopted by a majority of the best drivers over the National Road.

When a stagecoach driver did stop in a town or at a tavern longer than the minute or two just described, he was received as a personage. He was usually a well-dressed man, and one whose strong, masterly character showed in his face and quiet manners. He associated with the passengers when he wished. Eminent statesmen such as General William H. Harrison, Albert Gallatin, Andrew Jackson, Zachary Taylor, Sam Houston, Henry Clay, Lewis Cass, and

James K. Polk, as well as others equally well known, such as Jenny Lind and Phineas T. Barnum, travelled over the National Road and regarded many of the stagecoach drivers as their trusted friends. Governor Thomas Corwin of Ohio was at one time a wagoner.

One little sign of the superior recognition the drivers were accorded is that the whisky they drank cost five cents a glass instead of three cents as at the taverns where the wagoners stopped. The five-cent whisky may have been a fancy brand or, if the same, the higher price may have been a tribute to the great, but it is of record:

> The whisky of that day is said to have been pure, and many persons of unquestioned respectability affirm with much earnestness that it never produced delirium tremens.

An important feature of the Cumberland Road especially, and of the entire National Road, was the bridges. These were made of good material and were durable structures, as was necessary. As the heavily loaded swaying vehicles swept down upon these bridges from off the practically solid stone mountains, it was particularly important that they should be able to stand the shock and the strain. That they were properly constructed is proved by the fact that so many of them have lasted so many years.

Inns and taverns were found about every twelve miles along the Road. They were long houses substantially built of the prevailing local material, whether stone or wood (that is, logs). Their front stretched along the Road. They were conducted by a host who had a cordial welcome and an understanding heart, prompt attention, ample accommodation; and inexhaustible refreshment for all travellers. Many

A tavern host

From a drawing by Stanley M. Arthurs for "Scribner's Magazine"

of the innkeepers were retired wagoners or stagecoach drivers, or their widows. Innkeeper and wife were one, in fact as well as in theory, and when one died the other lived on and functioned efficiently for the two. Naturally many of the inns were located in towns, in towns where travel and trade originated, or where they met means for greater speed in transportation. But taverns located on the lonelier stretches of the Road were not the less appreciated and were in fact important in every way. A stagecoach was not lost until it failed to turn up at the next large town. City dwellers of the

Stagehouse on the National Road
From a drawing by John W. Thomason, Jr., for "The Adventures of Davy Crockett"

present must not indulge the notion that they have the only real system of regular living. On the contrary, so regular were the stagecoaches on their schedules that isolated farmers along the Road could correctly tell the time of day by their passing. If there was no checking up of the arrival of a stagecoach at its destination by stop-watch to the split second, there was a more public decision, more "openly arrived at," evident to all who lived along the Road, as to what stagecoach it was that arrived first at this town, at that inn, or at such and such a relay station. Two compass points only were of real importance in those days—on to the west, and back to the east. The idea of a greater America to the west permeated all of every age, dominated all ambition, all hope, and gave inspiration to the imagination of every youngster and every old man and woman. All lifted

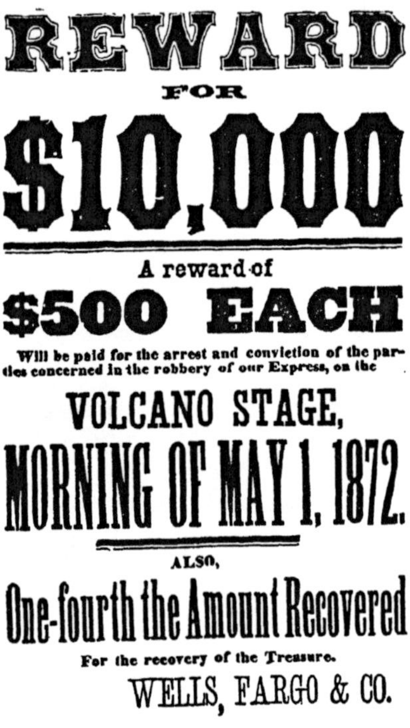

Reward circular

From the Jesse Charles Harraman Collection, in the Library of Congress

up their eyes to the hills; and as they came down into the prairie levels of the Mississippi Valley instinctively acquired the far-seeing eye.

So the great period of the Cumberland-National Road came to an end. It was never constructed through to St. Louis. That great period was from about 1815 to about 1840 or 1850. Its greatest service was to lead America over the mountains. The great commodity transported was America itself, the people. People, people, people, ever more people! Thereafter other means of transportation came. For the emigrants to the West, water transportation was waiting at the Ohio River. Water travel could not master the mountains. But when again the emigrants found water in abundant quantity and steady flood going their way to the West, they hailed it with joy, built rafts and broad flat-bottomed boats and floated on down the Ohio River to the Mississippi and into the great interior of the continent with its multiplicit opportunities and challenges.

The stagecoach and the Conestoga wagon even so were not losing their mission. Their task, inherited by the highways and the railways, was specialized more and carried on into a greater period of history and a vaster region, reaching out far ahead. One of the distinctive things about America is that it has always led forward into the unknown, into the new, and that its local life, wheresoever, whether in communities of few or of many people, has always trained up generations for the future with imaginations to respond nobly to the challenges farther along the road.

CHAPTER VI

Great Water Highways into the West

THE everyday things of the Ohio River and other rivers in their capacity as carriers of passengers and freight were somewhat similar to those of the National Road, and also progressively dissimilar. Accordingly life on the river was quite familiar to every boy and girl who went West, and no less was it intensely novel and exciting every hour of the day and night. The wagon of the road was on occasion a boat. Its successor of the actual river was so absolutely a boat that in many instances it was careless of its appearance and action as such. It was in fact a raft. It could be steered stern-end foremost; indeed it could be steered, if the proper skill were present, sidewise foremost also, which might be quite convenient in case of unexpectedly striking a dictatorial eddy in the current. Be it remembered, that in spite of these special abilities, the raft could still be steered fore-end foremost, and was so steered during large parts of the time. Men and women, boys and girls, in the great procession which constituted the section of the American population now under consideration, thrilled alike to the exciting education of the rivers and learned together the Western trait of stoicism under ever-new experience and recurrent surprise. And it all centered in the poker-faced art of steering your boat—which really was a raft!

Another important difference in the travelling conditions to which the raft adapted itself was in the packing of the traveller's goods. The Conestoga wagon ordinarily averaged at least 16 feet in length and 4 or 5 feet in width. It could be packed up to 6 or 7 feet above the bottom of the wagonbed, thus affording a "cargo space" on estimate of about 500 or 600 cubic feet at most. The raft might be 60 or even 100 feet long, and 20 feet wide. As to the height, quite literally the sky was the limit—within reason. It could easily carry ten times as great a load as a Conestoga Wagon. Indeed, it could carry the whole home place spread out on it. Not only food, seed for future crops, tools for starting their farms when they reached the haven where they decided that they would be, but also the horses, cattle, pigs, sheep and chickens—and dogs to round all up into their proper places at the proper times. All could be conveniently accommodated.

These figures might suggest that in not a few instances the rafts and their derivatives were larger than the rivers down which they floated. In one respect, which was an important one, this was the case—in the feeling the traveller had with regard to his journeying. Whether his craft was hardly larger than one of the river boats of the Eastern slopes and the earlier period, or in fact extraordinary in its dimensions, the immigrant felt he was floating on limitless currents westward into great possibilities and free opportunity. And that has been the special characteristic of all

Western Americans ever since. If they did not have that feeling of destiny before they went, they gathered it as they crossed the mountains and with the accumulating waters swept down the great river systems into a continental nationality.

All the boats in the rivers were more or less specialized, in construction, in operation, and in maintenance, from the raft. They were also, and even more, specialized to meet the needs, the facilities, and the desires of the particular families. They might be very distinctly *boats* and "not rafts at all," but they developed on the principle of the raft so as to render the peculiar service of the raft in some fairly efficient or even superior way. If the boat, whatever it may have been, be thought of primarily as a slightly or greatly modified raft, both the boat itself and the people who used it will be more readily understood. In the endless variety of these boats certain types were recognizable.

(1) The pirogue was a very large canoe. It was often 40 or 50 feet long and 6 or 8 feet wide. It could carry a whole family and several tons of goods. It cost $10 or $20, according to size.

(2) The bateau was a wide, flat-bottomed boat made of planks. It also could carry an entire family. It was propelled downstream by several pairs of long oars called sweeps; upstream it was poled. It was steered by another sweep at the stern. The cost was always over $20, and might reach $50. When small enough to use as a tender it was called a skiff, and cost only about $5.

(3) All the keelboats had a heavy timber, a four by four, running along the whole length of the bottom, to take the shock of collision with any under-water obstruction. From this they took their name. There were several types of keelboats, locally built and adapted to the conditions on their

Life on a keelboat

Redrawn from a lithograph published in "Fliegende Blätter," 1846

particular rivers. Keelboats were from 40 to 75 feet in length, often 9 feet wide, and carried a mast and sails. They usually had a running board on each side for use in poling upstream. They cost $2.50 or $3 per foot of the length. Keelboats were extensively used on all streams and came into general use with the increase in migration after the Ordinance of 1787 and long continued, probably because they offered a good average combination of simplicity of structure, durability, moderate cost, and adaptability.

(4) The ark was a heavy unwieldy boat, but durable; it was much in use on the Ohio. Its timbers cost all of $100. It was 75 or 100 feet long, often 20 feet wide and from 3 to 5 feet deep in its cargo space. Both bow and stern were broadly pointed and on occasion could serve somewhat as a ram provided the floating trouble-maker were not too heavy nor met in too swift a current. There was usually a house at one end for the family and an enclosure for the animals at the other. The steering oar had to be itself something like 40 feet long and required two men to manage it. The ark was always a difficult boat to manage and could never go upstream. On reaching its destination, it was broken up and sold as lumber, bringing sometimes $25. It was emphatically a one-way boat.

(5) "The flatboat was the standard water vehicle for travelling families and was a creation of the Ohio River valley," as Seymour Dunbar, the authority on American travel, has said. It varied greatly in size and in everything else. Its construction varied according to the nature of the streams to be navigated, the length of the journey, the freight to be carried, the probability of attack by Indians, if in the earlier days or in the more Western regions, and the purpose to which the timber would be put at the end of the trip. A flatboat 20 feet long and 10 feet wide was a very small one. Sometimes it was 60 feet long and 20 feet wide. The hull was made of square timbers of hard wood and

Upstream and downstream on a flatboat and two keelboats

From "The Keelboat Age on Western Waters," by Leland D. Baldwin. University of Pittsburgh Press when laden it often drew 2½ feet of water. Its hull rose 4 feet or more above the river. On top of the hull the side walls rose 4 feet higher. The whole was enclosed by heavy planks and covered by a roof. There were occasionally windows and a trap door in the roof. The flatboat was distinctly a downstream boat, and was steered by a great sweep as long as the boat itself. It was equipped with all domestic facilities. The livestock was kept in an open yard at one end of the boat. The family wash was hung out on the roof to dry, and the upper deck was often enclosed as a playground for the children, or if there were no small children, for all. Even in the names there was some variety. A Kentucky boat was a small flatboat destined for the Kentucky regions along the Ohio River. A New Orleans boat was an extra large flatboat going down the entire length of the Mississippi River. A broadhorn was a flatboat propelled by two great oars, one on either side of the boat, making the craft somewhat resemble the long-horn cattle of the West, with a third behind as a steering oar.

(6) The barge and the Ohio packet boat were express boats. They were used specially by business men who wanted to save time in their journeys. Practically smaller and larger sizes of the same kind of boat, the barge was 30 to 70 feet long and 7 to 12 feet wide. The Ohio packet boat was 75 to 100 feet long and 15 to 20 feet wide. Both had a mast, sails and rudder. They progressed generally at the rate of four or five miles an hour with the current, or about two miles an hour upstream, when they were propelled by men using

iron-tipped poles. Ohio packet boats went regularly between Pittsburgh, Cincinnati, and Louisville, carrying both passengers and freight before steamboats were introduced. By Ohio packet boat one could make the round trip between Pittsburgh and Cincinnati in a month and even have a day or two free for transacting business before starting back on the return trip.

The chief power for all this transportation was the simple one of natural floating. But floating had the strict limitation of being only one-way. Except in an eddy, there was no floating upstream. When the travellers decided they wanted to go up some tributary stream, whether of size to be recognized as a full-size river or merely as a little personal entrance to the future farm, new factors came into the situation. The active steady power of water-gravity had to be replaced by personal human power generated in the arms and legs of the travellers themselves; and the power had to be steady. The force of the current had to be felt and deducted from the force exerted by the travellers in the hope of making upstream progress. The result lay not on the lap of the gods, as it did in the gentle art of floating, but on the knees of the immigrants themselves. Needless to say the heavy part of the traffic went straight along down the Ohio and Mississippi rivers in journeys from 300 to 2000 miles long. This kind of travel flourished until 1840 and after, though the decline set in soon after 1830. The cause of this decline was the rapid multiplication of steamboats after that date. The steamboat endowed upstream travel with all the ease and convenience of downstream floating, making only a moderate deduction in the speed upstream—as a tax, so to speak—for the acknowledged privileges conveyed.

The period of danger from Indians ended much later in the Ohio Valley than on the Atlantic Coast. Nor were the Indians by any means the only cause of sudden death encountered by the immigrants. Accidents in the powerful currents were quite as serious and as ever-present a menace. Until the 1830s and 1840s this might appropriately be called the period of sudden death. And the travellers thought about it, incessantly—not nervously, but as a matter of everyday active concern. So too they thought about a future possible release from continual danger—at first only as a wish, then as a hope, until at last the beginnings of real release began to appear! When all was done, what did the westward-bound American think of the future? He knew his own personality as the dominant element in his life, indeed as quite a dictatorial element. Was there a similar dominant personality in all life, and did his own personality continue after that interruption at the behest of some Indian or of some snag in the swollen current? What was death?

We can now see that in those times, in those regions, the general attitude was a vivid one. They were vivid people. It should be noticed also that there was a definite outcropping forthwith of interest in religious questions, of co-operation with each other in that interest, and in the creation of religious organizations. All this went along with the increasing migration, and both downstream navigation and death-

endangered religion had the same general characteristics. The coming of steam brought a new freedom of thought, a new emotional and moral experience, a new religious viewpoint to the travellers as well as a new convenience in transportation. This new religious interest showed itself in various forms all the way from a rather crude though sincere spiritualism to a highly intellectual, indeed scientific agnosticism. General, however, was a large and practical morality, extending with its intellectual or moral sympathy over greater and greater and newer areas of population in the West. The most important fact is that it was all made up of the fibres of individual experience, and therefore *it was all everyday.*

It could not be treated as a merely general unrelated event when the father of a family was killed and the mother had to carry on and bring up the children alone. How was it the mother became strong in the emergency? Whence came her strength? as the travellers themselves were apt to express it. There was no *knowledge* whence, but to assert there was no life "future" to this life would hardly have seemed intelligent to the travellers. Conditions might be different after death—as in fact they were between the Ohio and the Mississippi, but there were conditions "there" and they would find out what they were "when they got there." Those conditions might be terrible (appropriately called Hell), or might be happy (appropriately called Heaven) but all were personal. There, in loving companionships true affection continued, and all that was not loving and strong faded. What was to come "in the future" was all exactly like life on the flatboat, and on the steamboat. Life on the rivers during this period of their migration cast their ideas of the future life and of their religion into the mold of their circumstances. Their religion became inevitably vibrant, genuine, and in the highest sense of the word everyday.

The age of steam was coming upon the great rivers to replace the native power of gravity, and the resultant change was miraculous. It had been coming as by inevitable destiny ever since the atmospheric steam engine had been invented by Thomas Newcomen in 1712; since James Watt had repaired the model of a Newcomen engine for the College of Glasgow in 1763; and since Richard Trevithick had built his first steam road carriage in the Cornish town of Camborne in 1801. But all these beginnings were in Great Britain and, so far as America was concerned, were prehistoric.

Means for adapting steam to water transportation was invented for the first time in America by John Fitch (1743–1798). Fitch was a heroic, sensitive and therefore a tragic figure. He had faults or shortcomings which proved fatal to him and unfortunate to the public. There are two elements in successful inventing: one is technical; the other commercial. There are times when it is difficult to say which is more important. Steamboat transportation could have been an everyday thing years before it was, except for the American predilection of the time for ridicule as an expression of profound wisdom. If John Fitch had had money at his disposal, or appreciated the importance of having money at his disposal, he might well have overawed the public, acquired a train of respectful followers, and established his steamboats as the great invention of his time and the invaluable means of developing the West—which they

John Fitch's second steamboat

From "Eighty Years Progress in the United States," by Eminent Literary Men, 1861

certainly were. But as things were, his experience was bitter and the story of his life sad.

In 1785 Fitch, living in Bucks County, Pennsylvania, began his work on steamboats. He applied to Congress for subsidies on the strength of what he was positive he could do. But Congress was not appropriating money on the basis of what to them were interesting theoretical assurances. The same was true of several scientific societies of the time. However, in 1786 the Legislature of New Jersey, and in 1787 the Legislatures of Pennsylvania, New York, Delaware and Virginia voted him the exclusive privilege for fourteen years of building and operating steamboats on the waters of those States. This seemed wonderful to him. With the inducement of these privileges Fitch managed to organize a group of Philadelphia men who brought him some support, and he started work on a 45-foot boat, propelled by 12 paddles, 6 on each side. This he successfully launched on the Delaware River at Philadelphia on August 22, 1787. In July, 1788, he launched and operated a 60-foot boat propelled by steam paddle-wheels on numerous voyages between Philadelphia and Burlington, New Jersey. On October 12, 1788, this second boat of his made the 20 miles upstream in 3 hours and 10 minutes. But the onlooking public demanded perfect operation on first trial on penalty of free sarcasm and scathing comment.

Fitch received a United States patent on August 26, 1791, and a French patent soon after. He had found money to build a still larger boat in 1790, but it was not convincing to the critics. His fourth steamboat, named the *Perseverance,* was wrecked before it was completed. He went hopefully to France for two years, only to return destitute to his birthplace, East Windsor, Connecticut. Then he built and launched a steamboat propelled by a steam propeller on the Collect Pond in New York City. Ridicule was the only reward of all his achievements. Utterly discouraged, he betook himself to the Kentucky forests to escape the jeers of the ignorant public he had tirelessly sought to benefit. There he saved up some pills, one by one, prescribed by a physician. He took them all at once, probably hoping in some kind of sleep "to end the heartache and the thousand natural shocks that flesh is heir to," but without the kindly understanding that Hamlet's great creator left to all the discouraged. His last prediction looks like a locomotive to draw carriages over the land on wheels. In the Ohio Valley, which should have been the scene of his triumph inaugurating a new period of transportation for America, crushed and broken-hearted, he died.

After the death of John Fitch the leaders in the development of the steamboat were Robert Fulton (1765–1815), Robert R. Livingston (1746–1813), John Stevens (1767–1838), and Nicholas J. Roosevelt (1767–1854). Later Thomas Gibbons (1757–1826) and Aaron Ogden (1756–1839), played an important contentious part in the history of the steamboat and brought the truly majestic and beneficent figure of Chief Justice John Marshall into its history.

Robert Fulton was an elegant international young figure at the time he first met Chancellor Livingston, and he was versatile withal. He started out in Philadelphia with a desire to become a painter of miniatures and portraits in 1782. He went to England in 1786 or 1787 continuing his study of painting. He exhibited at the Royal Academy of 1791. Then he turned his attention to canals and to torpedoes, getting steadily into a perspicacious interest in marine propulsion. Then he went to France. In Paris through Joel Barlow he met Edward Livingston, who introduced him to his brother, the former Chancellor of New York, Robert

R. Livingston, at that time Minister to France, "as just the man you want." Chancellor Livingston had negotiated the Louisiana Purchase and realized the character and the importance of the great rivers of the West. He had enough imagination and enough technical intelligence also to realize the possible importance of the steamboat, indeed he said that he had some ideas of his own on the subject but that his diplomatic duties would not permit him to give it prime attention. It was to this fact that Edward Livingston referred.

On October 10, 1802, Chancellor Livingston and Robert Fulton signed a legal partnership agreement. It provided that they should construct a boat 120 feet long, 8 feet wide and 15 inches draught, to carry 60 passengers, and to run 8 miles an hour in still water. Fulton was to build an experimental boat at a cost of £500, which amount Livingston was to advance; and Fulton was to take out a United States patent, the ownership of which and the profits from which should be shared between them equally for the duration of the patent, fourteen years. There were other appropriate financial and technical provisions.

The experimental steamboat was built and launched in Paris on the Seine instead of in England, so as to have the experimenting done with the advantage of consultation with Livingston. The machinery was, however, too heavy for the boat. During a stormy night the weight tore through the hull and sunk the whole thing in the river. A new and larger hull was at once built and the engine, which was not injured, was reinstalled. Fulton returned to America to carry out his agreement with Livingston in December, 1806. He at once proceeded to build the steamboat. The contract for building the hull was given to Charles Browne, a shipbuilder of Corlear's Hook on the East River, who pushed the work during the spring of 1807. When launched it was taken to Paulus Hook Ferry, where Fulton built the framing and gearing for the Boulton & Watt Engine that he had secured for it, and the engine was installed by April 23.

At first, until 1810, the boat was simply called the steamboat. It was not until that year called the *Clermont.* The boat was 133 feet long, 18 feet wide, and 7 feet deep; it was decked over a short ways both bow and stern. Behind the Boulton & Watt engine was the 20-foot boiler set in brick and housed over. Two side paddle wheels, 15 feet in diameter, propelled the boat.

Without delay, after his agreement with Fulton, Livingston through the influence of his friends had arranged for Congress to pass an Act on April 5, 1803, by which the rights of monopoly granted to John Fitch should be granted to him and Robert Fulton for twenty years on proof being produced within two years of the conditions being fulfilled. The two years was later extended to April, 1807. From the standpoint of the partners, it will be seen that Livingston was very wise, indeed shrewd. Through all the preliminary period, there was no uncertainty in regard to their rights. Fulton's first voyage on the Hudson River benefited by all the financial and business advantages that Fitch lacked. Furthermore, while Fitch could depend on little but his own personal confidence, Fulton had money at his disposal, technical understanding, business ability, political vision, and commercial statesmanship—all in the person of Robert R. Livingston—which was as it should be.

Fulton put the boat in motion in the water for the first time on Sunday, August 9, 1807, at about 12 o'clock noon, just four years after the steamboat trial on the Seine. He found certain lacks in the propelling apparatus, and supplied them. On the day he had appointed, Monday, August 17, 1807, he made the trial. Henry W. Dickinson has given a very concise statement of the notable event.

> At one o'clock the boat left her moorings at a dock on the North River; on board were about forty guests, almost wholly relatives and intimate friends. So quietly had everything been done that only one paper, the *American Citizen,* announced the coming event; nevertheless a large number of spectators were present. The excitement was intense, the incredulity, scorn, and ridicule that had met him at every turn while "Fulton's Folly," for so the boat was nicknamed, was being built, gave way perforce to silence first and then to shouts of applause and congratulation.[1a]

Robert Fulton wrote a letter to *The American Citizen* on Friday, August 21, 1807:

> I arrived this afternoon at 4 o'clock in the steamboat from Albany. As the success of my experiment gives me great hopes that such boats may be rendered of much importance to my country, to prevent erroneous opinions and to give some satisfaction to the

[1a]H. W. Dickinson: *Robert Fulton,* page 217.

friends of useful improvements, you will have the goodness to publish the following statement of facts:

I left New York on Monday at 1 o'clock and arrived at Clermont, the seat of Chancellor Livingston, at 1 o'clock on Tuesday; time 24 hours; distance 110 miles. On Wednesday I departed from the Chancellor's at 9 in the morning and arrived at Albany at 5 in the afternoon; distance 40 miles; time 8 hours; the sum of this is 150 miles in 32 hours—equal near 5 miles an hour.

On Thursday, at 9 o'clock in the morning, I left Albany and arrived at the Chancellor's at 6 in the evening; I started from thence at 7 and arrived at New York at 4 in the afternoon; time 30 hours, space run through, 150 miles—equal to 5 miles an hour. Throughout my whole way, both going and returning, the wind was ahead; no advantage could be derived from my sail. The whole was therefore performed by the power of the steam engine.

This was the great achievement of Robert Fulton and Robert R. Livingston, establishing in the public consciousness that the steam engine was the means for national development.

But why should Robert Fulton be generally regarded as the inventor of the steamboat when both John Fitch and John Stevens built and operated steamboats on American waters before he did? It may be that the popular recognition is justified on technical, legal, or other grounds. This book does not pretend to be competent to give an authoritative answer to the question, but it would suggest that a mere comparison of dates may not be enough alone to determine it. One who has a right to express an opinion on the point, Carl W. Mitman of the United States National Museum, has said:

While Fitch constructed four successful steamboats, he gave little or no attention to construction and operating costs, failed completely to see the need for demonstrating the economical aspects of steam navigation and accordingly lost all financial support. For this reason, the steamboat era may be said to begin with Robert Fulton, who launched his first steamboat after the death of Fitch.

Is not then the economic element in invention an essential element for the reader to consider?

The steamboat, soon called the *North River,* and in 1810 renamed the *Clermont,* repeated its successful voyage to Albany and so also did other steamboats, which built up a regular line of service between the two cities. Livingston and Fulton in later years worked to establish a monopoly for their partnership in the use of the waters of the State.

Nicholas J. Roosevelt was interested in steam engines from the standpoint of a manufacturer as early as 1793. He built factories at Belleville, New Jersey, which he named Soho after the Boulton & Watt factories in England. He had some success there at first. His affairs took a significant direction when in 1797 he signed an agreement with Robert R. Livingston and John Stevens to build a steamboat on joint account, though his great time had not yet come. In 1809 Roosevelt made a journey through the Ohio and Mississippi Valleys to study the river conditions for the use of steamboats. Livingston and Fulton were trying to get the Governor and Legislature of Louisiana to grant them the monopoly of steamboat construction and operation in the

From Lloyd's Steamboat Directory, 1856

First boat built on the Western waters, 1812

waters of the State, which meant in the lower Mississippi, and commercially the southern ports. They promised as soon as the monopoly was voted to send a steamboat down the rivers as soon as possible. On April 19, 1811, this assurance was given, and Livingston and Fulton immediately sent workmen to Pittsburgh under Nicholas J. Roosevelt to begin building the *New Orleans,* a small boat of only 100 tons burden, propelled by a stern paddle wheel and with two masts in reserve for auxiliary service.

The *New Orleans* started from Pittsburgh in October, 1811. As far as Louisville the voyage was a continued jubilation. It was the first steamboat to be seen on the Ohio River. People had heard that there were steamboats in the East, and they knew that one was being built at Pittsburgh. Here it was! It was true! The only persons on board were Nicholas J. Roosevelt, his wife and family, the pilot, a crew of six, and a few servants. At Louisville, low water over the Falls of the Ohio held the *New Orleans* up for three weeks. During this time the steamboat made several round trips back to Cincinnati. At the end of November the water had risen and the *New Orleans* was able to continue its voyage, reaching its namesake haven in fourteen days. After a reasonable time the steamboat made its return trip *upstream* using as fuel the wood Roosevelt had contracted to be cut and piled for that purpose on the way downstream. The voyage of the *New Orleans* was a great demonstration. One single steamboat in almost incredible contrast with a riverful of flatboats of all kinds, sizes, and descriptions. The great thing was that the *people* had changed. Now they had faith in the future!

Seymour Dunbar in his *History of Travel in America* shows the swift increase of speed in travel on the great rivers by a table giving the time taken by steamboat trip from Louisville to New Orleans in various years between 1815 and 1853. This table is herewith given.

Year	*Steamboat*	*Days*	*Hrs.*	*Min.*	*Year*	*Steamboat*	*Days*	*Hrs.*	*Min.*
1815	*Enterprise*	25	2	40	1840	*Shippen*	5	14	00
1817	*Washington*	25	0	00	1844	*Sultana*	5	12	00
1818	*Shelby*	20	4	20	1849	*Bostona*	5	8	00
1819	*Paragon*	18	10	00	1851	*Belle Key*	4	23	00
1828	*Tecumseh*	8	4	00	1852	*Reindeer*	4	20	45
1834	*Tuscarora*	7	16	00	1852	*Eclipse*	4	18	00
1837	*Gen. Brown*	6	22	00	1853	*Shotwell*	4	10	20
1837	*Sultana*	6	15	00	1853	*Eclipse*	4	9	30

Probably no one needs to be reminded that life on the steamboats and along the shores of the rivers during this period was vividly depicted by Mark Twain in *Life on the Mississippi.*

One cannot, however, get a complete and truthful picture of the times and forces that accelerated the westward expansion of America without the stalwart and versatile figure of John Stevens of Hoboken (1749–1838). In 1788 he first learned of John Fitch's work and saw his steamboat on the Delaware River. He recognized the importance of steam as a motive power at once and gave it special attention thenceforth in his researches and experiments. In 1791 he obtained one of the earliest United States patents, for a vertical steam boiler, followed in 1803 by a patent for a multitubular boiler.

In 1797 he met Nicholas J. Roosevelt and formed a business partnership with him for the manufacture of steam engines.

In 1802 his first steamboat was launched, the *Polacca.* Then in 1804 came his *Little Juliana,* with its twin screw propellers, which two of his sons ran across the Hudson River and back successfully. In 1806 he began work on a 100-foot steamboat for passenger and freight service, the *Phœnix,* which he completed in 1808. Meanwhile Fulton and Livingston had secured a state monopoly for operating steamboats on the waters of New York State and in 1807 had sailed the *Clermont* up to Albany and back. Fulton and Livingston had invited Stevens to join them in this monopoly, but characteristically he declined on account of his agreement with Roosevelt. Stevens was therefore precluded from operating the *Phœnix* on the Hudson River. Accordingly, in 1809 he sent the *Phœnix* around to Philadelphia and the Delaware River by sea. It performed the voyage with entire success, and in this way became the first seagoing steamboat in the world.

During these years the ocean commerce was carried by the winds of heaven, filling the sails of those Valkyries of the Sea, the clipper ships. Those winds were unremittingly subject to the will and skill of the skippers. In storms there were many times when to speak of them as the winds of heaven would be distinctly misleading. Triumphantly associated forever with the oriental trade to China and to India, the clippers were during most of the nineteenth century outside the direct experience of everyday life, except in those ports—

like Salem, Boston, New York, Philadelphia, and Baltimore —from which they cleared, and to which like high-strung race horses, they swept home. The clippers were things that Americans heard much about as they penetrated farther and farther west across the mountains and across the prairie seas.

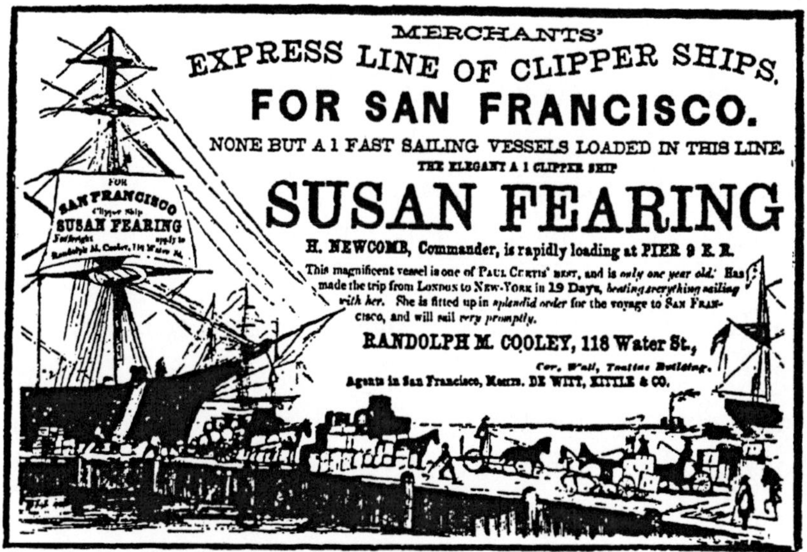

From the New York Historical Society Collection

Advertisement of the Merchants' Express Line of clipper ships

But circuses were closer to the everyday experience of most American families; and so were horse races. Every one had a horse, as every one has a car now, and every one raced his horse, some way or other, whether in set races at the County Fair, or just on sudden inspiration or feudal rivalry down the village street—any old plug! It is unfortunately not expedient to attempt the story of those marvellous vessels, the clippers, in this book. Their life, emerging in the time of the Revolutionary War[1] and, after the steamships *Sirius* and *Great Western* in 1838, and the first iron merchantman, the *Great Britain,* in 1844, yielding full right of seaway to the steamships only in the time of the Civil War, was all of it out on the ocean. This volume would better restrict itself to the development of America on land. The center of American population soon began to draw away from the Atlantic seaboard and to press on westward to Indiana and Illinois. But the reward for those who seek out the records and tales of the clippers, found in the logs and the yarns of the old salts, is ample, unfailing, and thrilling.

Meantime in the law courts a struggle had been going on, involving important issues, between the partnership of Livingston and Fulton and their legal successors against those who demanded the free right in all States to build steamboats and to steer them where they would, as their predecessors had had the right to build and to float or steer, if they could, their rafts and flatboats. Finally one Thomas Gibbons appealed his case against one Aaron Ogden, the heir of the monopoly, to the United States Supreme Court. Gibbons engaged Daniel Webster as his attorney. The case was decided by the full bench with an opinion written and delivered by Chief Justice John Marshall, on March 2, 1824, in favor of the freedom of the navigable waters of the entire United States. John Fitch, John Stevens, Robert Fulton, Robert R. Livingston, and others had done their work. Now all America could enter into their labors!

[1]See *Everyday Things in American Life,* Volume I, pages 223–228.

CHAPTER VII

When Canals Had Their Day

IT IS a significant fact that the *New Orleans* on that first voyage down the Ohio-Mississippi River was held up for three weeks at Louisville by low water over the Falls of the Ohio. Every one thinks of rivers like the Ohio as having a thousand times more water in them than was needed for the early navigation. But the volume of water in the river made little or no difference. It was its behavior that counted. Benjamin Franklin concisely stated the case for canals in a letter in 1772:

> Rivers are ungovernable things, especially in hilly countries, Canals are quiet and always manageable.

Advances in American life about this time were being fostered by a new element that was becoming evident. It was the general knowledge of the existence somewhere of greater things. It was purely ideal in character and needed not be tangible at all. A good instance was the knowledge in the towns and settlements down the Ohio and the Mississippi rivers in 1811 that there were steamboats in the East and that one was actually at the time being built at Pittsburgh. To some extent this was reliable report; to some extent, in some places, it could have been only mere gossip, correct or incredible in detail. But whatever its worth as early communication this crude knowledge became a real power in changing the attitude of western Americans toward the problems of migration and the development of those regions. Purely ideal and intangible as it was, such knowledge became a potent force and an everyday element in their life. In the influence of this new element is to be found the cause of

Robert Fulton's idea for a market or passage boat for use on canals
After a drawing in Robert Fulton's "Canal Navigation," London, 1796

such success as there was and of the industrial tragedy of the canal period.

Americans knew something about canals, the small canals of the Atlantic Coast, and also, at least by hearsay, the more important canals of England, associated by some of them with the name of the rising young American, Robert Fulton. Accordingly, to overcome the difficulties of river travel and traffic, not only leading men—Washington, Governor George Clinton, General Philip Schuyler, Elkanah Watson —thought of the canal as a solution, but the less prominent citizens who, when the leaders spoke, listened and gave effective support. The suggestion was logical and practical, provided it could be carried out with financial wisdom and on a large enough scale to meet the problems. So it was that canals grew up as corollary to the great natural water systems, spreading over the immigrant routes and reaching into all parts of the States formed from the Northwest Territory. First, rivers supplemented by auxiliary canals; later, the canals aspiring to be independent of the rivers and to take their place as trunk lines.

The canal period continued from about 1815 to about 1854. During this time there were three major canals built and maintained—the Pennsylvania, the Chesapeake and Ohio, and the Erie. This is almost a flat and deliberate misstatement. The Pennsylvania was only in part a canal, and that broken in the middle. The Chesapeake and Ohio was never completed. Only the Erie, of the three, was completed, has been maintained down to the present, and is still important. All three of these canals had their terminals at or near the edge of the Allegheny watershed, and their purposes were all alike to control the commerce of that central Mississippi basin and draw it to the ports of New York, Philadelphia, and Baltimore on the North Atlantic ocean front.

The Chesapeake and Ohio Canal had its origin in a plan urged by General George Washington in 1784. It was incorporated at about that time in Virginia and in Maryland under the name of The Potomac Canal Company with Washington himself as president. At the time of his death the active interest in the canal fell off, but in 1816 the interest emphatically revived. The idea struggled along through

State and Federal politics and finance until June, 1828, when it was organized as The Chesapeake and Ohio Canal Company. Ground was broken and construction begun on July 4. When all was ready, in accordance with the ceremony arranged, President John Quincy Adams took up a spade, stepped forward, and thrust it into the ground. But he struck a root. The earth of the first spadeful was not enough even for the purposes of ceremony. The incident seemed to be rather typical of the story of the canal to date. The action of President Adams was no less characteristic of the quiet determination of the man who endured four years of malignant hostility from his political enemies. On the present occasion President Adams laid down the spade, took off his hat and coat, picked up the spade again, and made another vigorous thrust into the ground. The work of excavation and construction had now been successfully begun. Localism was still powerful in public affairs, and was still snarling.

The great difficulty of canal building appeared in the experience incurred with this notable project of the Chesapeake and Ohio Canal. It was not one of engineering; it was primarily one of finance and of what financing involved. By the summer of 1831 twenty miles of the Canal had been finished from the Falls of the Potomac near Georgetown, but the company had taken on a controversy with the incipient Baltimore & Ohio Railroad. In another year the Federal Government had withdrawn from the project, and the State of Maryland was left alone with the whole responsibility. The depression of 1837, by which time construction had been finished to one hundred miles west of Georgetown, did not help matters. In 1841 the State of Maryland itself had to face the possibility of bankruptcy. At last, by 1850, persistent ability and public spirit carried the Chesapeake and Ohio Canal to Cumberland, Maryland. Beyond that it was never constructed. It was 184 miles long and 68 feet wide. Six feet deep, it accommodated by mid-century canal boats of 180 tons capacity. Its chief traffic was transporting coal from the Cumberland mines to Washington. It surmounted an elevation of 609 feet by means of 73 locks. The cost was about $14,000,000.

The Pennsylvania Canal came to its completion over physical difficulties rather than over political and financial difficulties. The first error was one of policy, of trying to canalize a succession of four rivers across the state, the Susquehanna, the Juniata, the Conemaugh, and the Kiskiminetis. A Pennsylvanian, Benjamin Franklin, had, as noted, long before stated briefly and clearly the trouble with this policy. In truth, no mountain river would stay put, and these four rivers were either primarily or secondarily mountain rivers. That the State of Pennsylvania could compete with the State of New York for the trade of the Ohio Valley by means of canals or by any other means was not to be questioned, but it remained a fact that while New York's Erie Canal had to surmount an altitude of about 500 feet by means of locks in a distance of 360 miles, the Pennsylvania Canal would have to surmount an altitude of something like 2300 feet in a distance of only 320 miles. Without unpleasant advertising it might simply be said that the cost of the Erie's 500 feet with attendant expenses came to more than $10,000,000, and 8 years of time.

The people of Pennsylvania, however, were determined, and that determination was becoming general and was reflected in the Legislature, which in 1824 voted a commission to investigate and report on the question. In 1826 this commission reported that a canal was practicable except for the highest ridges of the Allegheny Mountains, and the Legislature voted to commit the State to the construction of a canal, and to the use therefor of State money. Direct responsibility financially and direct consideration of the local conditions from the engineering point of view were thus insured. The individual character of the canal was the most important thing about it.

This attention to local conditions did valuable service every mile of the way from Philadelphia to Pittsburgh. After the work was completed the first section of the journey was made by a horse-drawn car over a rail way, 89½ miles, from Philadelphia to Columbia, a town on the Susquehanna River about 25 miles below Harrisburg and in the same latitude as Philadelphia. The local principle applied even to the extent of respectful heed to a hill that interrupted the route, on account of which the traveller was conveyed over an altitude of 187 feet secured by a hawser over an inclined plane 2805 feet long. Then literal horse power resumed its able service. The first 20 miles of this section was put into operation in September, 1832; the rest of the road to Columbia in October, 1834. The important distinction between the two sections was that those first 20 miles served as good publicity and argument for the entire project to the people of the State and especially to those living in and near the city of Philadelphia.

From Columbia the canal—a real canal, not a substitute—ran 172 miles to Hollidaysburg, up in the highest part of the mountains. It will be noticed that practically all the way, certainly after leaving the Susquehanna to follow the Juniata, the canal lay through genuine Scotch-Irish country, of whose determined character instances were given in *Everyday Things in American Life,* Volume I, Chapter VIII. The canal was itself an achievement, as any one will realize who nowadays travels comfortably by train or automobile through the region. It was 40 feet wide at top (wide for those mountains), 28 feet wide at bottom, and 4 feet deep. There were 108 locks in the 172 miles, a lock almost every mile and a half. Then came the great achievement! For here, between Hollidaysburg and Johnstown at the summit of the Alleghenies, the mountains rose to a height of 2300 feet above sea-level, and they did not do it gently. The distance was only 36½ miles, and the nature of the acclivity was mostly precipitous broken rock.

On account of its up-and-down character, the decision with respect to the construction of this short distance of 36½ miles was taken in 1831 to the Legislature so that, whatever was done, it might have public authorization. The summit of the mountain range was 10 miles west of Hollidaysburg. Five inclined planes were built to this point from Hollidaysburg and thence five more down to Johnstown on the western slope. The traveller took a seat in one of two cars on a rail road, and two stationary engines of 35 horsepower each at the top of every inclined plane by cables pulled the two cars up the total of 1398 and a fraction feet to the summit; and then lowered them down another total of 1171 and a fraction feet over the series of five more inclined planes to Johnstown. The traveller changed cars at every inclined plane. At Johnstown the traveller, with the pride of a survivor, re-embarked on a canal boat, surveyed the inclined planes behind him from the safer point of view, decided that descent was always more dangerous than ascent, and contemplated that he had surmounted a combined altitude of 2570 feet and lived. From Johnstown to Pittsburgh was a simple matter of a canal-boat voyage of 104 miles, though with 66 locks en route. But every sedentary reader of the present as well as the adventurous travellers of the time will agree that the Pennsylvania Canal was a resourceful piece of engineering, a triumph, in offering a trip of 394 miles always covered in four days!

Charles Dickens took the trip in 1842 and told about it in his *American Notes.*

On Sunday morning we arrived at the foot of the mountain, which is crossed by rail road. There are ten inclined planes, five *as*cending and five *de*scending; the carriages are dragged up the

> former and let slowly down the latter by stationary engines; the comparatively level spaces between being traversed sometimes by horse and sometimes by engine power, as the case demands. Occasionally the rails are laid upon the extreme verge of a giddy precipice; and looking from the carriage window the traveller gazes sheer down without a stone or scrap of fence between, into the mountain depths below. The journey is very carefully made, however, only two carriages travelling together; and while proper precautions are taken is not to be dreaded for its dangers.

There never was any record of serious accident on these 36½ miles. From Johnstown to Pittsburgh the traveller merely continued his journey. There was nothing to occasion special remark.

But extraordinary, thrilling, and inconvenient as this "canal trip" over the mountains was, it was not to be compared with an improvement thereon that was worked out by local enterprise as part of the everyday life and possibilities of the time. The incident in which it originated was truly great, and it was great because of the general attitude of the men concerned in it. A man, a Pennsylvanian, living on the Lackawanna River, whose name is lost to fame, decided, as many others did, to take his family and move out West, beyond the Mississippi. So, as the others did, he built himself a boat; it was like a small-sized flatboat. He put his family and all he owned aboard, and floated down the Lackawanna River. The women-folk had the meals hot and ready on time from the start. This was not in his opinion anything exceptional. Almost any day one could see families floating past down the river on the home-made boats that were their homes. No man would think of taking his family West that way now.

They floated down the Lackawanna to the Susquehanna and down the Susquehanna to Columbia and the Pennsylvania Canal. He got his flatboat transferred to the Canal and went on by the smooth canal and up the 108 locks through the mountains (sometimes called foothills) to Hollidaysburg. Here the Lackawanna man knew he must give up his boat, sell it as lumber, and go on over the mountains, "hiring" his way from others. He probably, in looking for a purchaser for his lumber, expressed his regret at having to sell. But the canal people there at Hollidaysburg were not asleep. Difficulties to them were challenges. They were no doubt waiting for a man to come along who had his nerve with him. Here he was! So they made a proposition to him. Would he take a chance on letting them try to rig up a car that would carry his boat and take it in "as is" condition up the five inclined planes and down the other five inclined planes over the mountain to Johnstown? There he could slip it off the car into the canal again and he could go on without extra expense to Pittsburgh, and on a thousand miles more in his own boat down the Ohio River to St. Louis or wherever he wanted to go. The Lackawanna man said he would take the chance. He did; they did. And there was no accident going over the inclined planes—nothing happened. It was forthwith an everyday thing, the proof of which was that canal people and transportation agencies made what changes in the equipment were necessary and ever thereafter, as the canal boats came up to Hollidaysburg or to Johnstown, they were lifted out of the water, divided into sections, put on wheels, and rolled along their way over the mountain, with reverse action and reassembling at the other place. That was in 1834.

Canals originally were meant for freight transportation,

From "The History of New Hampshire," by John N. McClintock, 1889

On the Amoskeag, one of the other canals

but very early there arose a decided vogue for canal boats as a conveyance for passengers. To the traveller of the present day, a horse-drawn progress of 3 or at most 3½ miles an hour would hardly be called speeding. But the people of those times were not inclined to be jittery. Their nerves were calm. They enjoyed a tranquil procedure through beautiful scenery, quite as some of us now prefer a walk through the countryside to an automobile drive at 50 or 60 miles an hour—and it is unquestionable that one can see more of the country walking. The boats on the canals, like the vehicles on the turnpikes, belonged to business companies or private individuals and were controlled and operated by them, not by the owner of the canal. The canal was another kind of public road. So like the Conestoga wagon high color became very popular. The first canal packet or passenger boat to reach the Ohio River from the East was appropriately named the *Pittsburgh*. It was 72 feet long, 11 feet wide, and 8 feet high. The underbody was painted red and black, the cabin white. The color was heightened by a row of 20 windows with green shutters on each side. A crew of 9 were in charge, and there were advertised accommodations for 150 passengers, but this was in the early years of the use of the word for sleeping places and eating tables and less was expected of the word than would be now or has been for many years. A guidebook in 1836, *A New Guide for Emigrants to the West,* published by J. M. Peck in Boston said:

> The Pioneer Line on this route is exclusively for passengers, and professes to reach Pittsburgh in four days—but it is sometimes behind several hours. Fare through, $10.00. Passengers pay for meals.
>
> Leach's line, called the Western Transportation Line, takes both freight and passengers. The packet-boats advertise to go through to Pittsburgh in five days for $7.00.
>
> Mid-ship and steerage passengers in the transportation line (*i.e.* the second-class passage, in the line boats) in six and a half days; merchandise delivered in eight days. Generally, however, there

Photograph from the United States National Museum

Grand Banks codfishing schooner "Open Sea," 1820

At the beginning of the Revolution, Marblehead had a fleet of more than one hundred and seventy of these schooners

Courtesy of the Peabody Museum of Salem

A model, made by Walter C. Leavitt, of the heel-tapper schooner "Hannah" of Marblehead

Courtesy of the Charleston Museum

An old South Carolina plantation boat

This boat was still in use in the latter part of the nineteenth century

Courtesy of the Mariners' Museum, Newport News, Va.

A Chesapeake Bay log canoe in the making

Courtesy of the Peabody Museum of Salem

A gundalow under sail on the Squamscot River, New Hampshire

From the Public Roads Administration

The first plank road open to travel in 1846 from Syracuse to Oneida Lake

Left, old tollhouse on the National Pike near Frostburg, Maryland. *Right,* toll-gate on the Maysville Turnpike. The Maysville Pike ran from Zanesville, Ohio, through Kentucky to New Orleans

From a painting by George S. Knapp, Syracuse, through the courtesy of the Onondaga Historical Association

Asa Danforth, Comfort Tyler (in center) shaking hands with Ephraim Webster, during the surveying for the Seneca Turnpike

From a sketch in the National Museum, Washington, D. C.

Stagecoach and Conestoga wagon stopping at the Eagle Hotel near Philadelphia, on the Lancaster Pike

Photograph by Blackington Service, Boston

Ledyard Bridge between Hanover, New Hampshire, and Norwich, Vermont

Photograph by courtesy of Alice H. Moore, Cambridge, Massachusetts

Bridge across the Lamoille River at Wolcott, Vermont

From "Picturesque America," edited by William Cullen Bryant, 1874

The covered bridge over Bellows Falls

Photographs by courtesy of the Landis Valley Museum

The Conestoga wagon

Top: A Conestoga wagon team. *Center right:* The wheel hub. *Center left:* Wheel hub with cover for sandy roads. *Bottom:* Hoop of bells for Conestoga team.

Photograph by Public Roads Administration

Jug Bridge over the Monocacy River on the Old National Pike, Maryland

Courtesy of the Southern Pacific Company

The Tombstone stage "Modoc," frequently held up in the latter part of the nineteenth century

From "Das Illustrirte Mississippithal" by Henry Lewis, 1857

Flatboat on the Mississippi

From "Les Voyages du Naturaliste Le Sueur dans l'Amérique du Nord, 1815–1837"

Interior of a family flatboat

From a painting by Stanley M. Arthurs in Scribner's Magazine

The Safety Barge

Introduced by enterprising promoters of a line of steamboats running on the Hudson in 1825, to make timid passengers less fearful of a possible boiler explosion

From a lithograph by Currier and Ives in the Library of Congress

The New Orleans packet "Eclipse" on the Mississippi

Photograph by courtesy of the Pennsylvania Railroad

Sectional canal boat being hauled over the inclined planes of the Portage Railroad in 1840

Photograph by courtesy of the Pennsylvania Railroad

Lower half of sectional canal boat leaving Third and Walnut Streets, Philadelphia

Pulled through the streets on trucks, the boats were placed upon the Philadelphia and Columbia Railroad and shipped to Columbia, Pennsylvania. There the sections of the boats were joined and they travelled by water over the Eastern Division of the Pennsylvania Canal to Hollidaysburg, Pennsylvania. Here they were placed on the Portage Railroad and hauled by eleven inclined planes over the east and west slopes of the Alleghenies to Johnstown, Pennsylvania, where they were placed on the Western Division of the Pennsylvania Canal, completing their journey by water to Pittsburgh.

From a section of a drawing by St. Memin

The "Clermont" at West Point during the trip from New York to Albany, 1807

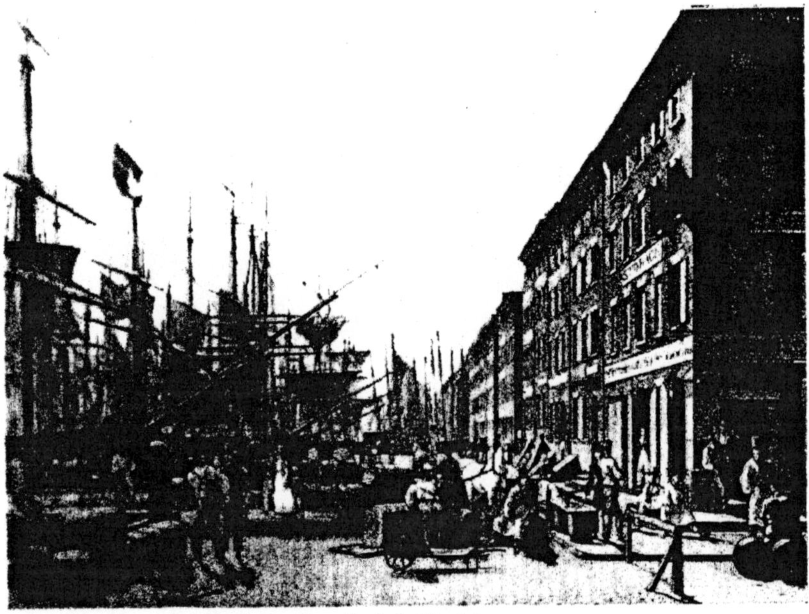

From the print collection in the New York Public Library

New York's waterfront, 1828. A view of South Street from Maiden Lane

From the diorama by the Public Roads Administration

Travel on the Erie Canal

Courtesy of the Onondaga Historical Association

Erie Canal Plate and Pitcher

The dates on the inscriptions indicate that they were placed on the market about the time of the Canal Celebration. The decoration on the plate represents the Erie Canal at the junction with the Hudson River in Albany

Photographs by courtesy of the Pennsylvania Railroad

Top: An old view of the Lemon House—a famous inn and station on the old Portage Railroad just at the head of plane No. 6 on the level between planes No. 6 and No. 5. *Center:* Model of "The Chief Engineer of Rome." *Below:* Entrance to the harbor at Lockport on the Erie Canal. From "Memoirs, prepared at the request of a Committee of the Common Council of the City of New York . . ." by Cadwalader D. Colden, 1825

The Village Post Office and Country Store
A painting by Thomas Wood in the Wood Art Galleries, Montpelier, Vermont

From the New York Historical Society

A jewelry and silversmith's shop in the Fifties

It was situated on Broadway, at the south corner of Murray Street opposite the City Hall, New York

A barber shop at Richmond, Virginia

A painting by Eyre Crow, exhibited in London and reproduced in the *Illustrated London News* of March 9, 1861 is some delay. . . . The price of meals on the boat is about thirty-seven and a half cents.

The following is from an advertisement of the Western Transportation, or Leach's Line, from Philadelphia:

Fare to	*Miles*	*Days*		*Days*	*By Packet-boat for Cabin Passengers, same line.*
Pittsburg	400	6½	$ 6.00	5	$ 7.00
Cincinnati	900	8½	8.50	8	17.00
Louisville	1050	9½	9.00	9	19.00
Nashville	1650	13½	13.00	13	27.00
St. Louis	1750	14	13.00	13	27.00

But the Pennsylvania Canal was not the only one in the State. The Union Canal, authorized in 1811 and owned by a private corporation, should at least be mentioned. Its 82 miles extended from Middletown on the Susquehanna River, where it connected with the Pennsylvania Canal, to Reading, where through the Schuylkill Canal it gave access to Philadelphia. Then, mingled with coal and iron mining, manufacturing and transportation of any kind, the Lehigh Canal of Asa Packer and Josiah White, 84½ miles long, showed a versatility of construction and operation which almost outdid the Pennsylvania itself. No canal system that was authorized by a State Legislature would fail to make evident an effort to reach all sections of the Commonwealth with its beneficial charters. By 1840 the State of Pennsylvania owned and operated 608 miles of canals!

The Erie Canal had a more simple, direct and natural development than either of the others. The interest of the people was aroused first, and the right technical aim and method were reached almost as if by experiment subject to the approval of the people. This was best. As far back as 1773 Christopher Colles, an Irish engineer, gave lectures in New York on Canals, and in 1784 proposed a plan of inland navigation for the Mohawk River. The Erie Canal later grew out of this plan. In 1788 Elkanah Watson saw and declared what might be done with such a system well equipped with canals and locks where desirable:

> Who can reasonably doubt but that by such operations the state of New York have it within their power by a grand stroke of policy to divert the full trade of Lake Ontario and the Great Lakes above, from Alexandria and Quebec to Albany and New York.

This far sight, this great purpose, was central and essential to the whole, giving lasting vitality to the entire project. Accordingly, in 1791 Elkanah Watson headed a campaign to convince the people of New York of the feasibility and importance of the plan. His grammar shows he realized the importance of his campaign. "State" is a plural noun referring to the people, not singular, referring to government.

In 1792 Governor George Clinton recommended to the Legislature that a commission be appointed to make a survey. Elkanah Watson was a member of this commission. The result was a system of river improvements or "canals" intended to reach from the Hudson to Lake Ontario, the Seneca Lake and Lake Champlain. General Philip Schuyler and William Weston, an English engineer, served on these works; the system was ready for use by 1796. Only by a stretch of present-day imagination could these be called canals, but considered from the standpoint of the people of the time, why insist on expensive construction when many reaches of flowing water afforded sufficient water for navigation?

The importance of the project, its possibilities, and the right conditions for it continued to seep into the consciousness of the people of the State. In 1808 Joshua Forman, an Assemblyman from Onondaga County, introduced a bill for a State-built system of canals. It was adopted and became a law. It was nine years before construction was begun under it, partly because of the War of 1812–14. A law authorizing construction was put through in April, 1817, by the influence of Thomas Eddy, the treasurer of one of the canal companies, State Senator Jonas Platt, and the powerful political leader, DeWitt Clinton, followed by the casting vote of Chancellor James Kent in the Council of Revision. There was at this time a natural effort to enlist Federal aid. DeWitt Clinton and Gouverneur Morris went to Washington to see the President about it. But the aid was refused. The effort was also made to enlist the aid of the States of Ohio and Indiana. The value of the Erie Canal to their people was appreciated but it was not found practicable to give any financial support to the undertaking. New York was therefore thrown upon its own resources, which probably was as well or better. The bearing of the responsibility and the making of decisions was in the one hand.

The work began at once under the direction of engineers

who became notable—James Geddes, Benjamin Wright, Charles Brodhead, Canvass White, Nathan S. Roberts, and others. The first contract for construction was let on June 27, 1817, and the work was begun at Rome, New York, on July 4. The first section of canal, between Utica and Rome, fifteen miles, was completed and opened with appropriate ceremonies on October 22, 1819. Thus politics was seen to be carrying out the will of the people.

The popular interest in this first opening on the Erie Canal is reflected in letters of the time. In every way the Erie Canal had entered into the everyday hopes and excitement and life of the people of the State.

> On the twenty-second of October, 1819, the first boat sailed on the Erie canal, from Rome to Utica. It was drag'd by a single horse, trotting on the embankment, in the towpath. [Another letter said that "The horse traveled, apparently, with the utmost ease."] It was an elegant boat, constructed to carry passengers, called the *Chief Engineer*—a compliment to Benjamin Wright, Esq. The president and the board of commissioners, attended by many respectable gentlemen and ladies, embarked the ensuing day at Utica, with a band of music, to return to Rome. The Scene was extremely interesting, and highly grateful. The embarkation took place amid the ringing of bells, the roaring of cannon, and the loud acclamations of thousands of exhilarated spectators, male and female, who lined the banks of the new created river. The scene was truly sublime.

A canal was still a river, or the child of a river.

> The interest manifested by the whole country, as this new internal river rolled its first waves through the state, cannot be described. You might see the people running across the fields,

climbing on trees and fences, and crowding the bank of the canal to gaze upon the welcome sight.

Canal Celebration.

On Wednesday last, the waters of Lake Erie were admitted into the Great Canal, and that stupendous undertaking completed. The navigation between the Atlantic and the Lakes is now open, and a direct intercourse established between this city and the fertile regions upon the borders of the Canal Friday next, the fourth of November, is fixed for the celebration of this great event. Preparations on a grand scale are making to commemorate the day. The details of the different institutions, societies, &c. have been published in the daily papers. These will form a grand aquatic procession, which will proceed to the Ocean, and having assisted in performing the ceremony of uniting the waters with the Ocean, will return to the Battery at three o'clock. National salutes will be fired from the different Batteries as the procession passes by, both in going and returning In the evening there will be a Grand Ball in the La Fayette Circus, which is to be considerably enlarged and fitted up for the occasion, in a style of taste and elegance never surpassed in this city We hope that no accidents will occur which may in any way disturb the rejoicings which are to take place.

From "The Truth Teller" of October 29, 1825

Newspaper announcement of the celebration attending the opening of the Erie Canal

As the construction of the canal progressed, other celebrations attended the openings of added extensions. The interest was not merely local. On April 25, 1823, the section between Utica and Rochester was opened. On June 26, 1823, *The Farmers and Mechanics Journal* of Vincennes, Indiana, printed an account, in which was the following:

On Saturday the Packet-Boat for Rochester left here [Utica] with eighty-four passengers, on her first trip. A boat will leave this place every morning, Sundays excepted, during the season and continue through to the Genesee River.

That first canal boat, the *Chief Engineer,* of Rome, was built from a model of which we have the privilege of showing a picture (facing page 133) through the courtesy of the Buffalo Historical Society, where the original model now is preserved. This model was brought from England in 1817 by Canvass White, and from it the boat was built. All canal boats were derived in form from the keelboats and barges of the river travel. As the unmanageable rivers became tamed, and the needed watercourses were reduced to subjection, there went a standardization of the boat to something of a unit size in the regular canal boat. This *Chief Engineer* is described in a letter of the time:

> The boat which received them is built for passengers;—is sixty-one feet in length and seven and a half feet in width;—having two rising cabins, of fourteen feet each, with a flat deck between them. The tow rope was sixty feet long.

With the construction of the Erie Canal there went certain accomplishments which may be mentioned to characterize the stupendous piece of work. There were the great aqueducts which carried the canal over the Mohawk River twice, one 748 feet long, on 16 piers; and the other 1188 feet long, on 26 piers; and still another, over the Genesee River, 802 feet long on 9 great beautiful arches. These were architectural as well as engineering achievements, in which the people all along the line of the canal, though they never saw them, took great pride. So too the designing and constructing of the group of ten locks at Lockport, in pairs, for passing the precipitous drop of 60 feet where the Erie Canal went over the Niagara escarpment. This was the work of Nathan S. Roberts.

Three mechanical devices may be mentioned which with the Erie Canal entered into the extension of the everyday life of the people, partly in their use by the hundreds and thousands of men who worked on the canal, partly by contributing to the speedy and proper construction of that work in which they took such pride, and partly by the after use in many ways to which they were put. One was a cable of which one end was attached to the top of a tree and the other wound on a wheel; by this one man could fell the largest tree. By a second seven laborers and a team of horses grubbed out forty stumps in a single day. A third was a plow with an extra blade for use in cutting small roots and underbrush. It will readily be seen how these became familiar to the workers on the canal and how they facilitated the economical advance of the work. Another economical incident was the finding by Canvass White, one of the engineers, of hydraulic lime on the route of the canal itself. This was essential for making the mortar used in the canal. This finding was most important, as otherwise the special kind of lime would have had to be imported across the Atlantic, which would have been very expensive. At that time it was not yet realized that the success of a canal was primarily a financial matter, and that even engineering considerations were secondary to that.

Such were some of the striking features that entered into the construction of this great work. The cost so far had been about $7,000,000. When completed, the Erie Canal was 363 miles long, from the Hudson River at Albany to Lake Erie at Buffalo. It was 40 feet wide at the surface and 29 feet wide at the bottom; and 4 feet deep. It will be seen from this that the canal was planned for flat-bottomed boats, of a type derived from the barge and the keelboat, and that the water displacement by weight of cargo could be only about 30 inches. The canal boat was a pretty long craft in proportion to its width.

The Erie Canal was completed, so to speak, and it was officially opened on October 26, 1825. On that day a fleet of canal boats started their voyage from Buffalo to go the entire length of the canal, to pass at Albany into the Hudson River, and then down to New York City, a distance of 500 miles. The beginning of the celebration was announced by a salute of guns, repeated along the entire route, taking ninety minutes as the signal was passed on from town to town. The fleet arrived at New York on November 4 and was formed in a circle off Sandy Hook, where Governor DeWitt Clinton performed the Marriage of the Waters, pouring a keg of water from Lake Erie into the Atlantic Ocean. Water from fourteen great rivers of North and South America, Europe, Asia and Africa also was poured into the ocean, symbolizing the future of Erie Canal commerce now made possible. New York City had been converted to belief in the canal, and well it might. It was the Erie Canal that made New York the greatest city in the western hemisphere.

But there was another current flowing west from the Erie Canal. The reputation of the great achievement and of what it would accomplish went on into Ohio, Indiana and Michigan, carrying a confidence that was less well founded,

Courtesy of the Bank of the Manhattan Company

New York's celebration of the opening of the Erie Canal

especially in view of the commercial situation in these less closely settled States. But canals did heroic service in opening up these States. Ohio we naturally think of as a square or at least lozenge-shaped State, quite evenly settled throughout, whether according to industry, mining or agriculture. In the canal days it was rather a stretch of wilderness between Lake Erie and the Ohio River with lines of population along the canals, constructed or proposed. Except along the canal lines the settlement was thin or did not exist. The Ohio and Erie Canal extended from Portsmouth on the Ohio River north to near Columbus, bending to the northeast to Dover in Tuscarawas County, then north through Akron to Cleveland on Lake Erie. Five branch canals were proposed to cut the band of territory between this canal and the Ohio, but only one of these, the one terminating at Marietta, was constructed, though not finished. A major canal was proposed also from Columbus north to Sandusky, but never built. The Maumee and Erie Canal extended from Cincinnati to Toledo. These were the main canals in Ohio at the height of the canal days.

The success, the prosperity, of the Erie Canal was based in the fact that the Erie Canal supplied an actual means of transportation and trade for a two-way commerce that already existed and reliably demanded that service. The Ohio and other western canals, as constructed, supplied an actual means of transportation and trade for a commerce that did not as yet exist and had in large measure to be created. They were a speculation. There was no steady business justifying the expenditure; the income did not balance the outgo, much less afford a justifying surplus. The depression that created the Panic of 1837 therefore was disastrous, and recovery was blocked by the coming of the railroads, which soon did the same work as the canals much faster and more economically. The story was repeated in Indiana, Michigan and other States that subscribed enthusiastically to the dream of the canal.

To be readily understood, the canal days must be studied in the large. While the canal, some particular canal, bore with poignant exhilaration or cruelty on the life of every person living along its line or within its range, it was really the whole system that was in touch with the local community. Population grew along the line of the canals for the simple reason that the canals offered the people by far the best way to get their supplies from the East, and the best way to send their surplus local produce, gathered into wholesale quantities, to market. The canals were not boundaries of populated territory. With a few miles on either side of them, they were themselves the populated territory with areas of wilderness between. Every man looked to the canal for the goods he needed and for the cash he expected to receive for his own produce. If he thought of moving to a new farm, he made his decision to a considerable degree on whether at the new location there would be a canal near enough to give him the necessary business contacts. The canal was between 1825 and 1854 in the everyday life of the people all that the railroad became later. It was of local value only in proportion as it reached the great markets of New York, Philadelphia, Baltimore, Lake Erie, the Ohio River and the Mississippi, and did the business of each farmer or tradesman where it could be done best.

A Yankee peddler

CHAPTER VIII

When Trading Was Retail

AS THE country settled, the trading naturally anchored in stores. First, as has been seen, each farmer bartered what he had raised for what he wanted and could get. Then came the peddlers, on foot, as indicated by their designation, with packs on their backs. Later they carried their goods on a wagon pulled by a usually bony horse. The Yankee peddlers hailed from New England along the turnpike and canal routes, with their stock of "Yankee notions," large in variety and small enough in size to carry on the back if need be. Needles, pins, hooks and eyes, buttons, scissors, all the way to spectacles, tinware, clocks, patent medicines and horse liniment, dry goods, hats, salt fish, and even larger items.

Following at short intervals, during the 1830s and 1840s, came the Jewish traders, hailing, most of them, from Germany as immigrants through Pennsylvania. They too came and went, on foot or leading a horse, conducting a barter or a cash business, according to the offer (cash preferred). Gradually they slowed down their pace and shortened the day's journey as they found a suitable abiding place where a group of farmers lived near together, or a village or town that promised an advantageous location for their business. In this way, one by one, their "peddler's packs" at last conveniently housed, the general merchandise stores of the Middle West developed.

The general store was inevitably located near the center of the town or village. It frequently had a porch, a step or two up from the road, on to which a horseman could dismount without first getting down on to the ground. There was also a back door, where barrels of flour and other heavy goods were discharged and where several barrels of salt were kept under a lean-to. In the main room of the store there was a stove in the middle, and two or three chairs, not necessarily of the best. Shelves lined the side walls, on which the stock was arranged in accordance with the average amount of sale and personal convenience. A counter ran along one, sometimes both sides, with occasionally a glass case on part of one. Here the men of the neighborhood frequently, not to say continuously, gathered to talk over the local gossip and to discuss the village or other public affairs. The focus of the whole place was the sawdust box, a subsidiary of the tobacco industry and of the art of marksman-

MINT WATER.

" Mint-Wa-ter !"

YEST.

To toot—to toot—too too—. East ! Here's East !"

BUTTER-MILK.

" Butter-Mil-leck !"

GRINDER.

" Any Knives, Razors, or Scissors to Grind ?"

From "The New York Cries," by Samuel Wood, 1814

Predecessors of the pushcart traders

ship. The humble target was always there, and it exercised commanding influence. It was understood the women did not need anything of the kind to polarize their opinions.

On one counter, near the front door, the post office was often placed, with its numbered, glass-partitioned "boxes" for sorting the mail by families or in case of lone importance by individuals, and the larger hole in the middle through which to hand out the mail when properly called for by number. The storekeeper was of course the postmaster, thus combining two useful services, and reaping recognition in the combined prestige. In such a post office-general store the storekeeper, descended from the peddler by only a few generations at most, with information derived from the popular postcard and from skillful conversation, did something to supply the place of the as yet nonexistent local newspaper, as the middle of the room did that of a local forum. The second story the storekeeper and his family usually occupied as their living quarters. Part of it he would often use as a storeroom, so as to keep the surplus of his supplies "close handy by."

Mrs. Josephine Young Case has given in her *At Midnight on the 31st of March* a remarkably live picture of the old-time general store, all the more clear and more faithfully vivid because it reverts to the past suppositiously from the present with our electrical conditions.

> By eight o'clock the farmer's milk is down
> And teams and trucks and cars have brought their cans
> To load on George's truck which, red and big,
> Travels the thirteen miles to Centerfield,
> The creamery and railroad. George is gone
> By eight-fifteen, and everybody comes
> To market at the store, to get the mail,
> And talk about the government or the weather.

. . . . .

Now outside the store the grey
Reluctant morning lightened up to show
The concrete road that ran straight through the town
White and untravelled. Everything was still
But for the few and quiet calls and cries
Of children walking down the road to school.
Bert rang again, and anxious rang once more,
While silence dropped around the stove and all
Listened as still as he.

. . . . .

Now George came in, that drove the big red truck
An hour before his time, and crossed the room
To warm his hands before the stove that showed
Such scarlet warmth in little window panes.

. . . . .

He sat down in a chair that creaked, and none
Replied.

. . . . .

No one said much, but finally Earl got up
And slowly went to get his car, and more
Went after, till a cavalcade of cars
Moved down the road as fast as they could go.
All went but Bent, who had to mind the store
Come Judgment Day.

The high time of the general store was before the Civil War, say between 1825 and 1860. But of course the general store was an impressive, if not a dominating institution in some regions as late as the 1870s and the 1880s. Indeed, in some regions it still is. It is too simple, too practical, and too American ever to be lost entirely from the land! It is not difficult to state its operation as an institution. All the trading of the general store was based on the inherited habit of barter. But it was not confined to barters by any means. The merchandise of the general store was exchanged for local

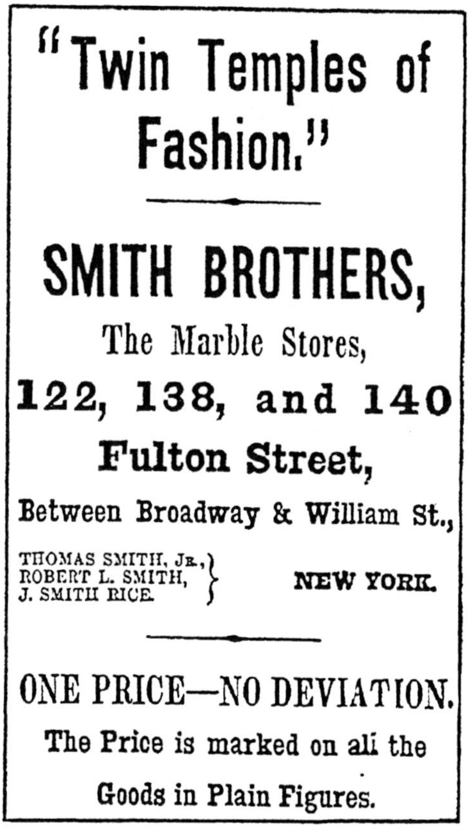

From "Harper's Weekly," July 9, 1859

Temptation for shoppers

goods, but there was some local produce, especially in fairly settled regions and in earlier times, that commanded cash, such as, for instance, furs, linen, beeswax, potashes and pearl-ashes, and deerskins. Also there were some imported goods, coming by wagon over the turnpikes or coming by canal boat that demanded cash, such as, for instance tea, coffee, leather, iron, gunpowder, and lead. The general store was the great bottleneck through which all trading had to pass. In addition to the limitation of these conditions, the general store had to take many of the commercial risks, of price-decline, and of loss in transportation, which justified the demand for cash for imported goods from the local customer, and justified a preference for exchange in buying local produce. Then too, in all the trading of the general store it was customary to give the local customer long credit, a custom that lasted through the nineteenth century. If a man settled up only once or twice a year, he was not claiming unreasonable privilege. The custom grew out of precedent conditions. The barter habit and all its works and derivatives, including the long-credit privilege, gave way before the simple and inevitable habit of the customers themselves in buying whatever they needed to get and selling whatever they had to dispose of on the same trip to the store.[1]

As the population became more dense in regions, the general stores had to serve larger bodies of customers in a wider range of goods than their facilities made practicable. Naturally then stores soon sprang up handling each only a single line of goods.

The full human importance of the general storekeeper in his community cannot be realized unless considered from the personal point of view. To every one of his customers,

[1]At two places in Connecticut my attention has recently been called to use of the expression, "Now I must go store-ing," for marketing.

From "Vanity Fair," 1860

Humor in the Sixties

"You should be women, and yet your beards forbid me to interpret that you are so.—*Macbeth*, Act I, scene 3" which means, to every one of his neighbors, the general storekeeper was not only the source of daily supplies; he was their banker by virtue of long credit, and adviser in the management of their resources, whether those resources consisted of cash or of produce. He was their friend, to whom they all went to discuss their problems and difficulties. Indeed, he occupied among them something of the place of the good lord of the manor in mediæval Europe and even in Biblical times, who at times "sat in the gate and judged between his people what was right" with horse sense and understanding.

As the population became more dense in regions, the general stores had to serve larger bodies of customers in a wider range of goods than their facilities made practicable. Stores then soon sprang up handling each only a single line of goods. These were the regular retail stores. At the beginning of the nineteenth century the general stores were truly general in being found in all parts of the country. These specialty stores were rare outside of twelve cities, all of which had a population of 5000 or more. The earliest of these special line retail stores dealt in bakery goods, which had to be fresh when sold, in stationery, which had a rather limited appeal, largely among the lawyers and people of the courts, boots and shoes, which everybody wore, and wore out, china and glassware, hardware, jewelry, ship chandlery, tobacco, millinery, and men's clothing; these last called "slop shops." As industrial communities developed, general stores decreased in those neighborhoods and specialty stores increased, both in number and in amount of business.

The manufacture of men's clothing began in New York about 1835. Soon there were retail stores specializing in it. But until about 1860 a gentleman still followed the old

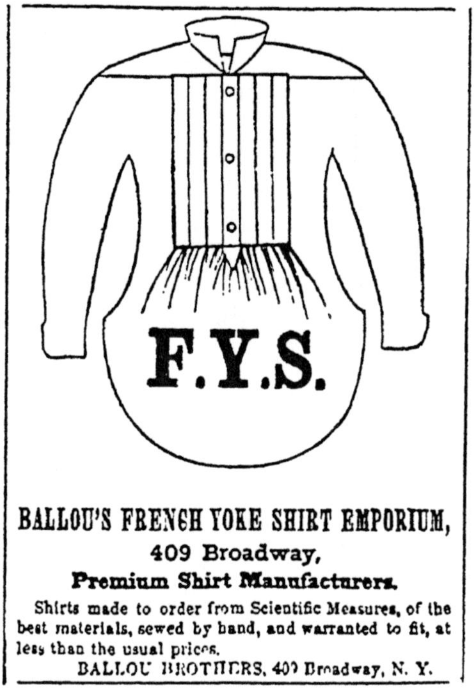

From "Harper's Weekly," March 26, 1859

Up to the minute in men's wear

custom-made way of going first to the cloth man to select the material and then to the tailor to arrange for making it up as he wished. Women's wear was still made in the home by dressmakers and other women employed for the purpose. By the same time, 1835, the local artisan in jewelry had started a specialty store in jewelry, sold it at retail and also repaired it, thus continuing his old handicraft. Shoes had always been sold in the general stores, though also made and sold by local shoemakers; before 1860 retail shoe stores were beginning to appear in the cities, but they did not interfere seriously with the sale of boots and shoes in the general stores.

Retail stores came to the service of the home quite noticeably in 1840 and soon after. In the matter of heat there were stoves before that time, but not coal stoves; neither were there stoves for cooking. Heat and cold go together. Before 1840 there was no ice on sale, neither were there iceboxes or anything predicting refrigerators. Letting the butter and milk stand in the cold springhouse, or lowering them in buckets or pails—according to the etymological latitude, by ropes down the well itself, was the country resource for refrigeration—and by no means a bad one at that, as many will testify! Lamps had been practically the same for many centuries, but even so people relied on candles to help in illumination. Carpets were not manufactured to any extent before 1840, but then soon found retail stores awaiting them. Also coal and wood, oil, and "paints-glass-oil" together. Not until 1855 were their retail furniture stores; before that furniture was the work of the local cabinetmaker. The crowning comfort and glory too among the neighbors for some time was hot and cold water, which came with plumbing in the year 1860.

Advertising in the newspapers greatly increased the amount of retail business, and also the variety in the lines of the retail stores. At about 1800 such an advertisement, one column in width, simply announced the location of the place of business, the kind of goods sold and what was accepted in exchange. About 1830 the price of paper was lower. The stores could afford to indulge in more expensive advertising, and authorized larger advertisements with something of illustrations, identifying the store by recognized emblems: groceries, a barrel of liquor and a chest of tea; a drugstore would show a mortar and pestle; a jewelry store a watch; and a bookstore an open book. In the 1850s there was a willingness to increase the advertisement still further, opening up the design and allowing more white space to show to the advantage of sales promotion. But advertising by window displays, in our sense of the term, was not thought of and was not practicable until long after 1850. That depended upon plate glass.[2] Store windows with their extraordinary expanse of glass, becoming themselves— glorious and practical!—an immediate and complete form of retail advertising, was not as yet, except in a very limited way.

The depression of 1837, the failure of the canals, and the ensuing panic combined to cure the American business man of financial recklessness, and to make him cautious. Within

[2]Plate glass was made in England, in Belgium, France, and Germany, but not in America. What was needed in America before the Civil War and for some years after was imported. The first to be made in America was produced by Captain John Baptiste Ford at New Albany, Indiana, in 1868, and he had to send over to England for trained men and for machines. The real development of this kind of glass here in America—its successful manufacture, its wide distribution, and useful adaptation to its market—did not come until the middle 1880s, after our period had gone by into the past.

a year or so a man by the name of Church established a bureau in New York to give wholesalers information about the financial reliability of their out-of-town customers. In 1840 the first mercantile reference book was published. The first mercantile agency was started in 1841 by Lewis Tappan; and a second in 1842 by Woodward & Dusenbury. The Bradstreet Company was started by J. M. Bradstreet in 1849. Later R. G. Dun took over the business of Lewis Tappan under the name of R. G. Dun & Company. These agencies did much to forward the business of the retail stores, eliminating much of the risk, reducing the losses, and increasing the profits.

According to the census of 1840 there were, in 1839, 57,565 retail stores in the United States, and the average investment in these was $4350. Of these 51 per cent were in the five States of New York, Pennsylvania, Ohio, Massachusetts, and Virginia. The proportion was smaller in the South, both in number of stores and in amount of business done, but this was attributable to the general economic system of the reign of King Cotton. Through those five states—especially New York, Pennsylvania, and Ohio—it will be recognized, ran the grand highway system of the canals. General business vitality, through the retail stores, was the great advantage the canals brought to the people along their towpaths. Despite all financial inexperience, despite the numerous business failures, despite the ruthless competition of newer and better kinds of communication and transportation, it must gratefully be acknowledged that the canals endowed the Middle West with just the kind and degree of success it needed for its wholesome advance, before, their destiny accomplished, like the worker bees they passed away. The farm boy, who nearly a hundred years ago looked across the fields and saw the horses of the canal boat lifting out of the morning haze as it hauled its cargo to the neighboring village at a speed of 3 or 4 miles an hour, really had something to remember. He was seeing a passing institution hauling in to the village the substance of an institution that would not pass, the general store, but that would remain and rapidly develop into the special retail store and the department store, the chain store and the mail-order system—dreams that were still for him far in the future, but which would grow upon him and his neighbors as swiftly and as imperceptibly as he would grow to manhood and to dealing with the problems of life.

The small beginnings led through the general stores up to the great emporia that to us now symbolize notable achievements in business and in trade, in the exchange of needs for accomplishments and possessions.

D. SAMUELS,

42, 44 and 46 Third Street, ***SAN FRANCISCO.***

Specialty in Ladies French Underclothing, Real Laces, Shawls, Saques, Sashes.

The Largest Stock of Real Laces in the City. Manufacturer of Kid Gloves.

From an advertisement published in 1872

CHAPTER IX

What's New and the Newspapers

AS A MEANS of communication, talk, polarized around the cracker barrel in the general store had one conspicuous advantage over simple conversation. It included in its range a greater number of people; it was comparatively wholesale. The talk also tended more and more to be such as would be of interest to all the people, and to unite them more and more, in their common information and in their general interests. There was no way quicker to reach every one in the entire neighborhood than to tell it around the cracker barrel in the general store. Indeed the cracker barrel was a true symbol of the coming national institution—the newspaper.

That the derivation was direct may easily be seen by a glance into New England during the Colonial Period. In those days as often as the post brought a newspaper, appropriately called a newsletter, to a village, all the people gathered around the minister and listened while he read the whole sheet to them, all four pages, from beginning to end. Farther west, in the turnpike and canal regions, where life was more commercial in its essential nature, the postmaster or the general storekeeper took the place of the minister as reader. With the arrival of more than one copy of the paper, the news began to be decentralized and its distribution multiplied. There would be more than one reader, and an outlying village could have its own reading.

When some enterprising man brought a printing press to town, the village soon found itself elevated to the importance of being a news center, with an incipient organization for gathering, writing up, printing and distributing the news, both local and "foreign," albeit the entire organization might at first be all in the person of one man. It was still essentially all talk, no more different from cracker-barrel conditions than moving one's lips when reading to oneself and keeping them still. So too in the subject matter there was from the beginning the distinction recognized between the facts themselves and the comment of the reader about those facts—between the news and the editorials. While it was all a case of natural development, that development was rapid, keeping pace with the successive generations in their time and places. The newspapers were the cracker-barrel talk of those later generations.

During the hundred years with which this volume deals the rise of the newspaper in influence and power was swift. The increasing availability of newspapers more than anything else accounted for the rapid adoption of the Constitution by the participant Colonies. It also accounted, with their increasing number, for the steady expansion of their influence, and for the shift of political power from the professional people to the common people. The curious second-hand way of choosing the President and the Vice-President of the United States provided by the Constitution, still literally followed but since 1832 actually ignored, reveals how great was this change in the power of the newspapers by the time of Andrew Jackson, in only forty years.

In 1776 there were only 37 newspapers in all the 13 Colonies. The difference in the newspapers of the colonial days is seen by comparing *The Boston News-Letter* in 1704 and Noah Webster's *American Minerva* in 1793, ninety years later. Yet how much the one looks like the other. The minister, the postmaster, or the general storekeeper can readily be imagined reading either one of these sheets to his neighbors. At the end of the Revolutionary War there were naturally only a few more, 43 in all the States. War conditions do not foster peacetime developments. The swift increase in the number of newspapers thereafter is clearly seen by a table in the census of 1880.

The presses on which these newspapers of the earlier period were printed were of the old wooden hand-press type, the same kind that Benjamin Franklin used. The power for making the impression was supplied by a wooden hand screw. The labor of working one of the old screw presses, according to Robert Hoe, was about equal to that of a plowman in the field. The parts that bore the strain of the work and in which the strength of the press inhered were all of wood, and were of course all jointed or otherwise fastened together. The practical use of these presses was therefore distinctly limited. The newspaper one of these early

GROWTH OF NEWSPAPERS FROM 1776 TO 1840

State	1776	1810	1828	1840
Maine	—	—	29	36
Massachusetts	7	32	78	91
New Hampshire	1	12	17	27
Vermont	–	14	21	30
Rhode Island	2	7	24	16
Connecticut	4	11	33	33
New York	4	66	161	245
New Jersey	–	8	22	33
Pennsylvania	9	72	185	187
Delaware	–	2	4	6
Maryland	2	21	37	45
District of Columbia	–	6	9	14
Virginia	2	23	34	51
North Carolina	2	10	20	27
South Carolina	3	10	16	17
Georgia	1	13	18	34
Florida	–	1	2	10
Alabama	–	—	10	28
Mississippi	–	4	6	30
Louisiana	–	10	9	34
Tennessee	–	6	8	46
Kentucky	–	17	23	38
Ohio	–	14	66	123
Indiana	–	—	17	73
Michigan	–	—	2	32
Illinois	–	—	4	43
Missouri	–	—	5	35
Arkansas	–	—	1	9
Wisconsin	–	—	—	6
Iowa	–	—	—	4
Total	37	359	861	1,403

From the Census of 1880, VIII, page 47, reproduced in George Henry Payne: *History of Journalism in the United States*, page 393.

printing presses printed—from the importance and nature of its subject-matter called a newspaper—was a sheet not larger than 16 x 20 inches, printed into four pages with five columns to a page. About the year 1798, in England, the Earl of Stanhope made a decided improvement by having the frame of the printing press made all of one piece of cast iron. This strengthened the press and enabled the printer to bring more power to bear in the printing of woodcuts. The future of the printing press obviously lay along the line of reducing the amount of labor in the use of the press; of meeting the increasing demands of the industry (as for printing larger sheets of paper); and of gaining speed in the printing so as to turn out continuously larger editions of newspapers.

In the twenty years between 1816 and 1836, there were a goodly series of improvements in the printing press. In 1816 George Clymer of Philadelphia made an iron printing press in which he dispensed entirely with the screw, and made other changes. He took it to England, and it was there known as the Columbian press. In 1822 Peter Smith of New York, who was connected with the firm of R. Hoe & Company, made a press which was in many respects better than anything up to that time. For the screw he substituted a toggle-joint. In 1827, however, Samuel Rust of New York made an important improvement on Peter Smith's press by having the cast-iron side uprights hollowed for wrought-iron bars which were riveted at the top and the bottom. This increased the strength, reduced the weight and simplified the construction. In the regular course of business competition R. Hoe & Company bought Rust out and proceeded to make further improvements on his press. Hoe called the result of the purchasing and inventing the Washington press, and manufactured many of its type until the

Courtesy R. Hoe & Co.

Peter Smith's press (1822)

cylinder press near the end of the nineteenth century preempted its field for all but fine proof work.

The first application of steam power to the printing press was made by Daniel Treadwell of Boston in 1822. The frame of his press was of wood. While he was actually the first, there is no record that he ever made more than three or four of them. The outstanding man of the early steam printing press was Isaac Adams of Boston, who patented his presses in 1830 and 1836. After Robert Hoe had established the cylinder press in America, R. Hoe & Company bought the entire Isaac Adams business in 1858.

In the early days, say, before 1840, it was usually the function of a newspaper to be the voice of a public man. It was his means of "talking" with the people. During the Revolutionary War General Washington availed himself of the services of just such a man, and with great effect—Thomas Paine. Paine met Benjamin Franklin in London and came to Philadelphia with letters of introduction from him in November, 1774. He was in Philadelphia during both the First and the Second Continental Congresses, supporting himself largely as a writer for *The Pennsylvania Magazine,* which was a periodical coming out rather less than more frequently. So he came to know personally and to be known by the leaders of the time, Washington included. Early in the summer of 1776 Paine enlisted in Washington's little army, under General Roberdeau, in a Pennsylvania division of the Flying Camp, a body that was to be sent wherever needed. After the term of service of this organization expired Paine went to Fort Lee where General Nathanael Greene was in command and enlisted under him. General Greene on or about September 19, 1776, undoubtedly with the approval, possibly at the suggestion, of General Washington, appointed Paine a volunteer aide-de-camp. During the day Paine served in the same way as all the other soldiers; in the evening he listened to the consultations of Washington and his generals, with whom he associated personally. The morale of the army was very low.

Courtesy R. Hoe & Co.

Top: Treadwell press of 1822

Bottom: Hoe ten-cylinder rotary press of 1846–1848

Discouragement was everywhere. To Paine Washington looked for emergency service as a writer. At night around the campfire he wrote a pamphlet which began with the famous words, "These are the times that try men's souls." With an almost hopeless letter from the commander to his relatives in Virginia, the copy of *The Crisis* was sent to the printer in Philadelphia. It was first published in *The Pennsylvania Journal* for December 19, 1776. It was then issued in a little pamphlet and ordered to be read to every corporal's guard in Washington's army. The effect was electrical. It put heart and determination into every man. The army had retreated across New Jersey on Newark. With his revitalized force Washington went into Pennsylvania, recrossed the Delaware River on Christmas Eve and captured Trenton. During the remainder of the war Paine wrote a dozen more numbers of *The Crisis*. It is no exaggeration to say that these papers were General Washington's means of "talking" to his soldiers. *The Crisis* was his newspaper!

When Alexander Hamilton, James Madison, and John Jay sought to bring popular pressure to bear in favor of the adoption of the Federal Constitution, they wrote that extraordinary series of eighty-five essays which has been called "the most profound treatise on government that has ever been written," and published them all under the *nom de plume* of Publius in the newspapers. The first appeared in *The Independent Journal* of New York on October 27, 1787. Thereafter, until April 1788, two or three numbers of *The Federalist* appeared every week and were copied in other newspapers throughout the States. It is curious that this notable series of papers, written for the purpose of commanding popular opinion, should have been published under a *nom de plume.* Times were different even if human nature was the same. Professional men did not busy themselves in those days with newspapers and printing presses, except in the most general way of policy, and maybe in finding means to meet deficits. But it does not therefore necessarily follow that every one did not know who Publius was.

Alexander Hamilton was a progressive man. He realized the power of the press, and availed himself of it. He had a newspaper. It was *The Gazette of the United States.* He had an editor for it, John Fenno, whose salary he guaranteed. The first number appeared on April 15, 1789. In 1791 the seat of the government was moved from New York to Philadelphia. *The Gazette of the United States* and John Fenno went thither also, in fact because as Secretary of the Treasury Alexander Hamilton went thither.

Thomas Jefferson, who agreed with Hamilton in little or nothing, found when he returned from France and was appointed to the Cabinet by President Washington on March 22, 1790, that he needed a newspaper to answer the arguments of Hamilton's *Gazette of the United States.* This was in no sense pro forma. Trying to enlist the active assistance of James Madison in the situation, Jefferson wrote to him, "Hamilton is really a colossus. For God's sake, take up your pen and give him a fundamental reply!" Aaron Burr, who was certainly not prejudiced in his favor, said of his controversial power, according to the famous lawyer, Jeremiah Mason, "Any one who puts himself on paper with Hamilton is lost." Jefferson's paper, *The National Gazette,* appeared for the first time on October 31, 1791. The editor was Philip Freneau, whose financial uncertainties were steadied by a salaried appointment from Thomas Jefferson as a translating clerk in the office of the Secretary of State.

The election of Thomas Jefferson as President of the United States automatically retired Alexander Hamilton from politics. Soon with John Jay and a few other Federalists he founded *The New York Evening Post,* the first number of which appeared on November 16, 1801. The editor was William Coleman, who came from Massachusetts. Of him Jeremiah Mason said:

> Another of the extraordinary men who then ranged that country was William Coleman, afterwards so greatly distinguished as the editor of *The New York Evening Post,* under the patronage of General Hamilton, that his opponents gave him the title of Field Marshal of Federal Editors. . . . His paper for several years gave the leading tone to the press of the Federal party. His acquaintances were often surprised by the ability of some of his editorial articles, which were supposed to be beyond his depth. Having a convenient opportunity, I asked him who wrote or aided in writing those articles. He frankly answered that he made no secret of it; that his paper was set up under the auspices of General Hamilton and that he assisted him. I then asked him, "Does he write in your paper?" "Never a word." "How, then, does he assist?" His answer was, "Whenever anything occurs on which I feel the want of information, I state the matter to him, sometimes in a note. He appoints a time when I may see him, usually

a late hour of the evening. He always keeps himself minutely informed on all political matters. As soon as I see him, he begins in a deliberate manner to dictate, and I to note down in shorthand" [he was a good stenographer]; "when he stops my article is completed." At that time the first and ablest men in the country directed the course of the political press.

Equally fundamental was Thomas Jefferson's belief in

Courtesy of "The New York Evening Post"

One of the first reforms urged by *The New York Evening Post* was to clear the streets of pigs

newspapers as essential to the sound development of the democracy. In a letter dated January 16, 1787, he said:

The way to prevent these irregular interpositions of the people is to give them full information of their affairs through the channel of the public papers, and to contrive that those papers should penetrate the whole mass of the people. The basis of our government being the opinion of the people, the very first object should be to keep that right; and were it left to me to decide whether we should have a government without newspapers, or newspapers without a government, I should not hesitate a moment to prefer the latter.[1]

[1] *Writings of Jefferson*, Monticello Edition, VI, pp. 57–58.

The people of the United States became politically more and more democratic as the years passed. This was incident to their natural growth. It followed the leadership of

encounter the perils and hardship
interesting service.

From the London Observer.

The Velocipede, or Swift Walker—This truly original machine was the invention of Baron Charles De Drais, master of the woods and forests of H. R. H. the Grand Duke of Baden—The account given of it by the inventor, of its nature, and properties—is,

1. That on a well-maintained post-road, it will travel up hill as fast as an active man can walk.

Courtesy of "The New York Evening Post"

The first illustration used in *The New York Evening Post*

Thomas Jefferson and his party, and came to a height with the election of Andrew Jackson to the Presidency. The newspapers were an important instrument in this democratic development. This means not only that the people, more and more of them, read the newspapers avidly, becoming familiar with the news of each week and considering the comments of the editorials, but that the producing

UNITED STATES WEEKLY TELEGRAPH

WASHINGTON, NOVEMBER 5, 1832.

VOL. VI..............$2.50 PER ANNUM.....BY DUFF GREEN. ....No. 28

Politics in the press

of the newspapers and the determination of their policies fell more and more into lines consonant with the opinion of the "common people." The people were taking over from the political leaders the control of the newspapers. Naturally one of the last leaders directly to "have" a journal for its political usefulness was Andrew Jackson. With the picture of Alexander Hamilton dictating at the beginning of the period, we have a similar picture of Andrew Jackson at the end.

When President Jackson was inaugurated in 1829, *The National Intelligencer* and *The National Journal* of Washington lost their semi-official standing; *The United States Telegraph* became the official newspaper of the administration. But the President further established *The Globe* in Washington as his own newspaper, and "more directly than had Hamilton or Jefferson he made the paper a vehicle for the expression of his personal views." Amos Kendall had been an assistant on *The United States Telegraph.* He soon became a confidential advisor of Jackson's, and one of his Kitchen Cabinet. Then he became an editorial writer on *The Globe* and nightly had private conferences with Jackson, at which the President would lie down and smoke and dictate his ideas "as well as he could express them," while Amos Kendall wrote them out and rewrote them until by dint of continued editing and changing he got the articles in the form the President wanted.

Alexander Hamilton and Andrew Jackson; William Coleman and Amos Kendall! Coleman was an able newspaper man, but neither he nor any one else ever was the superior of Hamilton in directing newspapers. From the strict journalistic point of view Amos Kendall was unquestionably more influential than President Jackson in the shaping of *The Globe.* Amos Kendall was such a man as could conduct a newspaper independently of direction from any political superior. He was a born leader and a newspaper afforded him the right instrument for wide public influence. John W. Forney, who had a shrewd knowledge of the men of his time, found it hard to believe that so soft-spoken a man as Kendall could have written those nervous editorials which aroused so much resentment among the Whigs and so much enthusiasm among the Democrats. To a considerable extent Amos Kendall got to be a statesman himself. As an administrator and as a writer he rendered effective public service under Jackson, service which fully entitles him to recognition as a political servant of high and independent importance. Nor was Kendall's effectiveness limited to the fields of journalism and politics. In a short time he became one of the business leaders in the new electrical communication, the telegraph.

Alexander Hamilton started still another newspaper, for which we must go back to 1793. With this the change from statesmen to editors as the predominating element in the newspapers was begun. The newspaper was *The American Minerva* of New York. The editor was the capable Noah Webster. For Hamilton's purposes, with Webster as editor, it was not necessary for the paper to be in Philadelphia where he himself was; it was better for it to be in New York. Noah Webster had the comprehensive Federalist point of view; he had experience, having personally advocated the copyright law through all the States; he was an active man, having travelled all over the country on that mission. It was sufficient if Hamilton kept in touch with Webster. This he did. Alexander Hamilton in Philadelphia, the capital, and Rufus King in New York financed *The American Minerva.* The statesman and the editor were in their ultimate relative positions. *The American Minerva* became a newspaper of strong influence.

The interest of Americans in what was happening elsewhere and in what concerned themselves required that the news and newspapers be spread evenly through the country. County newspapers, certainly one, usually two, one for each party, were published at practically every county seat, whither every one went once a week on market day, sometimes oftener. The news in these papers was distinctly local and reminiscent of the old talk around the cracker barrel. Expansion to include national and foreign news came about the middle of the nineteenth century through what was commonly called "patent insides," received from some large city newspaper. Through the industrial and populational development of the country, cities sprang up among the towns and villages that were provincial in their function and importance. These had newspapers which reflected the provincial character.

Springfield, Massachusetts, was one of these. Thither in 1824 migrated a young, twenty-seven-year-old printer, Samuel Bowles, up the Connecticut River from Hartford, in true pioneer style, his wife, baby, and printing-press all on a flatboat. Encouraged by a small group of Springfield Anti-Federalists, he came with journalistic intent. He brought out a newspaper on September 8, 1824, a weekly, called *The Springfield Republican.* The name through the gyrations of political nomenclature has come to mean exactly the opposite of its original significance, but in all the years no one ever need fail to understand what Samuel

From a drawing by A. B. Frost for "Scribner's Magazine"

Payment in farm produce for a subscription was not unusual

Bowles meant and what *The Springfield Republican* stood for.

With the completion of the Boston & Albany Railroad in 1839 Springfield grew rapidly into a manufacturing city and railway center. The newspaper also grew rapidly, rising on the solid foundation laid for it by its able editor in the local news. Under all three editors of the same name, Samuel Bowles, *The Springfield Republican* began, worked up, and maintained a remarkable system of local news correspondence which covered every town and village in the upper Connecticut River Valley, and which made the paper indispensable to the people of western Massachusetts. Indeed, *The Springfield Republican* made the local newspaper to be an acknowledged national element in direct effect and in general influence.

Samuel Bowles, Sr., insisted all his life on entire editorial independence. He declared he had several times refused "with scorn" offers of financial aid for *The Springfield Republican* if he would allow the backers to use the paper for causes in which they were interested. The proposals came from men who recognized a good newspaper man and they were simply offering to put his paper in the unworried position of most of the regular newspapers of the time and of the previous fifty years. Samuel Bowles was an editor of the advanced type, but their offers did not deserve to be answered with scorn.

Expansion of the paper by the addition of a daily edition to the weekly was suggested. Business friends thought it unwise. Samuel Bowles, Jr., urged it. Samuel Bowles, Sr., finally decided in favor of the idea and put the daily under the management of the son. On March 27, 1844, *The Springfield Daily Republican* appeared for the first time with an area of four small pages. When the father died in

1851, the son inherited the editorship and with it the independent attitude of the father, which he in turn duly handed on in 1878 to Samuel Bowles, III. *The Springfield Republican* became an intensely personal institution. Under the editorial Bowles dynasty the paper became widely known for great ability and fearless independence throughout the country.

The growing interest in what was happening everywhere and anywhere also required a spreading of the opportunity to learn the news through all classes of the people. Classes might mean various degrees of education or intelligence, or might mean various incomes. Sixpence (6 cents) for a newspaper seemed to many people large a hundred years ago. The natural consequence was that many of the people did not read papers. Certainly they did not buy papers. Good business usually comes by increase of the sales and decrease of the price.

Benjamin H. Day brought out the first number of *The New York Sun* on September 3, 1833. It was a four-page paper; each page 8 x 11¼ inches in size. It was a penny paper. It was not the first penny paper. *The Cent* of Philadelphia, *The Bostonian* of Boston, and *The Morning Post* of New York, all preceded *The New York Sun,* but they all died in a short time. Day not only put the price where it would attract attention to his paper but took measures to insure increased sales. At the outset he declared that the object of *The New York Sun* was "to lay before the public, at a price within the means of every one, all the news of the day." At the outset he hired a reporter, George Wisner, to help him gather the local news; he paid him $4 a week. Further, he hired boys to hawk copies of *The Sun* around the streets. A little later Day stimulated the enthusiasm of his newsboys as salesmen by selling *The Sun* to the boys at *The Sun* office for two thirds of a cent apiece and had them sell it on the streets at one cent. Still further, Day made sure that *The Sun* should be interesting simply as reading. *The Sun* printed the news in which the common man and the laborer were interested, police court news, and such. This was a new departure, and made *The Sun* popular among the numerous common people.

The extreme instance of this "interesting reading" was the Moon Hoax. On August 25, 1835, *The Sun* printed a story three columns long, purporting to be a reprint of a report by the great astronomer, Sir John Herschel, of seeing life on the moon from the Cape of Good Hope through a new and specially large telescope. The inhabitants were described as winged human beings and biped beavers from whose houses smoke issued. The articles continued for four days, and so cleverly were they written that not a few scientists were deceived and many readers believed them to be true. To not many of them was the literal truth of the articles at all a serious matter. They were delightful reading and the penny-paper readers enjoyed them. They were written by a reporter by the name of Richard Adams Locke, who was receiving $12 a week. Wages had gone up in the three years since George Wisner drew $4, and Locke's honorarium went up again at once.[2]

The circulation of *The New York Sun* increased rapidly under the stimulus of these varied devices even during the first two years from the founding:

January 1, 1834,	after four months	4,000
April, 1834,	after it had become a daily	8,000
August 28, 1835,	after the issue of the Moon Hoax	19,360

Benjamin H. Day, as he said foolishly, sold *The Sun* in 1840 for $40,000, but three *Sun*-men, Arunah S. Abell, William M. Swain, and Azariah H. Simmons, started newspapers along the same line as *The New York Sun* in other cities—*The Philadelphia Public Ledger* and *The Baltimore Sun*. Typical of these newspapers and of others that followed in that line of journalism are these maxims to be found among those laid down by William V. McKean,

[2]Richard Locke's "Moon Hoax" was an effective incident in the development of the American audience for fiction. The epithet "hoax" sticks because that was a hundred years ago, and people "ought to have known better." It is a very pleasant conviction that we cannot be fooled: *we* have too much common sense. Certainly! But those who cannot accept the imaginative as vividly as the literal lose much. We have had fictional experiences recently. The Hayden Planetarium in New York and the Franklin Institute Planetarium in Philadelphia both vividly advertise voyages to the moon. Oh, but these are scientific! True, and also skillfully fictional. Then there were the Jules Verne romances, which have proved to be far more scientific than was believed at the time they were issued. And Orson Welles skillfully prepared for Hallowe'en, 1938, a radio broadcast of an invasion from Mars. Some literal-minded people in northern New Jersey, the supposed "location" of impact, tuned in after the broadcast had begun, and accepted it too vividly. They almost started a panic.

managing editor of *The Philadelphia Public Ledger:*

Do not say you know when you have only heard.

Before making up judgment take care to understand both sides, and remember there are at least two sides. If you attempt to decide, you are bound to know both.

Plain words are essential for unlearned people, and these are just as plain to the most accomplished.

By 1836, only three years after its first number was issued, *The New York Sun* claimed a circulation of 27,000, which was 5600 more than the combined circulation of the eleven six-cent newspapers. Two years later, with journalistic modesty, *The Sun* said what was nonetheless probably true:

Since *The Sun* began to shine upon the citizens of New York there has been a very great and decided change in the condition of the laboring classes and the mechanics. Now every individual, from the rich aristocrat who lolls in his carriage to the humble laborer who wields a broom in the streets, reads *The Sun.*

Already we perceive a change in the mass of the people. They think, talk, and act in concert. They understand their own interest, and feel that they have numbers and strength to pursue it with success.

The Sun newspaper has probably done more to benefit the community by enlightening the minds of the common people than all the other papers together. (June 28, 1838.)

A stream is shunted back and forth by the banks of its bed until its swift current has pretty well taken its own way and has fixed its own course for good. So was it with the twenty-year-old Scotchman, James Gordon Bennett. The effect of his contact with politics and other relationships was that when on May 6, 1835, he brought out the first number of *The New York Herald* by his own personal labor, he declared characteristically:

> We shall support no party, be the organ of no faction or coterie, and care nothing for any election or candidate from President down to constable. We shall endeavor to record facts on every public and proper subject, stripped of verbiage and coloring, with comments when suitable, just, independent, fearless and good-tempered.

Bennett naturally had the fighting blood of a Scottish clansman in him. This was also a fighting period in the history of American manners. This may be illustrated from the Diary of Philip Hone, who was Mayor of New York in 1825. While shaving one morning he witnessed from his front window on Broadway an encounter between William Cullen Bryant, the poet, and William L. Stone, the historian, editors both, which Mr. Bryant started by hitting Mr. Stone over the head with a cane. Some will be specially glad to hear this of Mr. Bryant. The pictures of him make him seem so much like one of the older prophets, and this makes him seem somewhat human like his fellow-men. Such were the habits of the times. It will be noticed that Mr. Hone did not stop his shaving on this account. So too Mr. Bennett lived and rose in accord with the ways of the time. On occasion he was clever enough and original enough to get even, usually not with a stick over the head but with a few sticks in the paper. This also helped his circulation, for there were many who dearly loved such a paragraph in the news.

The times were such as to supply abundant news for a newspaper that wished to dethrone politics from editorial pre-eminence, from railroads to matches, or locofocos, as they were called then. Every man was most interested in

BRITISH STEAM PACKET SHIP GREAT WESTERN.

NEW YORK TO BRISTOL.—The new and splendid steam ship GREAT WESTERN, Lieutenant James Hosken, R. N. commander, was intended to sail from Bristol for New York about the middle of this month, and will return from New York to Bristol within fourteen days after her arrival here, probably about the 15th of May next, but the precise day will be announced in a future advertisement.

This new and magnificent ship has been built by the Great Western Steam Ship Company, as the first of a line of packets expressly designed to accomplish the object of a regular steam communication between America and Europe, and every thing that science and practical knowledge can furnish has been provided to render her a safe, and in every respect eligible conveyance for passengers and goods.

Her length over all is 234 feet, beam 35¼ feet, depth 23¼ feet, admeasurement 1340 tons, her engines of 450 horse power.—Her accommodations for passengers are of the most superior description. She has state rooms, &c. for 128 first class passengers, besides 20 good secondary berths, and, if required, 100 more sleeping berths can be conveniently arranged.

For freight or passage, or further information, apply to

RICHARD IRVIN, 18 Front st.

New York, 17th April, 1838 a19-1m*

Advertisement appearing in April 20, 1838, issue of *Morning Herald* at New York

how he could earn his living, support his family, and make a fortune. This was Bennett's reliance from the start. He introduced such news into *The Herald* from the beginning. For example, in his second number, on May 11, 1835, he printed a money-market report; and on May 14, a report of sales on the stock exchange. He was also the first to print reports of religious conventions—not from piety, but because there would be many people who would buy that number and who would buy again to see if there were more.

James Gordon Bennett consistently kept on an independent course in all public affairs. He extended the journalistic interests of his paper widely. He speeded up the process of converting events as they happened into printed news. And whenever there was opportunity he made news. These characteristics are evident in what he did, without advance

MORNING HERALD.

FRIDAY, APRIL 20, 1838.

☞ No Steamer last night, when we went to press. What? what? what? what?

"Lost to an anxious World and an expectant America"

notice, on the first day that steamboats effected the crossing of the Atlantic ocean, April 23, 1838, which appropriately was St. George's Day. The *Sirius* arrived in the Upper Harbor in the morning; the *Great Western* in the afternoon, but Bennett had his newspaper out before the *Great Western* sailed up the Bay. A few lines from this sheet will present a brief but vivid impression of the man.

ARRIVAL OF THE SIRIUS STEAMER IN SEVENTEEN DAYS FROM CORK

THE BEGINNING OF THE NEW AGE IN STEAM POWER—THE BROAD ATLANTIC BRIDGED AT LAST—ANNIHILATION OF SPACE AND TIME

This morning the city was thrown into a state of glorious excitement at the announcement of the *Sirius* steamer, Capt. Roberts, in 17 days from Cork, Ireland, consigned to Messrs. Wadsworth & Smith of this city. To these gentlemen we are indebted for copious files of London and Liverpool papers, magazines, etc., down to the latest dates. . . . The news by this arrival is not so important as the arrival itself. . . . She is now up and anchored off the Battery, where thousands were down gazing at her, early in the morning.

That James Gordon Bennett was a man of quick decisions will be seen from the next quotation, taken from the same morning paper:

We will take several days before we get over our delirium and think soberly. One thing is now certain—I mean to go to London in a few days, partly to see the coronation of Queen Victoria, which takes place on the 21st June, and partly to establish agents in Europe, so that I can outstrip all other papers on this continent. I shall also purchase a press, like that used by *The London Times* capable of throwing off 5000 sheets in an hour. The power of Steam applied to the press must move *pari passu* with the same mysterious agent as applied to navigation in the example before us. More of this anon.

With the *Great Western* arriving that afternoon Bennett had a grand follow-up in *The Herald* the next morning.

As *The Herald* grew and he had large means and facilities for its work, Bennett made lavish use of the telegraph for his domestic news, and kept dispatch boats sailing about, 59 miles or more outside of Sandy Hook, at times 250 miles out, to meet the steamers from Europe and hurry the news in. But he was concerned also with the general interests of the profession and co-operated in them with other papers. He represented *The Herald* personally at the meeting when the Harbor Association was formed; and again when the New York Associated Press was formed to gather the news in large cities. The service of Bennett's correspondents in Europe was exceptionally able; and during the Civil War

The Herald's war correspondents were rivalled only by those of *The New York Tribune.* But as Samuel Bowles left his greatest legacy in his son, Samuel Bowles, Jr., so was it with Bennett. James Gordon Bennett, Jr., carried *The New York Herald* on into the new period, invented exclusive news, and continued the paper as an ever greater journal.

Consideration; co-operation; communism: all are forms of co-ordination, slight, moderate, extreme. By activity or by restraint one can be efficient and businesslike in each degree. So comes much sociology. Think and work! is an old maxim. In the 'Laborare et orare" of the Benedictines it goes back at least 1500 years. Noted learning was one result thus long ago; model farms were another. Brook Farm, founded in eastern Massachusetts by the Reverend George Ripley, Nathaniel Hawthorne, Reverend William Ellery Channing, Reverend Ralph Waldo Emerson, Henry D. Thoreau, Margaret Fuller and others, in 1841, was just such an ideal model farm, with the theory strong. But all the uplands of New England were instinctively strong on Think and Work. With those born in that region the thinking and working were inseparable. There, in the village of Amherst, New Hampshire, in 1811, was born one Horace Greeley. It may be only a coincidence—but if so it is a striking one—that in 1841, after some miscellaneous journalistic experience, not all fortunate, Horace Greeley determined to start an independent venture and founded *The New York Tribune.* The connection was emphasized when in 1844 Brook Farm came under the influence of Horace Greeley, and when Albert Brisbane wrote a series of articles about the co-operative ideas of Fourier in *The Tribune.*

Purpose was strong in Greeley's mind and character. Greeley did not simply want to start another newspaper. There were then eleven dailies in New York City for a population of something like 250,000. Purpose was strong in Greeley's mind, and a high standard. He wished to combine the live quality of Bennett's *Herald* and the propriety of William Cullen Bryant's *Evening Post.* There was no penny paper of Whig allegiance. When Greeley issued the first number of his paper he had about $1000 worth of printing equipment and $1000 of cash which he had borrowed from a Whig friend, Jason Coggeshall. His intake for the first week was only $525. But he was travelling light. Everything counted. The name he selected, *The Tribune,* was reminiscent; it rang with classic associations with the Gracchi. Intellectual interests and high standards took form in a broad range of departments and a fine group of assistants. His political news was as specific as that of any paper in the city. His editorials were well-informed and positive. Literature, art, music, lecturing—which in those days included oratory as oratory—were taken care of by competent writers. The news-gathering covering all of these subjects was energetic and superior. The people and the number of people he took on his staff from the Brook Farm community were extraordinary: Henry J. Raymond, later of *The New York Times,* Charles A. Dana, later always associated with *The New York Sun,* Edwin L. Godkin, who later was with *The*

New York Evening Post, Albert Brisbane, George Ripley, Bayard Taylor, Solon Robinson for agriculture, the young George William Curtis, and Margaret Fuller, with Whitelaw Reid coming along a little later and rising to the succession in the days when *The Tribune* had become a jour-

Courtesy of the New York Historical Society

Horace Greeley's room and desk at *The Tribune*

nalistic institution and was no longer the embodiment of Horace Greeley. Greeley had his eccentricities, which cost him sore, as in the case of Henry J. Raymond, who split off and founded his own more moderate newspaper, another great institution, *The Times.* Greeley was described as "that farmer in the city," but he realized his great dream of high-minded influence in public and in home life. He made a human and practical form for the spirit of Fourier, more durable than the Brook Farm could be. And he attained it speedily. In circulation beginning at scratch, he began his 4th week with 6000 and his 7th week with 11,000 sales. On the eve of the Civil War the circulation of his three *Tribunes* (daily, semi-weekly, and weekly) was 287,-750. He sought only the attainable, but he was only half interested in money. Accordingly he had to suffer. Not only *The New York Tribune* had national influence; *The New York Tribune* was a great national influence. As long as Horace Greeley lived, he was *The Tribune*. It was a great personal newspaper. After he died it became an institution.

From a drawing by A. B. Frost for "Scribner's Magazine"

"Well, let's see what old Horace says this week"

CHAPTER X

Home-Life: Downstairs

FROM the center of these and other activities radiated the home life of the American people, sometimes shining in a single circumscribed kind of life, sometimes in many, but itself always essentially the same simple wholesome life. The character of this home life was like that of light. It was to be seen only reflected in the places where it was to be found, in the houses and furnishings, the everyday things that have gathered around that life, and that have together taken to themselves the name of home.

The chief room of the home life in the nineteenth century, all considered, was the dining room. Here the whole family gathered regularly three times a day for food. Here they talked, parents and children, in a family equality. Here they welcomed friends and guests. Here they celebrated the feasts of the year and all special occasions, birthdays and other anniversaries, with the eating of an extra good and usually extra large dinner.

The dining room was a good-size room, sixteen by twenty feet or more, according to the size of the family and the frequency of its use for social occasions. In the middle stood the large dining-room table of some hard or imported wood, usually carved somewhat, making a handsome piece of furniture, especially between meals. It consisted of two semicircular ends with sliding arrangements for increasing the table by inserting one, two, or three leaves on temporary or permanent occasion. At other than mealtimes a decorative centerpiece or colorful dish of fruit stood in the middle. Around the table stood the chairs. The father's and the mother's chairs stood at either end, somewhat larger than the others and dignified with arms. The other chairs, without the dignity of arms and naturally called side-chairs (see Volume I, page 34), stood along the sides of the table, for the children at ordinary meals, the place on the mother's left being reserved for the high chair, inherited collaterally by the youngest child. On formal occasions the ranking gentleman guest sat on the mother's right, and the ranking lady guest on the father's right. The father always carved the roast, and the mother always served the coffee and tea; she also always served the dessert at the end of dinner. Formality increased with wealth and social pretentiousness. Therewith on "occasions" the younger children were relegated for the meal to the kitchen, according to their years. But most families retained their informality, and emphasized their welcome to their friends rather by their heartiness.

The only other important piece of furniture peculiar to the dining room was the ponderous sideboard, with its ornamental back-piece, on which or in front of which stood the silver service. The top was often of marble. The body of the sideboard consisted, above, of two drawers for the silver and the table linen, and below, of an ample cupboard. In the opinion of the younger majority of the family one of the

From the dining-room table

From "Eighty Years' Progress in the United States," by Eminent Literary Men, 1861

most important things kept in the sideboard was the big round cookie tin, which contained sugar cookies in the spring and summer and doughnuts in the fall and winter. This made the sideboard a point of much resort for those in the family who were most of true taste and appreciative appetite.

Sometimes there was a serving table near the door to the

kitchen in the larger houses, but usually the pantry in no man's land, between the dining room and the kitchen, where indeed only women were allowed, served all the purposes of minor and final preparation of the food for eating.

The food, all of it prepared in the kitchen under the same roof, wherewith the family progressed through life with appetite and health, differed from the food of the present day mainly in three respects: 1. The diet as a whole was much heavier; 2. the small farms came much nearer to the larger settlements and towns than now, so the country produce was more personal in its raising and delivery; and 3. science and large industry had not as yet made their great contribution to health, offering a greater variety of foods (of cereals, for instance), and a greater adaptability to the work or physical activity of the members of the family, beside merchandising conveniences for their supply.

Breakfast, not infrequently, starting off with a good bowl of oatmeal or cornmeal mush, in order to begin the day right, presented meat in its lighter forms, which they understood to be beefsteak, mutton chops or veal cutlet, or sausages, or in Pennsylvania and its derivative regions, scrapple, and of course eggs, usually boiled, for the eggs in those days had harder shells than now and could stand bouncing around in the boiling water. Bread, cut in thick slices (baked the day before) with plenty of butter; and especially in the south, hot bread: rolls, muffins, soda biscuit, really yellow inside, and Maryland beaten biscuit (literally beaten with a mallet or hammer for an hour). These items will testify to the joys of that first meal of the day, and to the able digestions prevalent in those generations. It will go without saying that the mother or whoever did the cooking got up a couple of hours before the breakfast bell rang. But all the cooking of the breakfast was not done beforehand. The triumph of that early meal was the griddle cakes!—uncounted, no record remaining of their number, and cooked while eaten—sometimes of wheat flour, more often of Indian meal (corn meal was called Indian meal when you were talking about griddle cakes), but the height of all and glory of the nineteenth century was buckwheat cakes with Vermont maple syrup! (Vermont or any other state of the same latitude.)

Post Script:—*In New England,* and wherever New Englanders went—(which was where not?)—on Saturday night, baked beans and brown bread, with cider vinegar and black New Orleans molasses—(yes, that is right!), and cod fish cakes for Sunday morning breakfast.—That prepared any one for Eternity!

Coffee and tea were the abundant beverages, served by the mother. The milk pitcher was always kept full. Thus also were the children. The tea, boiled to attain all that was in it, predominated exclusively in families of recent English derivation. The coffee was often closely akin to local produce by virtue of the indigenous chicory, but just the same it made a good hot dark-brown drink and many cups of it could be drunk for breakfast, and were. Arabia and Brazil were farther away in those days than now, and that made a difference. It will be remembered that in the colonial days, when coffee and tea were first introduced, the pioneers said they were only slops and did not stick to the ribs.[1]

Dinner came in the middle of the day, at noon, except among those formal, somewhat wealthy people in the cities, who were more pretentious in their ways, who had it late, at seven o'clock in the evening. But then with these families, the grown men of the family were getting into the habit of going "down-town" or somewhere at a distance for a good part of the day, and did not, as was invariable in the smaller towns and villages, come home for dinner. With them also the idea was getting hold that a man could do a bigger and a better day's work on a light meal in the middle of the day instead of a full meal. So was born the lunch! And the general habit of lighter eating became pervasive and proved beneficent.

But it may be noticed that during the nineteenth century the men grew stout, even heavy, more and more. This may be accounted for quite naturally. They married by the time they were twenty-five. Their wives had grown up in a long established idea that taking care of their husbands meant feeding them. Wifely devotion was attested by the loading of the table with quantity and variety, rather than by skill in attaining a balanced diet. Thus was the queen of the kitchen to be recognized. What result could be more inevitable? Farm life in the early years afforded daily exercise that would stand the strain of so much eating, but as

[1]*Everyday Things in American Life,* Volume I, page 122.

AMERICAN COOKERY.

A Prevailing National Want.

To the Editor of the Press:

SIR:—The concessions made by many of our hotel keepers to the Duke Alexis, and recorded by him in his book, to the effect that there are no American dishes, and that we have no American cooks, do not surprise me.

During the Centennial, some foreign visitors criticized American food, while others, in this case royalty, criticized the lack of native foods and cooks

From "American Dishes at the Centennial," by James W. Parkinson, King & Baird, Printers, 1874, and from "Harper's Weekly," May 13, 1876

new and personally more sedentary occupations came in with mechanical inventions and commercial developments, the eating continued and accumulated around the waist. Later, the Civil War imposed general restraints which in dietary habits were never completely removed.

Accordingly the dinner, whether timed in the middle of the day or in the evening, was a considerable meal! It began with soup. Then came meat. Without plenty of meat a man was starved. Roast beef, or mutton, or ham, with a rich brown gravy. Fish on Fridays by general custom as well as by religious habit. Then chicken or the superlatives of chicken—duck, wild game, or turkey. Jellies, jams or/and cranberry with any or all meat or fowl. Salads were of later introduction; it was genuine imported olive oil that gave salads their permanent place in the menu, in the days of lighter diet. The dinner closed with a dessert—a pudding or pies, or both. Indian pudding of corn meal, bread pudding, using up the left-over crusts, or plum pudding with hard or soft sauce, or both (hard by virtue of its consistency and by virtue of the brandy in it). Such a dessert might indeed put a close to any meal. Coffee (large cups) was served all through the meal. As we look at the daguerreotypes or the early photographs of the 1840s and 1850s, who would not say, "Why not?" And who would not gladly submit to such hospitality?

As has been said, many of the farms on which the food of the townspeople was raised snuggled in close to the towns themselves. Indeed the towns reached out into the country along the divergent roads. Considered from the standpoint of commercial distribution, there was no middleman for much of this farm-truck. It came straight from the producer to the consumer in the farm wagons and was sold at the door of the house, as well as through the store down in the center of the town. In *The Legend of Sleepy Hollow* Washington Irving wrote a charming account of such a farm. The story was supposed to have happened much earlier, soon after the Revolution, but it was written and published in 1820, and the conditions it described lingered long after that. Farm life is not sudden and jumpy in its changes and developments.

Old Baltus Van Tassel was a perfect picture of a thriving, contented, liberal-hearted farmer. He seldom, it is true, sent either his eyes or his thoughts beyond the boundaries of his own farm; but within these everything was snug, happy, and well-conditioned. He was satisfied with his wealth, but not proud of it; and piqued himself upon the hearty abundance, rather than the style in which he lived. His stronghold was situated on the banks of the Hudson, in one of those green, sheltered, fertile nooks in which the Dutch farmers are so fond of nestling. A great elm-tree spread its broad branches over it, at the foot of which bubbled up a spring of the softest and sweetest water, in a little well formed of a barrel, and then stole sparkling away through the grass to a neighboring brook that babbled along among alders and dwarf willows. Hard by the farmhouse was a vast barn that might have served for a church, which seemed bursting forth with the treasures of the farm; the flail was busily resounding within it from morning to night; swallows and martins skimmed twittering about the eaves; and rows of pigeons, some with one eye turned up, as if watching the weather, some with their heads under their wings, or buried in their bosoms, and others, swelling, and cooing, and bowing about their dames, were enjoying the sunshine on the roof. Sleek, unwieldy porkers were grunting in the repose and abundance of their pens, from whence sallied forth, now and then, troops of sucking pigs, as if to snuff the air. A stately squadron of snowy geese were riding in an adjoining pond, convoying whole fleets of ducks; regiments of turkeys were gobbling through the farmyard, and guinea-fowls fretting about it like ill-tempered housewives, with their peevish, discontented cry. Before the barn door strutted the gallant cock, that pattern of a husband, a warrior, and a fine gentleman, clapping his burnished wings and crowing in the pride and gladness of his heart—sometimes tearing up the earth with his feet and then generously calling his ever hungry family of wives and children to enjoy the rich morsel which he had discovered.

Such were many of these farms, not only along the Hudson River but all over the country. A name might be important for the identification of a place but it could not limit the characterization to that one place. Even in the towns themselves there was a good deal of the farms, dove-tailed in, and in fact all through; the country spirit was pervasive. When a town grew to be a city, it lost a great deal, even if it did also gain much. Out beyond the farmsteads came the fields, the pure country part of the farms, though still centered in the farmsteads, and still responsive to the centripetal power of the towns. In another paragraph Washington Irving described the fields as Ichabod Crane, the schoolteacher of the community, rode through them.

As Ichabod jogged slowly on his way, his eye, ever open to every symptom of culinary abundance, ranged with delight over the

MAY-DAY IN THE CITY.

From a drawing by Winslow Homer for "Harper's Weekly," April 30, 1859

Moving day never changes

treasures of jolly autumn. On all sides he beheld vast store of apples, some hanging in oppressive opulence on the trees, some gathered into baskets and barrels for the market, others heaped up in rich piles for the cider-press. Further on he beheld great fields of Indian corn, with its golden ears peeping from their leafy coverts and holding out the promise of cakes and hasty-pudding; and the yellow pumpkins lying beneath them, turning up their fair round bellies to the sun, and giving ample prospects of the most luxurious of pies; and anon he passed the fragrant buck-wheat fields, breathing the odor of the beehive, and as he beheld them, soft anticipations stole over his mind of dainty slap-jacks, well-buttered, and garnished with honey or treacle.

But Ichabod Crane was sensitive not only to vistas of agricultural scenery. He was an eater, and looked toward the future with gustatory anticipation. So Washington Irving has given us also a comprehensive account of the above farm produce as it would look and smell and taste after it had passed through the magic realms of the kitchen.

The pedagogue's mouth watered as he looked upon this sumptuous promise of luxurious winter fare. In his devouring mind's eye, he pictured to himself every roasting pig running about, with a pudding in its belly and an apple in its mouth; the pigeons were snugly put to bed in a comfortable pie and tucked in with a coverlet of crust; the geese were swimming in their own gravy, and the ducks pairing cosily in dishes, like snug married couples, with a decent competency of onion sauce. In the porkers he saw carved out the future sleek side of bacon and juicy relishing ham; not a turkey but he beheld daintily trussed up, with its gizzard under its wing, and peradventure, a necklace of savory sausages; and even bright chanticleer himself lay sprawling on his back, in a side-dish, with uplifted claws, as if craving that quarter which his chivalrous spirit disdained to ask while living.

But the kitchen itself, where deeds like these were done! Between the kitchen and the dining room there was almost always a small special room, the pantry. Part of its purpose

From a drawing by Winslow Homer for "Harper's Weekly," November 26, 1859

The Apple Bee

Peel it in one curl and see the initial of your true love

at least was to keep the odors of the kitchen from penetrating to the family and their friends in the dining room before the exact appointed moment when the roast, or the turkey, or whatever it might be, was borne in with a keen sense for climax to have its turn in appreciation and attention. In its way maybe this little pantry was the most artistic room in the house, not in its decoration—it was not decorated at all—in its service. The precision of the dramatic progress of the meal was insured by this little architectural item. Without it one would be enjoying two or three courses all at the same time; and the senses would get confused. The pantry was also made use of in the ordinary sense of the word. Here on glazed shelves the glassware and the china were kept, and here in a nice special sink, often with running water, the dishes were washed.

The kitchen!—It has a long and noble history. In America much of it has been in the nineteenth century. Its rise is rooted in the colonial days, when it was the common room of the house. Its development has been largely by elimination.[2] First the beds were taken out and put in rooms of their own. Next the great eating or dining table was moved out, possibly in part to make the honor of guests more impressive. Then the gathering place for all and sundry was given a special abiding place, and forthwith glorified by the exotic designation of the parlor. What remained of the original common room was the kitchen. All this eliminating was undoubtedly done at the exigence of the cook, who did not want people around, talking, while she was exercising her skill in the esoteric art. Her wishes would certainly come to pass. For nearly one hundred and fifty years now she has been the actual potentate. Her will has been unquestioned,

[2]*Everyday Things in American Life,* Volume I, pages 18–19, 24, 25.

A

B

C

D

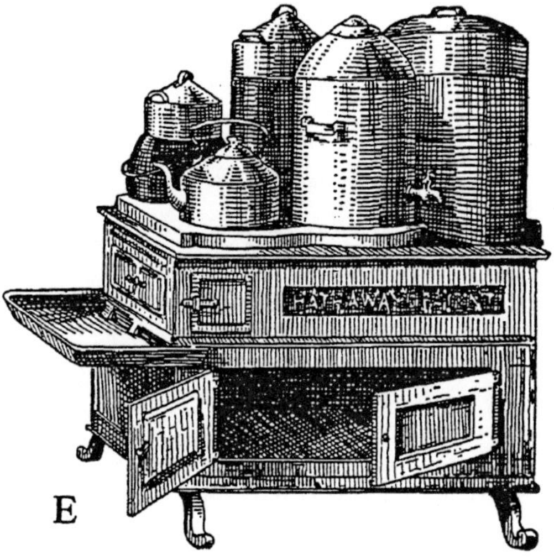

E

A. The old-time stove salesman with his "Portfolio" on his back

B. In this elevated oven type of stove, the housewife had to step up in order to do her baking

C. A fire scoop used to carry coals borrowed from a neighbor in pioneer settlements

D. A cast iron fire pot stove of the type used on fishing and whaling ships

E. The original whole-meal cooking set of about 1840

Drawings by E. G. Lutz after illustrations in stove catalogs, 1841–1850, courtesy of The American Stove Company

her processes not even discussed. The men and other women all this time have ever been well-content to eat, staying on the other side of the pantry door.

Earth, air, fire, and water! By skillful handling of these primal elements of the ancients, the cook has accomplished her wonderful results. Fire, supreme ever since Prometheus brought it down from Heaven, rapidly outstripped the other three in culinary importance. The equipment for the use of fire had a rapid development as soon as stone coal was discovered and made available, both the kind called by the geologists and mineralogists anthracite, and the kind called bituminous, soft coal for short. In colonial times fuel for the fire was brought in horizontally through the door; in the nineteenth century it came into the house through the cellar-way, and then up to the kitchen, vertically, from a bin in the cellar. A marked differentiation came in cooking when the oven was joined to the kitchen range and baking became an indoor process. The extreme size of the oven would seem to have been reached in the days of the "Underground Railway," when Mrs. Bronson Alcott put a Negro refugee into her outdoor oven to hide him until he could successfully be forwarded to Canada. He needed plenty of air, for they knew not how long he would have to stay there quiet, so it must have been a large oven indeed. The Alcotts were a hospitable family and fed people properly when they came to their house. Roasts and pies had to express an Alcott welcome at any time. The Alcott oven may have been of exceptional size but it was by no means the only exception;

there were others as large through the country, as for instance several in thickly settled Bronxville, New York, dating back a hundred years or more.

The necessary air for cooking was supplied through the outside door, which admitted that essential, summer and winter, as well as all the supplies. The earth contributed its quiet service by keeping the supplies cool in the cellar until iceboxes were invented and installed, and later, the stage of fancy names having been reached, refrigerators came into preferred use. Water, in the colonial days, was carried in buckets through the door from the spring. Then, as in the kitchen of the farmhouse at Graeme Park, near Philadelphia, built in 1810, it was piped into a large stone sink, large enough to do a washing. Thence a hole through the wall of the house allowed the water to drain out again. Later, in the 1850s, water was pumped up by a windmill into a tank in the top of the house, whence it ran down through pipes into the kitchen sink, the pantry, and other convenient outlets in the house, provided the tank was large enough to supply so many.

To justify this exclusiveness on the part of the kitchen, it should be noted that by this time the kitchen fire had been encased in iron, whether in a stove or a more amply developed range, and was easily hot enough not only to cook every meal to a crisp brown but to render the whole kitchen uncomfortable for any other use, whether for eating, for conversation, or for sleeping. A large table with a heavy top, sometimes with a butcher's block beside it, whereon lay a ferocious cleaver, offered conveniences for kneading bread and for cutting up the steaks and chops and other meat. But even fierce as some of these items may appear, and imperious as might be the studied atmosphere of the place, it could readily be felt instinctively that all that was done here was nonetheless lovingly wrought with tact and understanding and kindness. The mother was more times than not the cook. Of the kitchen in the very house in Concord that contained the aforementioned capacious oven, in December, 1860, Louisa M. Alcott, she of *Little Women,* wrote in her diary:

> A quiet Christmas; no presents but apples and flowers; for Nan and May were gone; and Betty under the snow. But we are used to hard times, and as Mother says, "while there is a famine in Kansas we mustn't ask for sugar-plums." All the philosophy in our house is not in the study; a good deal is in the kitchen, where a fine old lady thinks high thoughts and does kind deeds while she cooks and scrubs.

But the productions that came forth daily from the kitchen—in fact three times daily! Before the days of the vitaministry of modern cookery, the preparation of the food was, as has been noted, entirely in the hands of her who presided in that sanctum. Sincere appreciation was expressed in emotional superlatives, but not in objective recipes. The priestess did not often write down how she did it; and the habitués of the dining room did not know. It was largely a matter of the personal magic of incommunicable homely genius. It was as personal and transient as is real conversation. Who would think of asking for a recipe for good conversation! It is the finest, most intangible result of true education, whether formal or unconscious, by association with people of genuine character and living culture.

HOW TO

Keep a Husband,

OR

CULINARY TACTICS.

Title-page from a San Francisco cook book of 1872

From a cook book published by Cubery & Co. in San Francisco, 1872

How personal good cooking was may be illustrated by an actual instance which occurred in Virginia back in the 1850s. A young lady went to the darky mammy who did all the family cooking and who was indeed an exceptional cook, and said to her, "Aunt Chloe, I wish you would tell me how to make that cake we had for supper!" With arms akimbo Aunt Chloe began, "Well, Miss Agnes, ah don' know 'z ah *can* tell yo'. Well, yo' tak's a half dozen aigs—ef yo' got um—an' then—yo' jest goes ahead, as yo' knows, an' makes it." Miss Agnes became a wonderful cook by the old-time instinctive method, long before recipes and cook books came into their present universal career. There are still mothers and cooks, whatever the title, who express their care for the family and their hospitality for friends with dishes "made out of their heads." Any one who has eaten of these dishes will agree that certainly "magic" is the right word for it.

No doubt many housewives kept blankbooks in which they wrote their own recipes. Julian P. Boyd, Librarian of Princeton University and formerly of the Historical Society of Pennsylvania, says:

> There is a manuscript cook book, of perhaps two hundred pages, in the Historical Society of Pennsylvania which is commonly called *The Martha Washington Cook Book*. Actually it was a volume compiled by her mother-in-law, Mrs. Custis, who gave it to her. Martha Washington evidently used it during most, if not all, of the time that she was Mrs. Washington.

Probably such blankbooks were used a good deal in the kitchen, and may have been lent around to friends who did not all have as strong an instinct for returning books as for borrowing them, with the general result that few of these manuscript books have been preserved. Some of them however did get into print. From the recipes of *The Martha Washington Cook Book* Mrs. Fiske Kimball has recently made an ample selection, translating them so far as advisable into the equivalents and kitchen customs of the present. She has further preceded them by a vivid and interesting account of the home life of the Washingtons from their daily habits to their trouble with the servants.[3]

Another later blankbook that worked its way into print was *The Virginia Housewife* by Mrs. Mary Randolph. It went through several editions, the first in 1824. In her preface Mrs. Randolph recounts the inception of the book:

> The difficulties I encountered when I first entered on the duties of a House-keeping life, from the want of books sufficiently clear and concise, to impart knowledge to a Tyro, compelled me to study the subject, and by actual experiment to reduce everything to proper weights and measures. This method I found not only to diminish the necessary attention and labor but to be also economical; for when the ingredients employed were given just proportions, the article made was always equally good.

There is also a little book in a stiff marbled paper cover, with pages 3¾ x 5¾ inches, entitled *A New Collection of Genuine Receipts,* etc., and dated 1831. The American Antiquarian Society in its bibliography of early American cook books says there were two editions of this little book printed in 1831, one in Boston and one in Concord, N. H.—in order, it would seem, to facilitate distribution and to serve different regions. In the compass of eleven of its 102 pages it becomes for the nonce an incipient cook book, but there is not a word about cooking on the title-page. The Genuine Receipts pass on, true to blankbook habit, without the interruption of a new chapter or section heading from "To

[3]Marie Kimball: *The Martha Washington Cook Book,* 1940.

clean paper hangings" (wallpaper) to how "To fry meats &c." Two recipes betray the taste of the time: "To make a rich plum cake," which calls for a glass of brandy (how big was a glass in those days?) and "To make a rich seed cake," which however plain still called for a glass of brandy. Then the Genuine Receipts pass unobtrusively again from "To keep gooseberries" to "Cream of Roses," "Pearl water for the face," and in crescendo to such practical directions as "An astringent for the teeth," "To prevent tooth ache," and "A radical cure for the tooth ache."

Good food was not uncelebrated in epic song. Joel Barlow (1754–1812), foreign-living American poet and friend in Paris of Robert Fulton, cooked as well as ate with keen pleasure. While he delighted in French cooking, as who would not, he did not therefore forget the old home dishes of his native America. He wrote a poem on "Hasty Pudding," which the American Antiquarian Society includes in its bibliography of early American cook books as a sufficiently practical recipe even if was expressed in a verse-form characteristic of the times. With some humor it reminds us that the mind of a cook may indulge in moral reflections at the same time that his breast is swelling with anticipatory emotions and his hands are preparing the feast. An extract is given here. The title-page says: The Hasty-Pudding. A Poem, In Three cantos. "Omne tulit punctum qui miscuit utile dulci." He makes a good breakfast who mixes pudding with molasses. (Does not one need something besides Latin to make this translation?) Written in Champerry in Savoy,

1793. By Joel Barlow, Esq. It was probably first printed in New Haven, Connecticut, in 1796, and was reprinted in a number of editions until 1856, or it may be later. With lines gathered here and there a characteristic passage may be accumulated. It begins:

Ye Alps audacious, thro' the heav'ns that rise,
To cramp the day, and hide me from the skies;
Ye Gallic flags, that o'er their heights unfurl'd,
Bear death to kings and freedom to the world,
I sing not you. A softer theme I choose,
A virgin theme, unconscious of the muse,
But fruitful, rich, well suited to inspire
The purest frenzy of poetic fire.

I sing the sweets I know, the charms I feel,
My morning incense and my ev'ning meal,
The sweets of *Hasty Pudding*. Come, dear bowl,
Glide o'er my palate and inspire my soul.

Dear *Hasty Pudding,* what unpromis'd joy,
Expands my heart, to meet thee in Savoy!

But man, more fickle, the bold license claims,
In diff'rent realms to give thee diff'rent names.
Thee the soft nations round the warm Levant
Polanta call, the French of course *Polante;*
Ev'n in thy native regions, how I blush
To hear the Pennsylvanians call thee *Mush!*

Thy name is *Hasty Pudding!* thus our sires
Were wont to greet thee fuming from their fires;—

Yet may the simplest dish some rules impart;
For nature scorns not all the aids of art.
Ev'n *Hasty Pudding,* purest of all food,
May still be bad, indifferent, or good;
As sage experience the short process guides,
Or want of skill or want of care presides.

Attend the lessons that the Muse shall bring—
Suspend your spoons, and listen while I sing.

The earliest of all American cook books, so far as known and a printed one at that, was *The Compleat Housewife*, published in 1742. It is now a very rare book, possibly only one copy remaining, the one owned by the American Antiquarian Society. It is well to notice it, because most or all of our social customs (and eating is a social custom, only excepting bolting the victuals) come down from those courtly days, and also on principle, as they can most truly understand the present and most clearly look into the future, who are most familiar with the past. Therefore it is that in all history first things come first, though in this instance we are putting them last.

The American Antiquarian Society quotes *The Compleat Housewife* as claiming that its contents were "never before made public in these parts; fit either for private families, or such public-spirited gentlewomen as would be beneficial to their poor neighbors." It was printed and sold by William Parks at Williamsburg in Virginia, in 1742. Like the earliest architectural books[4] *The Compleat Housewife* came

[4]See *Everyday Things in American Life,* Volume I, pages 129–131.

from England, where an edition was printed in 1727, which may have been the first or may have been the fifth English edition. There were several American editions. Martha Washington may have had one; it is not known; but it was to be had in her day.

One year this early cook book boldly aligned itself, in the matter of spelling, with the future. In 1761 it presented itself as *The Complete Housewife.* That was, however, for one year only. Faint-hearted, in 1764, with the next edition, it resumed the *Compleat* spelling. *The Compleat Housewife* was an authority far back in the prerecorded age of American cooking, before the period with which this volume is specially concerned. Acknowledging the gracious smile with which for a moment the book looked forward to our time and spelling, we can properly only turn and salute its writer with the assurance that we are certain every dish she sent in to the feast was a feast in itself indeed.

But we have been intruding into the mysteries of the kitchen! Thither none but those by nature, by heredity, or by duty privileged, may ever successfully penetrate. (And most of those are women.)

The hall, the hallway, or the front hall, was one of the essential elements of the house in the nineteenth century. Deriving its name untouched from mediæval times, despite the entire change in its character, this remnant of the hall of the old English manor became chiefly a mere passageway. It was a passageway between indoors and outdoors, a passageway between upstairs and downstairs, a passageway to and from the various specialized family rooms. Architecturally it was comparatively long, yet still somewhat broad, for it had to reach from the front to the back of the house and it had to contain a fairly dignified front stairs, yet allow for convenient passage past them.

With the front door the hallway provided the grand entrance to the house. This consisted of the door itself, larger—that is, broader and heavier—than any of the other doors, and usually with a narrow window on each side to admit light and to permit a glimpse of who was there. Privacy was ensured by thin curtains in front of these windows; one could see out but not in. (There was also, unacknowledged, but almost all houses had one, a mirror fastened to the frame of an upstairs window set at such an angle that one could easily see who was at the front door.) Outside there was a large step surmounting the two or three rising from the level of the sidewalk, whereon the visitor could wait until allowed admittance. The old brass knocker on the middle of the door was gone. In its stead, on the right-hand door jamb was a brass bell pull, a round knob two inches wide, attached by a stout wire through the wall to a bell on the inside close to the ceiling, or at the farther end of the hall. A pull on the knob set the bell a-jangling. It could be heard all over the house and every one knew there was some one at the front door. There was also a foot scraper, and later some kind of doormat on the outer step, so that the visitor could clean the mud off his shoes while waiting and not track it into the house.

A. Gateway with lantern overthrow; *B*. Suffolk type of latch; *C*. A carefully fashioned shutter fastener; *D*. A fish vane with "tulip" finial, characteristic of many early vanes

Redrawn by E. G. Lutz after drawings by Albert H. Sonn for "Early American Wrought Iron"

Conspicuous and convenient in the hall stood the hat-rack, a tall piece of carved wooden furniture, probably black walnut, distinctly erect, some six feet high or so, and three feet wide. This comprised a mirror, on either side of which were strong pegs on which to hang hats and coats, and below, an umbrella-stand with its pan to catch the drippings when it was raining. There was also a grandfather's clock, almost always placed here in the front hall, unless it was on a landing halfway up the stairs. It was where every one could readily see what time it was, especially before every one had a watch. A chair or two completed the furniture.

The stairway was in its glory in colonial days. Always noteworthy, though now usually much simplified, it was still the most prominent feature in the hallway, whether to one coming in through the front door, or from any of the rooms.

The highest dignity attained through this specialization came with the parlor. In some regions, in the early days, the dignity attaching to this room was so high that it was used only for funerals, and was closed the rest of the time. As dignity is under such conditions, the room was usually pretty musty. It is no doubt true, and certainly more just, to remember that even in the most dignified instances the parlor was also used for other occasions, for weddings, for instance. But the little airing-out it got, if any, did not eradicate the mustiness that maintained the continuing dignity of the chamber. It should further be borne in mind that the

From Ballou's "Pictorial Drawing-Room Companion," 1855

An evening party in Boston

room, in respect to its musty dignity, conformed to the temper of the family. On the one hand, many, very many families used the room for family and social purposes a great deal, and were used to fresh air to a considerable extent. On the other hand, of those who did not so use it many did not notice anything exceptional or different in the room from the ordinary, any more particularly than the difference in coming into the house from outdoors.

The parlor was always located at the front of the house, the parlor door opening into the hall usually to the right of the front door. The dining room was often on the opposite side of the hall. In the colonial days the parlor was one of the "fire-rooms," that is, it had a fireplace in it. Over the fireplace, in the nineteenth century, was always a marble mantelpiece, whereon stood, in the middle, a good-sized clock, also of marble, of a contrasting color, as of black marble on a white marble mantelpiece. As the family got into the habit of using the parlor more and more the convenience of having the time easily available in that room increased and the necessity for the great grandfather's clock in the hall decreased. So the mantel clocks increased and the grandfather's clocks diminished in number. At either end of the mantel stood one of a pair of large decorative vases, which might hold masses of showy flowers, or which might prove themselves quite sufficient unto all possible decorative requirements of the situation.

The chief piece of furniture in the parlor was the marble-topped center table. On this stood a large and handsome kerosene lamp, sometimes of the kind called a student's lamp, around which the family could gather in the evening. Also on the center table there were one, two, or even several books, which not only *could* be read, but could serve as symbols of literary standards and taste. Among these—and the one, when there was only one—was the Holy Bible, large, impressive, and illustrated, insistently suggesting that there was no book with which the family was more familiar—and sometimes this was the fact. This family Bible was also the place through which the stream of vital statistics originally flowed. Herein were recorded the dates and the data of all births, marriages and deaths in the family or among their kin. Whether read or not, in the recording of American history, local or general, it was an important volume, an important institution.

A large armchair was to be found beside the center table, in the best light—frequently two, one on either side, for the parents or the grandparents. And along the wall, between the windows, waited the ample sofa, holding three *fairly* comfortably, or holding two more comfortably with a certain amount of space between them, to ensure not being too forbidding for the conversation, and yet on the other hand not too informal. The sofa was indeed well adapted to follow in the progress of friendships between the stage when each one sat on one of the rather straight-backed side chairs, of which there were several at hand, and the stage when they didn't.

Not infrequently, especially among the more literary

people, and as the years rolled on, there would be a nice-looking bookcase, with glass doors, in the parlor. People were not yet really in a hurry to get a book. Such bookcases were not more than three feet wide, and five shelves or six feet high. The books were of family selection or such as were chosen by friends and other wedding-present donors. Sets of Shakespeare's *Works* (frequently Bowdler's strictly proper edition), Gibbon's *Decline and Fall of the Roman Empire,* and other standard authors were there to be found—under lock and key.

In one of the outer corners of the parlor, almost without fail, there stood a whatnot, a set of shelves, literally named, to hold—what not indeed. Often triangular, so as to fit into the corner, on its receding shelves, reaching high toward the ceiling, were exhibited all sorts of curios from all over the world—branches of coral, pink and white, sea-fans, large conch shells, anything that was not local and that might attest a foreign origin or seafaring connection. For all this contributed to create a cultured atmosphere, which in many, many homes, throughout the country, was very sincerely and definitely desired.

Family and visitors were further characteristically reminded and assured that the religious spirit underlay the life of this home by the framed mottoes, of which one at least adorned the walls. "God Bless Our Home" worked in colored worsteds often found a fitting place over the parlor door. Nowadays these framed mottoes would probably be called crude and sentimental, but fifty years from now the

Drawings by E. G. Lutz

Home Furnishings

Top left: Framed motto. *Right:* Whatnot. *Lower left:* Hat rack. *Right:* Forewarning of approaching visitors sophisticated, as likely as not, will be seeking them out, as they do samplers now. Sentimental they were, *i.e.,* appealing to the interest of some personal or extraneous circumstance rather than to pure form and color. The mid-nineteenth-century sentiment did go to an extreme, however, in its framed wreaths made of human hair, tresses from the heads of relatives gone to join the dear departed. Family portraits by fine painters, of whom America has long had an increasing number,[5] were surely preferable in point of both personal sentiment and artistic beauty to either hair wreaths or mottoes, and these portraits gradually took over the wall space that the wreaths and mottoes had previously occupied.

In the homes of professional people—ministers, teachers, doctors, and frequently lawyers, though lawyers more often had their offices downtown in the business part of town, where their clients were apt to be—there was usually still another room, the study. This was the special sanctum of the professional man himself. It was often located in an ell of the house, and had a separate entrance from the street all its own, so that all the professional work and interests, to which it was devoted, might be kept quite separate from the domestic interests and the family life of the house proper. There was of course inside access from the house.

[5]See Oskar Hagen: *The Birth of the American Tradition in Art.*

CHAPTER XI

Home-Life: Upstairs

STANDING out in the hall, the dominant feature was the stairs going up to the second floor. Everything else—walls, doors, windows (if any), furniture—all stood and stayed in their places. Even when you wanted a door to open, you had to do something about it. But the stairs went up, all by themselves, not in the stand-still way that a ladder offered its services, but with a silent graceful curve, like an airplane of a later period taking off, which not only took you up to the second floor but landed you quite a ways farther back in the house, and in very truth up into another region. That graceful curve of the stairs also came down with a thrill all its own, as the small boy of the family specially appreciated, he more than any of the others. The down curve seemed to be concentrated in the banisters. By an imaginative facility that outsped time and eluded the eye of the dignified grandfather clock on the landing, the young girls of the family, as they neared the end of their teens, seemed to appreciate the up-curve of the stairs in an anticipatory way of their own. While recognizing that the stairs consisted of steps, they felt they were walking on air, as they went up the stairs, all in white, and from the top of the steps threw a bouquet of flowers, orange blossoms, down into a smiling happy crowd of sweet faces and outstretched arms.

It goes without saying that when guests were to be received or friends welcomed, it was down these stairs that the hostess came. And when one of the family, having lived through as many years as one naturally would, left the home for the last time, it was by these same stairs he came, and so out the front door into the outdoors under the deep blue starry sky. Immediately, it is true, he came from out of the parlor, that formal center of the house. But that was only a pause. In the real fact, he came down the stairs from the mystery of the upper rooms out into the all-pervading mystery of the night.

It was literally true, a certain elusive mystery pervaded the upper rooms, the second floor, and to some extent also the third. If there was a fourth floor, or more, the mystery seemed to have faded, and one floor was just the same as another. This did not apply to the garret, or attic, as it was called in some parts of the country. Many people would say they had never noticed any mystery. That is just it, they had never noticed it. It was elusive, as the mystery of life itself, the greatest mystery of all, is elusive. It is so easy to take life for granted. This mystery of the upper rooms began inevitably in those stairs and the feeling they gave of uninterrupted motion. Every piece of wood in them was nailed firmly into place and did not move an inch as long as the house might last. The whole region was called after the stairs, thereby attesting their subtle pervasive influence—upstairs.

These rooms were all alike called bedrooms, which distinguished them from the parlor, study, dining room, and kitchen. There was a bed, one at least, in every room, and some one habitually slept in each bed. But there the generalized unity stopped. Every room was the focal habitat of a different member of the family. It was *his* or *her* room, to be his or her individual self in. The furniture might be standardized somewhat and only adapted to the tenant, but the general atmosphere and the reminiscent decoration were absolutely of and characteristic of the inhabitant. In fact, these rooms were all alike and all entirely different. That in itself is a mystery, and yet the necessary key to the true appreciation of domestic architecture. Only by approach through this personal mystery does a room become to one not merely another room but a certain particular room, So-and-So's room. Whether this element in the home inhered specially in the house would be hard to say. In the period under consideration Americans lived only in houses; there were no apartments. But even so, who ever heard of a haunted apartment! Ghosts never recognized apartments and distinguished them with their ostensible presence. But a ghost was not essential in any way to this mystery of the upper rooms—whether one believes in ghosts or not. That mystery came from the virile personalities of the members of the family who lived in these rooms. There might be ghosts too, if so be there were, upstairs much more often than down.

During most of the nineteenth century, the assignment of the bedrooms was quite established. Father and mother naturally had the best room, and it was on the front of the house. They shared a large double bed. Single beds were given only to adolescents. In the rivalry for the next best room two sisters of winning age assuredly won. The older sons had a special room, in a wing or maybe on the third floor, aloof from any area subject to the influence of the feminine, a room where they could live their own lives in masculine independence.

The small boy of the family usually got a room by himself, for some reason, and usually on the second floor. A room on the third floor was too far from parental influence, and too near to his older brothers, if they were installed in that still upper region. There was no clamor from those older brothers for his intimate companionship until he was sixteen, was distinctly *of them*. He knew time was on his side and that he would be received later if he was "a good kid" meantime. He also knew there were advantages in having a room by himself, however small, on the rather feminine second floor. Somehow or other it happened that all small boys' rooms had a window opening out on to the kitchen roof, or on to a shed roof, or on to the roof of an ell. Gutter-pipes also as by a kind fate were built stronger than might have been expected; and trees reached out their branches, as judged by squirrels and small boys, quite near. This informal means for juvenile exit and entrance has been immortalized by Mark Twain in *Tom Sawyer,* to whom many and many a man claims kinship, gladly recognizing bits of his own youthful experience.

With such a structure and such a use of the house over the length and breadth of the expanding country, and through the duration of the hundred years, there was also a developing change of conditions which intimately affected

A bona fide pioneer residence which might be called a forerunner of the present-day trailer

From "Beyond the Mississippi," by Albert T. Richardson, 1867

the very structure of the house itself and the nature of the home both in general and in local detail. One of these conditions was heat. Heat was not only the means of preparing the food for eating and of subduing the weather to obviate seasonal migration and abbreviation of the activities of living. Heat insured relaxation of nerves and bones in personal comfort and the lifting of strained attention from physical conditions. It made possible the rescue of sedentary occupations and the development of the intellectual life. In no way did a red nose, chattering teeth, and aching bones betoken intellectuality. The chief home of civilization and of human achievement has always been the temperate zone. The mission of heating and cooling devices has ever been to offset the extremes of the weather and practically to modify the climate of winter and summer into the equable conditions and adequate variety of the temperate zone.

Heat in the colonial days was secured by means of the fireplaces, whether in the kitchen or in the fire-rooms, and the burning of wood as the fuel in them. The result was of course a tremendous advance in warmth and comfort, compared not with what has been realized since but compared with what had gone before.[1] It should be recognized that, speaking generally, the colonial days were in America times of decided individual self-reliance. The farthest that heating could go under those conditions was with the fireplaces and the wood stoves. Coal was much better, a great advance, but coal could not be used for heating whether for general warmth or for cooking, until coal had been discovered, until organization had effected co-ordination of men sufficient for the mining of the coal, until facilities had been devised for the transportation of the coal from the mines to the people who wished to use it in their kitchens, fire-rooms and other places. Then the fireplaces acquired grates, which sat in the fireplaces without a rebuilding of the chimneys, and held the coal while it burned. So grates followed the and-

[1] *Everyday Things in American Life,* Volume I, pages 18–26.

irons. But superior as the grates were, there was something about the andirons and their wood fires that has withstood the encroachments of all practical considerations, even to the present day, if only one can get the wood. It is no longer a matter of picking up the axe and stepping out to the wood lot for a little exercise and an armful or two of oak for the backlog, or of maple, or of apple. The open fire is now to be counted not as a necessity but rather as one of the spiritual assets of the home.

Progress declared itself in the main line of descent first in the receptacle for the fire, in the wood stove, probably derived by collateral descent from the roasting kitchen of five or six generations before. Then as coal became available, the stove was improved and advanced from being a mere wood stove to being a coal stove.

There was in due time another effect of progress in the fireplace, but it was really a minor one, for it was in fact only a luxury; it affected the spiritual atmosphere of the home but little if any. It required a change in the construction of the chimney, providing for a hole going down from the back of the fireplace to the cellar below. The ashes were simply pushed down this hole and cleaned out in the cellar without tracking them through the house in defiance of breezes from drafty doors and windows. It was called the ash dump. There was no suggestion of spirituality about that name. To be sure these were wood ashes. But wood ashes were no longer recognized as precious. They were no longer saved for the making of soap. They were merely lighter and more blowy than coal ashes. The ash dump was a convenience; it was practical; also it marked the end of the triumph of wood as a family fuel.

Stoves had their day—coal stoves, of course. There could be a stove in any room in the house. The only condition was that it be placed on that side of the room that would permit of access to the chimney for the smoke flue through a round hole in the wall. The circle always was the emblem of Perfection, and it had in connection with these stoves something of the same significance. Stoves, even coal stoves, attained their superiority with the unlimited access to chimneys represented by these round holes in the walls of the rooms. There were seldom if ever stoves in the bedrooms, for stoves would make the rooms too hot for sleeping. In the northern latitudes, in the winter, the beds were heated by soapstones or bricks, wrapped in flannel and laid between the sheets. This was ideal, barring the chilly process of undressing—a minor but personal art in which the dwellers of the northern latitudes all gained speed. But once in bed the condition—warm as toast within, and nipping cold outside—was beatific! But those ashes still had to be carried down through the house.

The stove had to go! It was moved down into the cellar, made bigger and somewhat more complicated; a pipe went up through the walls to every room, emerging through a square hole in the floor covered by ornamental iron work, called a register. The real reason for this name is by now probably lost in the sands of time. The register was equipped with iron slats behind the grill work which by means of a simple ratchet could be opened to admit the warm air into the room, or closed to shut it off. The collection of coal stoves, with being moved down into the cellar, had been reduced in number to one, but that one greatly increased in size. The heating of the house had become a system. This made a new name appropriate. The heating system was called a furnace. The size of a furnace, as compared with a mere stove upstairs, seems to have impressed the name-givers. The unabridged dictionary says a furnace is "an enclosed place in which heat is produced by fuel combustion." An enclosed place! There sounds in that no tone of compromise with anything.

As long as success in heating the house was not complete and entirely under control, there was effective recourse to accessories to supplement the heating apparatus, whether that consisted of fireplaces, wood stoves, coal stoves or furnaces. The most effective were the carpets and rugs on the floors. Under the carpet was laid a layer of matting or of straw. This doubled the warmth of the carpet. In summer matting took the place of the carpet, and in the fall fresh straw was laid before the carpet was replaced. In the winter up north storm doors and double windows contributed much to the comfort of the family, usually with one pane of glass in each window on hinges so that the room could be readily ventilated and fresh air supplied for the health and greater comfort of the inhabitants.

In time differentiation crept in among the furnaces. There

were hot-air furnaces, steam heaters, and hot-water plants. The system of pipes was the legacy of the hot-air furnace to its successors. When steam came and there had been opportunity to adapt it to the heating of the house, the large tin pipes leading up to the registers were discarded and a system of steam pipes was substituted, leading up to radiators. When it was thought advisable to circulate hot water instead of steam the necessary adaptation was made and hot water went through the pipes and warmed the house much less emotionally. The water now had to be raised only to about 200° Fahrenheit to get good hot water that would circulate well, instead of to 212° to generate steam. Steam, if compressed too much, will explode. Of course the old hot-air furnace was dangerous too, if the young stoker had the idea that tending the furnace was, like tending a stove, merely a matter of shovelling in coal and shovelling out ashes, and having in reserve a little knowledge of kerosene, in case he tried to save time in bringing his fire back after some youthful neglect. But steam was known to be a powerful force and to require technical understanding in its management. Accordingly the tender, to start with, was never so young as in the case of the hot-air furnace. So there were less property loss and fewer deaths. But we are getting too near to the end of our period, even considering the most advanced communities.

Another condition which intimately affected the developing house and home in the nineteenth century was light. With this continuing moderate warmth there came into the everyday life of Americans an extension of time. In the northern winters, for instance, it was no longer necessary for people to hibernate all the hours of the dark night in order to restore their nervous resistance to the cold. They could use more time in the work and in the enjoyment of life. So artificial lighting came into appreciation. From being an economized luxury it was promoted to being not only a generally used but even to being, by benefit of applied science and technical engineering, a squandered and taken-for-granted necessity.

The development of lighting in America was even more swift, more sudden, than the development of heating. As the colonial period was left behind, the use of candles was increased and then abandoned. From one candle, and then several candles, there came the multiplication of candles in chandeliers. The ambition of heat through this colonial period was to attain to an artificial warmth that insured a perfect luxury of comfort. The standard of light on the other hand was the natural daylight. More than that was not desired at whatever time of night.

Two elements were regularly essential to a light-producing fire, for heat and light since prehistoric times have steadily been akin, the gaseous fuel and the consuming oxygen—in its native state, air. With the candles, between times of use the fuel, wax, was hard; this fostered their preservation. When the lighting of the wick started combustion, the hard wax of the candle was melted, and as the flame became hotter, the melting of the flowing wax proceeded into an inflammable gas, which burned with a steady bright light-giving fire, blue around the wick encased in a yellow spear-head. With a single candle, however slender or thick, the melting of the wax around the wick was circular; when the candles were more numerous, the heat from the other candles increased the melting of each candle, increasing the fuel-element in the combustion, and created a larger, general glow which lighted the whole room or a larger part of the room more brightly—and also wasted the candles away more rapidly.

With the passing of pioneer conditions from large areas of the territory of the United States, chiefly through the advent of the canals and railroads, oil lamps came into more general use for lighting in America. During the nineteenth century oil lamps were the prevalent form of lighting, in the small town and country districts continuously, and in the cities until gas offered greater convenience and better light. Whale oil was not the only oil used for lighting, but until 1860 the whaling industry supplied the increasing American market, both for house and for street lighting.[2] The first street lighting in America, thanks to John Clifton and Benjamin Franklin, was in Philadelphia in 1756,[3] but street lighting could not become an everyday thing in American life until there was sufficient fuel of the right kind. One advantage of oil over candles for outdoor lighting was

[2]*Everyday Things in American Life,* Volume I, pages 216–219.

[3]For Franklin's account of this see *The Practical Dr. Franklin,* published by The Franklin Institute, Philadelphia, page 47.

that oil lamps were not as easily blown out by the wind. An early use of oil lamps was in lighthouses.

The existence of mineral oil was known. There were "burning springs" where the gas seeped to the surface, but its practical value was not recognized. After August 27, 1859, when Edwin L. Drake (1819–1880) found mineral oil by drilling near Titusville in western Pennsylvania, it began to be obtainable. Drake lacked the business wisdom to make him personally successful. But by 1865 mineral oil, kerosene, was generally available. With kerosene there came also a change in the form of the lamps the better to accommodate the more easily flowing liquid.

At first the lamp wick was flat, rising up out of the oil in a receptacle below. Adopting a device invented by Aimé Argand of Switzerland in the latter part of the eighteenth century, the light was greatly improved by the Argand burner, which had a cylindrical wick and supplied a current of air for the combustion of the oil on the inside of the wick as well as on the outside. An excellent reading lamp in common use was called the Student's Lamp. It had a cylindrical wick and the oil supply in a reservoir above the level of the burner on the other side of an upright standard, from which the oil descended steadily through a pipe.

Gas lighting brought a great change in domestic lighting. Gas became a general and everyday thing in the cities, but naturally not in the small towns and country districts. However, the number of cities in the United States was increasing rapidly. The gas was manufactured by baking coal in retorts, drawing off the gas and leaving the coke, which was valuable for other purposes. The gas was supplied from a central source through a system of pipes to the houses in the city and also to street lights where the gas was burned in what were still called "lamp-posts." At the ends of the pipes, where light was desired, there were gas fixtures, which consisted of a steatite tip to flatten the flame into a "fish-tail," and a glass globe to diffuse the light and give a more decorative appearance. The business accounts were automatically kept by aid of a system of gas-meters. "Lamp-lighters" went the rounds through the streets with their ladders at sunset and in the early morning to light the lights and to turn them off. Gas lighting in American cities was first installed about 1816. By 1875 it was in general use wherever a town was large enough to justify the expense of plant and operation.

Still another of these civilizing agencies was water. As life goes along, too much of anything is certain to turn to poison. "All work and no play makes Jack a dull boy," as Jack will see to it that we remember; and "All play and no work" will make him an unhappy, irresponsible nitwit. Water in sufficient quantity on Saturday afternoons was for Jack the sure cleansing agency and moral corrective; and as a special remedy to have the mouth washed out with plenty of water—with soap added—worked the sure cure of small boys for dirty talk. Vulgarity—dirt—is at a disadvantage with plenty of water around. Good fresh water, whether in the tub, at the swimming-hole, or at the seashore, will wash any soul back to the love of clean beauty, sane merriment,

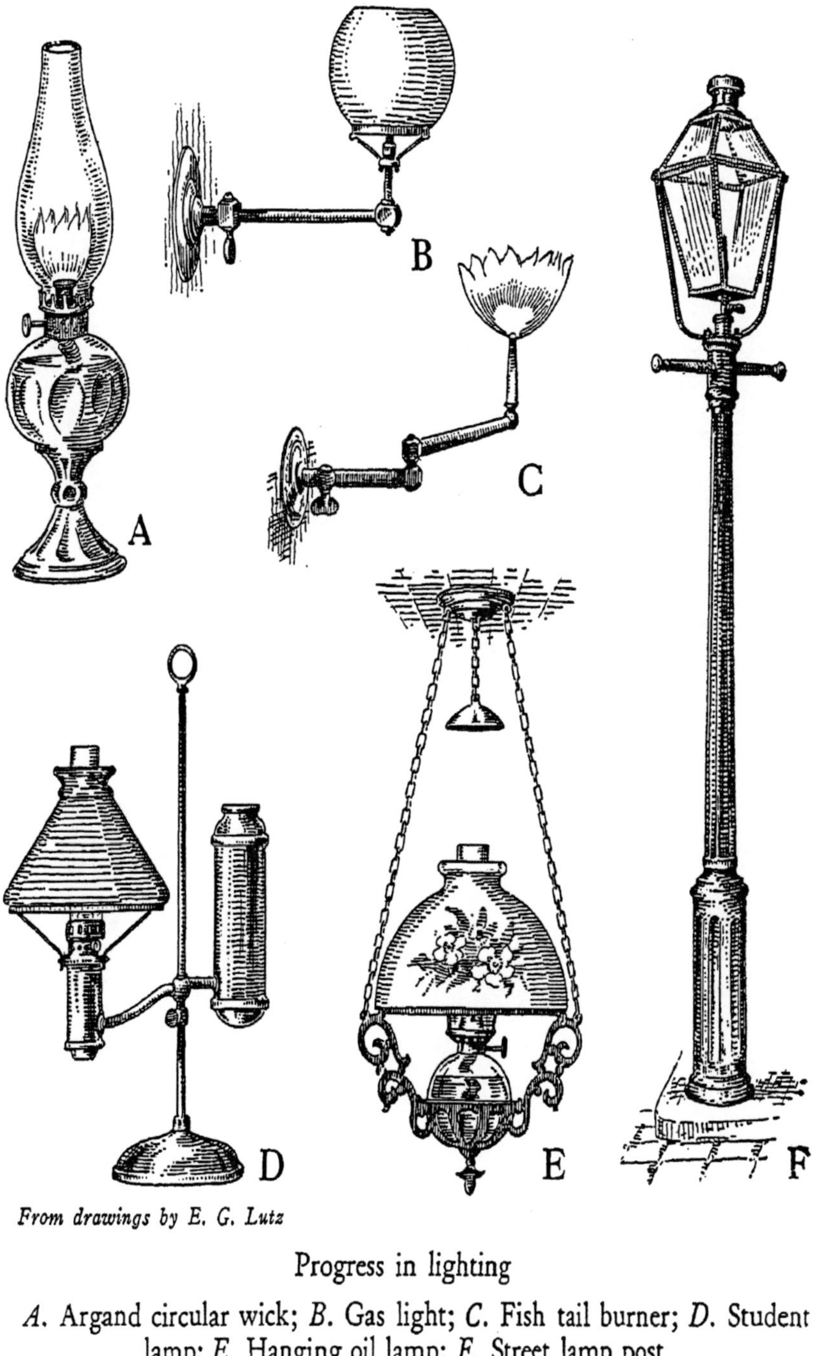

From drawings by E. G. Lutz

Progress in lighting

A. Argand circular wick; *B*. Gas light; *C*. Fish tail burner; *D*. Student lamp; *E*. Hanging oil lamp; *F*. Street lamp post and resourceful vigor, just as running water will cleanse itself of any and all physical impurities in seven miles.

But water, at least as represented in the bathtub, had some peculiar incidents in its history. The small boy, if he knew his history, could fairly claim full legal justification for his aversion to taking a bath. Bathtubs were never even mentioned in America, in public or in private, before 1820. Bathtubs were first installed not earlier than 1832, when a row of model houses was built in Philadelphia, the water supply coming through the Schuylkill Water Works at the rate, in 1836, of $36 a year per tub. For part of the same year the use of bathtubs was prohibited by Philadelphia city ordinance on sanitary grounds; and their use was prohibited in Boston in 1845 except on advice of a physician. However, water had its way and found its own high level. In 1836, despite the legal frown, there were 1530 bathtubs in Philadelphia, and by 1860 most of the hotels in New York had them. Further, in the middle of the century the luxurious "rain bath" arrived. And a little later when new industries brought with them social poisoning during the industrial revolution, the rebalancing science of sanitation, based on water, made its appearance and rapidly, persistently produced its great contribution to a clean, a healthful, and a delightful American life.

A radical and welcome improvement came with the introduction of running water into the house by means of a water system similar to the heat and lighting systems. The first element in this was a pump, in many districts run by a windmill, to send the water through a single water pipe up to a tank in the attic. Thence the water descended by gravity through the smaller water pipes down to the kitchen sink, and to the sanitary glory of the bathroom on the second floor. Indoor baths had formerly been taken in a large round tub on the kitchen or bedroom floor. Now a special oblong tub was devised with faucets admitting the water at one upright end, the drain pipe opening out immediately underneath, and a sloping end opposite for luxurious reclining and soaking. These bathtubs were made of tinned iron and were the subject of many progressive improvements, and contributed greatly and steadily to the development of cleanliness and health.

In the bathroom at about the same time was placed the sanitary seat. Formerly this necessary convenience was a separate little closet back of the house, and so in America called by simple abbreviation the backhouse. It was an earth-closet, into which from time to time dry earth was poured to cover and to absorb the fetid substances. When water was piped into the house and the bathroom was invented, the sanitary seat was moved thither, and water was piped to a special little tank for flushing. The name of "water-closet" was naturally given it.

Water pipes and running water in the bedrooms did not come until later. Municipal water systems with large reservoirs adequate to supplying the whole town or city also came later. In regions where there was not an abundant surface water supply the artesian well water from great depths, and heat-coils of pipes in the kitchen range or in the furnace and a tall copper boiler standing alongside made the hot water plentiful.

Ice for preserving foods, in succession to the cold cellar and the springhouse, was cut on the frozen ponds and

Courtesy Gifford-Wood Company, Hudson, N. Y.

Ice harvesting

lakes in the north and stored in special cellars, whence it was shipped all over the country and to some extent even abroad. One of the peculiar instances was how the Honorable Timothy Dexter of Newburyport, Massachusetts, who was as peculiar as was his luck, made a considerable fortune by sending ice to Greenland and warming-pans to India. Ice became a great industry and lasted for many years.

As the Federal America grew up through the colonial, so in its architectural aspect it grew up through the stately Georgian. The advance seemed at first to consist of putting a classic portico with Doric, Ionic, or Corinthian columns, surmounted by a pediment, in front of every building—state house, church, bank or residence. But there were no professional architects in America during the first quarter of the nineteenth century, and this was fortunate. Architectural progress was carried forward in America by amateurs. This correctly understood is a title of honor; its accurate synonym is enthusiast. As these amateurs lacked the emphatic professional training, they were not so strict in obedience to the precise rules of the art, and allowed themselves more originality in special circumstances. As skill increased a fine new style grew up, the Greek Revival, which originated in America and thence spread to England.

The prime leader of this movement, as noted, was Thomas Jefferson,[4] although, as also noted, he was rather inclined to remain rigidly loyal to the Roman phase of the art and to the model of Palladio. Among the definitely amateur and so more original leaders were Benjamin Henry Latrobe, with his Bank of Pennsylvania at Philadelphia and his Bank of the United States (carried out by William Strickland) and his Catholic Cathedral at Baltimore, Ithiel Town, and William Thornton, who designed the National Capitol at Washington.

While the architects of the Greek Revival were not bound

[4]*Everyday Things in American Life,* Volume I, page 130.

by traditional practice in details, they did not escape, naturally (nor did they want to), the working out of the classic principles.

To realize how this freedom saved the art from stereotyped formality it should be noted that the Greek column was a section of wall thinned down to the least requirement in order to support the burden above, and evidently to appear to be able to support it. In the column this section of wall was itself made beautiful with the flutings which emphasized the stress of the support; with the base with its horizontal lines from which the support sprang (except in the Doric, which seemed to spring spontaneously to meet its burden without any preliminary preparation of a base); and with the capitals where the supporting columns met their burden, and where the support was glorified by the simple Doric, or the more decorative Ionic or Corinthian.

In the American Greek Revival it should no less be recognized that the section of wall may be used in accordance with the same principle by simple acceptance of equal sections symmetrically disposed in a treatment that for simplicity out-Dorics the Doric, or in a treatment that restrained the beautifying of the section of wall to the austere pilaster. The intensity of shadows between the columns, fostered by the depth of the main wall in from the columns or wall-sections also asserted the lean virility of the support. This was often beautifully emphasized by balconies and wrought-iron grill work. The appearance of the steam railroad in about 1825 gave the iron-foundry business a great impetus and added this quite original subsidiary art to the attractive features of the Greek Revival.

It is merely tantalizing to touch on this subject as slightly as is practicable in a book as general as this book. The reader who is interested in this subject should be sure to read, leisurely and with abundant time given to the illustrations and diagrams, the books listed in the bibliography.

The interior decoration of the house was inevitably directed by the fact that the home was a human place. The faces of the father and the mother and the grandparents were to all the kinsfolk and acquaintance the most interesting and the most treasured things to be seen in a house. When therefore the art of oil painting became available to duplicate those faces, portraiture became the chief decoration of the home and dominated it all the nineteenth century.

In 1839 Louis Jacques Mande Daguerre, a Frenchman, brought to success his invention of the heliographic picture, which has been called after him the daguerreotype. This greatly increased the number of good portraits that could be made and greatly reduced their cost, though also greatly reducing their size, even to that of the little oil paintings, of only three inches or so, which were appropriately called miniatures. Experiments to improve the process of making daguerreotypes by many artists were brought to success in 1840 by John W. Draper, a professor in the University of the City of New York, now New York University, when in 1840 he took an excellent "photograph" of his sister,

Dorothy, on the roof of a house on 4th Street, New York City. This still further extended the number of small-sized portraits that could be had, and still further reduced their cost. The difference in degree of improvement no doubt then was soon so great as to amount to a difference in kind. In the past one hundred years photography has become a great art, a popular amusement and a recognized industry. Meantime, however, portraiture in oil paints has held its own. For character study and for the representation of personality, for those who can meet the unavoidable expense, it is still supreme.

The house was made beautiful also by the beauty outside, the gardens and trees and lawns surrounding it, and inside by the views of the landscape framed by the windows. The development of this type of painting had lagged behind portraiture, as was natural. But there was one phase of the landscape art that during the first half of the nineteenth century in America took on a special form—the wallpapers. In brief this art simply distinguished between the landscape vistas looking out the windows and the landscape vistas supplied by the imaginative art between the windows. In these wallpapers landscape and classic elements were commonly combined and made the scene of geographic panoramas, or the scene of mythological or historical stories. Sometimes actuality was cleverly challenged by a paper balustrade running around the room in the design of the wallpaper and secured in the house by the strong shadows of the perspective. These papers were at first imported from

Europe where they were designed and made in France and England. The most prominent of the wallpaper artists were probably Jean Zuber, of Mulhouse in Alsace, and Joseph Dufour, of Paris. Later on fine wallpapers were made also in America, in Boston and other places, and there was an excellent market for them until about 1850.

One result of the leeway inseparable from the amateur development of domestic architecture was that in not a few instances the householder adapted a panoramic wallpaper to his house by inserting some sections and omitting other sections. Truly as such a practice might cause pain to the artist, if he knew of it, nonetheless there did occasionally result some original and striking, however sudden, effects in the architecture of the landscaping represented in the design. Nonetheless, with all these irregularities, wherever found, and whether fortunate or unfortunate, the art was fascinating indeed. As an art, rare now, the panoramic wallpaper soon after the middle of the century withdrew before the decorative wallpaper, designed in simple repetitive patterns and readily reproduced by the roller presses at moderate cost. The art also yielded before the rise of the inexpensive, mechanically reproduced landscape and genre art such as the Currier and Ives prints. These were easily framed and hung up in the middle of a wall space instead of having to be spread over the whole of it.

CHAPTER XII

Clothes and Their Material

THE brooks and other small streams descending the hills and merging into larger streams, and into rivers, at last empty into the sea, where for a while their currents are distinguishable but soon are lost. So was it also with the making of cloth and of clothes. The making of cloth in America began early, early in the colonial period and inevitably followed certain racial lines. In the early times the material to be used for clothes was not a matter for personal selection and choice. The Colonists as a matter of course wore and made to wear what had been common in the parts of the old countries from which they came. Because they could not obtain silks, satins, and brocades, they did not refuse to wear what they could get in adequate quantity and what they could soon learn to make—the same that the common people at home made and wore. The small streams of the home garment industries have long since flowed on into the seas of the vast cotton, woolen and linen manufactures. Of their original courses only a little information now remains, but this, so far as it is authentic, is suggestive and interesting.

The cotton industry had flourished in England for a

long time, England with its wide-flung commerce bringing the raw material home abundantly. So in the earlier years of American nationality the working up of cotton centered in New England, developed by the men who came from cotton-manufacturing England. Even though the Southern Atlantic States proved to be a great cottton-producing region, the cotton mills remained in the New England States. England imported her raw material from India; New England imported her raw material from the South.

The growing of flax and the making of linen had been a flourishing industry in Ireland, and, among English-speaking people at least, with Ireland linen was at one time associated the world over. Indeed the north Ireland city of Belfast has been gratuitously accorded the high-sounding supername of Linenopolis. It was the Scotch-Irish immigrants in the early eighteenth century who brought flax and the manufacture of linen to America. Considering the difficulty of raising flax and the difficulty of its manufacture into linen at every recurrent step of the process, it seems certain that only people as dogged in character as the Scotch-Irish could have succeeded. In the later colonial days every farm had its patch of flax. Flax and linen found a foothold in the states of Kentucky, Virginia and New York, Indiana and Ohio, and considerable flax was grown there during the years about 1840, but in the latter States much of this was for linseed, and as the years passed, about 1850 to 1860, the crop for linseed increased over the crop for fiber. Cotton was the crop natural to the United States, and the cheap cotton was the chief reason ascribed for the failure of linen to maintain a prominent position in the textile industry.

The Scotch shepherded the wool industry into America. There had been a woolen industry, with weavers' guilds in the southeast of England ever since the reign of Edward III, but America owed her sheep and her woolens to the Scotch. Sheep-raising and woolen cloth-making had long had a center in Scotland, colder and windier than England, where tweeds were named after the river that flowed through the sheep district in the south of Scotland. Woolens were not only made there but almost universally worn there too, all except below the knees until the warm socks were reached. But pure wool did not wear well enough to satisfy the thrifty Scot. However the Scot was resourceful as well as thrifty.

Linsey-woolsey, as is evident from its name, was a combination of linen and woolen, and the vernacular form of the name asserts its Scotch derivation. In the cold home country of Scotland linsey-woolsey well filled all serviceable requirements for the kilts—durability (supplied by the linen) and warmth (supplied by the wool). So in weaving, the strong linen threads were used for the warp, and the woolen, warm and full-bodied, for the weft or filler. Some of the linsey-woolseys, in America as well as in Scotland, were fine materials, but later, in America, the name came to refer to a rather cheap coarse material. In general, linsey-woolsey in the earlier part of the nineteenth century was common to those parts of America that had been settled by the Scotch-Irish. The name is said by some to be derived from the English village of Lindsey in Suffolk. This may be, but a guess may be hazarded that quite as likely it came from the noble Scotch line of the Lindsays in Lanarkshire, which lay between Edinburgh and Glasgow, or rather, which rose between and overlooked the sheep and woolen district to the south. The Lindsays were famous even back in the twelfth century. Probably most Americans are familiar with that member celebrated at length by Sir Walter Scott in "Marmion" with the bare resounding title, by appointment of King James V,

> Sir David Lindsay of the Mount,
> Lord Lyon, King-at-Arms.

Flax and linen occupy a traditional position in the general field of manufacture. The Scotch-Irish brought the flax spinning-wheel to America, to New England, as surely as the German brought fractur and painted flowers to the eastern part of Pennsylvania. This does not mean that the spinning-wheel was not used elsewhere before it was in New England—positive dates are often uncertain—but that the vital spark was struck out there in New England and that the spark has stayed vital there all through the course of manufacturing. All colonial life did not sing to the accompaniment of the hum of the spinning-wheel. The Dutch women were not great spinsters, yet they were busy and thrifty all day long. Accordingly, as they did not use flax to any extent, but little flax was raised in New Netherland.

On the other hand, after about 1670, when English people began to settle in New York, flax and the flax spinning-wheel promptly came in too.

The Scotch-Irish planted flax in New England in the first part of the eighteenth century and installed the little spinning-wheel there too at the same time. Thereafter what is called linen manufacture was in every instance a personal and individual piece of work and bore the stamp of an art, as truly as does embroidery or painting, in spite of the word "manufacture." The word means "making by hand," but that is not what it is. It is "making by machinery." It is no more making by hand than the brief gesture of the hand with a lever in its hold to start the machinery going. For the purposes of quantity production, machinery's work is magical, but to use the same word for both processes is to obliterate the distinction between them and to breed confusion, and to despoil each of its distinctive quality: an art and an economic achievement.

The process of the making of linen out of the flax was not simple. It was distinctly complicated and, until one got accustomed to it, difficult. It protected the art. From the first step of all, the ripple-combing, to get rid of the seed-polls; and the retting or rotting, to separate the fibers from each other lengthwise; through the heavy breaking, to break the fibers crosswise into manageable lengths; the carding, to get the fibers all to lie parallel; the spinning, to twist the comparatively short fibers into durable and really long threads; and the weaving, to cross-hatch the fibers into

Breaking

Swingling

From drawings by E. G. Lutz

Hackling (or hetchling)

Spinning flax into thread

From flax to linen thread

linen cloth—it was all in the colonial times a process that was largely done personally, by hand or by foot. Bleaching followed. Bleaching was a supreme operation, or rather series of operations. Alice Morse Earle says that in all over forty bleaching operations were employed upon "light linens" and that sixteen months passed from the sown flax-seed to the finished linen. How could a machine be expected to give personal care to this bleaching! The artist's instinctive sense was in control and the fine quality of the product was as much a personal matter as is the making of a fine wine, or of a beautiful garden, or of a poem.

As the march of the States began, westward from the original thirteen, flax was planted in considerable quantities in Kentucky, Virginia, and New York. This extension was favored by the fact that flax grew wild in Virginia, and in New York and Pennsylvania it was more or less a matter of natural similarity of agricultural habit and of family industry. The flax industry of Kentucky was advancing over the mountains, still as the dominant textile craft. Cotton and wool were not yet rising to supremacy, but their time was near. A good deal of flax was planted in Ohio and Indiana, but it was not for the making of linen; it was for the production of linseed oil. Some home-made linen might be made, but that was a poor affair compared with the old linen industry; the importance of the great market was not reflected in it, nor the magic of quantity production. Still later flax travelled up into the mountains of North Carolina and Tennessee, and farther west into Missouri. But, as in

1850–60, the purpose was decreasingly for linen and increasingly for linseed. Paint was the resulting commodity, not handweaving or embroidery.

The way the people themselves felt about it was testified very early by a couplet, stating that the Pennsylvania folk felt the work with the flax was something to take pride in, referring to their region,

> Where live High German people and low Dutch
> Whose trade in weaving linen cloth is much.

In form linen was made, into sheets, tablecloths, personal linen and underwear, with a mixture of wool into bedspreads, and into summer clothes. Linen was prepared from the beginning, and spun, and woven as an art. A yard of linen was itself a masterpiece. Better industries would arrive, bringing practical benefits in all textile work applied to wool and to cotton. In the initial period of the factory, there were said to be, in 1827, seven flax mills in America with a total of 2620 spindles. These mills used imported flax and disappeared under the high tariff of 1828. Hardly a powerful industry! A revival came in the middle of the nineteenth century, when in 1846 a linen mill was started at Dudley, Massachusetts; and when in 1852 the American Linen Company started up at Fall River, Massachusetts, with 10,500 spindles. In 1850 there were nine mills in Massachusetts alone, but in 1860 only three remained.

With a pioneering people like the Americans continually moving into new country as they were during all the nineteenth century, wool had the decided advantage over linen in that it was warm, whereas linen was cool. Another great advantage was that wool could travel on its own feet. With the necessity for quantity production it was fortunate that wool was easy to spin into thread, even by hand. This made the passage from the family industry of handwork into the machine industry of the factory by no means difficult, but on the contrary very encouraging. The multifold reward of the quantity product stimulated the whole community, the workers, the merchants, and the consumers.

Steam was first used in any of the textile industries as early as 1801, though this was merely a record date. Steam was applied to transportation both on water and on land some time before it was applied to the textiles. This was very advantageous to the factory industry; it facilitated the transportation of the finished goods to the markets and to a wider and wider range of markets. It helped in an essential way the social miracle that was swiftly sweeping through American life.

What machinery, by grace of the inventors, did to the wool industry may be seen in the concise statement of a few statistics. During the handcraft period, before the factory came, the average amount of wool in use per capita in the United States was not more than 3 pounds. In the middle of the nineteenth century it had increased to 4 pounds; by the end of the century it had reached 8 pounds per capita for the entire country. In travel wool had gone from Vermont and the Berkshire section of New England and New

York, through New York and Pennsylvania to Ohio and the Kentucky bluegrass and on toward a large multi-state area later, extending from Montana, Idaho, Oregon and Wyoming, down through California, Utah, Colorado, and New Mexico to Texas. And the increase of the number of sheep in these areas had been as great as its westward extent.

During this period several types of sheep had been popular with the sheep-raising farmers of America. The Merino was originally a Spanish breed, and by tradition was descended from sheep salvaged from the defeat of the Spanish Armada on the coast of Scotland in 1588. In colonial times the American sheep was a coarse wool animal of a hardy but not productive type. Between 1800 and 1815 there were decided efforts to improve the breed by importation. Colonel David Humphreys of Derby, Connecticut, in 1802 imported 21 Merino rams and 70 Merino ewes from Spain Robert R. Livingston of New York also imported Spanish sheep to improve his flocks. There developed in the East a well-known Merino craze, with high prices for sheep and for wool. In 1814 wool sold as high in Ohio as $2.75 a pound. In 1810 Robert Livingston sold 4 full-bred Merino rams for $1000 apiece; and Colonel Humphreys sold two rams and two ewes for $6000. By 1816, after the War of 1812–15, this Merino craze died down, and in 1821 the wool industry began to recover, Saxony sheep now becoming popular among importing breeders for five or six years. By 1830 the interest in sheep settled into a steady prosperous business with Southdown sheep from England the popular type, with prices high and demand constant for fifteen years or more, until the Civil War. By this time the high records were in California, Texas, and New Mexico.

But the sheep industry did not exist for its own sake. It existed mainly for the purpose of supplying woolen clothes to the multiplying people of the expanding nation. Instead of the spreading of sheep, read the preceding paragraphs as of the spreading of a steady supply of woolen clothes over the new continent that was being opened up, and the significance of these developments will be recognized.

Americans take machinery as a matter of course. They want to read about machinery either only in the simple unexplained results, or in the complete technical details. Nothing in between. That John and Arthur Scholfield and others of the name; that Captain Nathaniel Stevens of North Andover; William Crompton, coming to America in 1836; John Goulding, careful to say he did not invent any part of his carding machine, but did devise the combination and arrangement of the parts; and E. I. DuPont de Nemours, great inventor of human machinery, otherwise of organization—that these and others worked out in one way or another the machinery that produced the woolen miracle is a simple fact. It is quite impracticable to tell their stories in these limited pages. The reader should resort to Victor S. Clark, to Percy Bidwell, and to Arthur H. Cole. The simple result was that by the period of 1820–30, but not until then, the factory had become the characteristic way of changing sheep's wool into warm cloth for daily wear;

and that by 1850 all the important improvements which had been invented in textile machinery had been adapted to the woolen industry. The carding machine was the nucleus of this. The first public carding mill was started in 1790 in Pittsfield, Massachusetts. The achievement of the industry during the succeeding sixty years may be noted in the following figures of factory output:

1820	$ 4,413,068
1830	14,528,166
1840	20,696,999
1850	49,636,881

There is however one technical detail which is essential to the American kind of satisfaction in the study of the manufacture of wool. The wool of the sheep is unique in that the fibers are covered with overlapping scales on their surface. Accordingly when these sheep's wool fibers rub across each other, these scales catch in each other and mat together, making a sort of felt. The hair of no other animal has these scales; nor has any vegetable fiber—not flax, not cotton. Wherefore—woolen suits and dresses, especially in winter!

The manufacture of wool forthwith divides into two branches aimed at the making of woolens, and the making of worsteds. In the manufacture of woolens the curliness and the tendency to felting of the fibers is strengthened and developed by the manufacturing processes, so as to produce a soft cloth with the fibers well matted together and the weave covered with a nap of short fibers and so slightly visible. In the manufacture of worsteds the fibers on the contrary are straightened out and laid parallel, the main long fibers are twisted very hard and the short fibers, that would make a nap, are combed out. In this way there is produced a smooth wiry yarn and a cloth in which the weave is clearly evident and a variety of design is entirely feasible in the weave itself.

In the study of the large industries, and of the industries after they grow large, there is inevitably risk of losing sight of the personal element. The personal element is never got rid of in achievement. Great achievements are slow grown; it is seldom that anything of telling importance is done at one stroke. When it is, it is usually only apparent, not really the fact. Everyday facts are the abiding truths, and they are built up gradually, a little every day, every year, every generation. The accumulation of character and of ability may be unrecorded, but it is not unexistent. Accordingly, to get a true glimpse of the development of textile manufacture the only practicable way is to take some instance, purely as an example. For our illustration of textile manufacture we will take wool; and for our illustration of woolen manufacture we will take the Stevens Mills at Andover, Massachusetts; and in the Stevens Mills we will focus on Captain Nathaniel Stevens, 1786–1865.

Nathaniel Stevens was born of a long line of able Stevenses, being the fifth generation from John Stevens, who was living in Andover in 1641. He went to the local academy, and was then bound out to a farmer, John Carleton, until he was twenty-one. This practice of the time did not indicate any inability on the part of the parents to bring up a son, but rather was meant to insure him the important discipline of living with other people and working with them. A boy who was bound out was seldom spoiled; duty was not often denied its right-of-way.

On attaining his majority, Nathaniel worked for three months in a livery stable in Danvers. Danvers in those day was something of a center. The educational value of that three-month period will be correctly appraised by remembering that the phrase "horse sense" at that time meant something real.

By this time young Nathaniel Stevens was ready for a foreign course. So he made a sea voyage before the mast, going to Leghorn, where he bought a quantity of Leghorn hats, famous then and famous still. These he sold on his return, his first independent business venture. It was an all-round practical education he received, no hit-or-miss affair. Then his regular development was interrupted by the War of 1812, in which he served as a lieutenant. Thereafter he served as a captain in the Massachusetts militia. The title sounded so obviously like him, expressing authority and yet personal interest in all his men, that it stayed with him all his life.

In 1815 Nathaniel Stevens married Miss Harriet Hale of Chelmsford and settled down. Her father, Moses Hale, was one of the pioneering spirits of the State and a man of enthusiasm in his business and in everything. Through his influence Nathaniel Stevens made up his mind to embark in manufacturing, and once so resolved, manufacturing became the abiding determination of his life. Accordingly in 1813 Stevens formed a partnership with two neighbors, and engaged James Scholfield, an expert textile man and younger brother of John and Arthur Scholfield, to run for him a mill which he built of wood on the site of the first sawmill on the Cochichawick Creek in Andover. As they prospered and were able to improve their property, they substituted brick walls for the wooden ones and progressed into permanence. An important change in manufacturing policy was to give up the making of broadcloth, with which they had started, and to specialize, from 1817 on, in flannels, for which the market was larger and steadier. Another early master stroke of Nathaniel Stevens was to bring all the women in the town who were weaving in their homes into the mill, thus gaining the great advantage of co-ordination, the forerunner of co-organization. In 1830 he introduced water power for their looms, making their work much easier and more productive.

Stevens realized that to be permanently successful a manufacturing business must be strongly centered and independent of transient circumstances. Once when Stevens had carried a load of flannels to Boston, a prominent merchant warned him not to try to compete with British manufacturers. "Take my advice. Sell out your mill and go into some other business." "Never," Stevens replied, "so long

In the J. Pierpont Morgan Collection at the Library of Congress

Illustrating War News

During the Civil War, A. R. Waud, an artist with the Union forces, made the sketch, shown at the top, of Grant's position at Cold Harbor on June 2, 1864. A wood block was made from the drawing and it was reproduced as shown below in *Harper's Weekly* of June 25, 1864

From the print collection in the New York Public Library

British steamship "Sirius," first to make the westward crossing of the Atlantic Ocean by steam, arriving in New York April 23, 1838

Courtesy of the Metropolitan Museum of Art

A spoon case of about 1825 used for carrying silver while travelling

Courtesy of Mrs. Welsh Strawbridge. Photo by C. V. D. Hubbard

A stone kitchen sink at Graeme Park, in continuous use since 1810

From the New York Historical Society

Coming to the Parson

This or other Rogers groups decorated many a parlor of the Seventies

Kitchen of 1833

Two of the group of miniature kitchen scenes exhibited by the American Stove Company at the World's Fair, Chicago

Kitchen of 1860

In the Metropolitan Museum of Art

An Eastman Johnson painting of a family group in the library of a New York house, 1871

The Laurence House

A portrayal of the wealthier type of Victorian drawing room was made for and used in the moving picture of *Little Women*

Photographs by courtesy of Hobe Erwin, Decorator

The Alcott House at Concord, Massachusetts

Living room of Meg, Jo, Beth, and Amy in *Little Women*

A Belle of the Diamond Horseshoe at the opera

A drawing by Harper which was "engraved especially for *Graham's Magazine*, June, 1849, by W. E. Tucker"

Courtesy of the Plumbing, Heating Industries Bureau

Changes in Bathtubs

A. The Saturday night bath of the early days. *B*. An early form of tub which folded up against the wall when not in use. *C*. Shows the same tub when ready for use. *D*. Is a crude portable shower bath supported on two wooden poles; a hand pump forced water to a tank at the top. *E*. Tub and shower in the Josiah Quincy house, typical of the period of wood enclosed plumbing. *F*. This bathtub was in the home of James Whitcomb Riley, at Indianapolis, Indiana

An engraving by Alfred Jones after the painting by R. N. Bass

"I've Thought of Something"

The Literary Emporium of 1845 takes a fling at would-be feminine authors and incidentally the movement towards women's rights

Courtesy of the Museum of Fine Arts, Boston

The Seasons

A wallpaper which was formerly in the house of Professor Young of Dartmouth College

Courtesy of the Philadelphia Museum of Art, Philadelphia

A section of the Captain Cook wallpaper

A famous and most picturesque wallpaper, close in effect to a tapestry. It depicted the life of Captain Cook, the explorer, on the Island of Tahiti. A set of this paper was placed in a house in Augusta, Maine, in 1807

SKIRT SEWING MACHINE.

EYELETING MACHINE.

A SKIRT IN PROCESS OF MANUFACTURE.

SKELETON SKIRT.

QUEEN ANN SKIRT.

EMPLOYMENT OF WOMEN.

ARTICLE III.

DOUGLAS & SHERWOOD'S HOOP SKIRT FACTORY.

We illustrate herewith one of the largest manufacturing establishments of this [illegible] Douglas & Sherwood's Hoop Skirt Factory; an establishment [illegible] which 800 women are employed, and 3000 hoop skirts turned out daily.

Five years ago Messrs. Douglas & Sherwood began the manufacture of skirts. At that time haircloth and other heavy materials were the substances most used in the manufacture; but the weight of several such skirts, and the heat generated proving injurious to health, the attention of makers was directed toward the discovery of a substitute, and hoop skirts were invented. When hoops were first introduced, to turn out six skirts per day was considered a fair day's work; now the several factories engaged probably produce over 20,000. In 1855 Douglas & Sherwood removed to Broadway, and set up 200 sewing machines (Wheeler and Wilson's); in 1856 they found the premises too small, and hired three houses in White Street, where they continue the manufacture. They consume a ton of steel per day; of other materials they use, monthly, 150,000 yards muslin, 300,000 feet whalebone, 24,000 spools of cotton, 2,000,000 eyelets, slides, hooks and eyes, etc., 300,000 yards of tape, 225,000 yards of jute cord, and 10,000 yards of haircloth.

THE FINISHING ROOM.

We are happy to add that Messrs. Douglas & Sherwood have not been forgetful of the mental welfare of their employées. In a building on White Street, adjoining their factory, they have established a free library for the girls, containing 2000 volumes. This will prove a good investment, and is an example well worthy of being followed.

THE KNIGHT'S LEAP AT ALTENAHR.

"When the Baron has fired the gate, men of mine,
And the water is spent and done;
Then bring me a cup of the red Ahr-wine;
I never shall drink but this one.

"And fetch me my harness, and saddle my horse,
And lead him me round to the door;
He must take such a leap to-night perforce
As horse never took before."

He harness'd himself by the clear moonshine,
And he mounted his horse at the door,
And he took such a pull at the red Ahr-wine
As never man took before.

He spurred the old horse, and he held him tight,
And he leapt him out over the wall;
Out over the cliff, out into the night,
Three hundred feet of fall.

They found him next morning below in the glen,
And never a bone in him whole;
But Heaven may yet have more mercy than men
On such a bold rider's soul.

A page from *Harper's Weekly*, January 29, 1859, showing how hoop skirts were made in Douglas and Sherwood's factory in White Street, New York, which employed eight hundred women, used two hundred sewing machines and turned out three thousand hoop skirts daily

From "Godey's Lady's Book," March, 1843

Fashionable children and their fashionable mamas

The Young Lady Chronicler of Fashion's prediction in 1860 of the incoming large hats for women which would hide the faces, and large neckties for men inspired these cartoons which appeared in *Harper's Weekly*, Christmas Supplement, 1859

By courtesy of the Onondaga Historical Association

From the Jesse Charles Harraman Collection at the Library of Congress

Left: William F. Harndon, the forerunner of the express business, conceived the idea of carrying small packages between New York and Boston, using a carpet bag and travelling by stage. steamer and railroad. Henry Wells and William Fargo were in his employ at one time. *Top right:* Wheelbarrow used to deliver express packages at Syracuse, New York, in 1847. *Below:* An early one-horse express wagon used in San Francisco about 1875

Courtesy of the Historical Society of Pennsylvania

The first railway train in Pennsylvania, 1832, at the Philadelphia, Germantown and Norristown Railway depot at Philadelphia

Courtesy of the Pennsylvania Railroad

Relic of the old Portage Railroad (near Hollidaysburg, Pennsylvania) across the Allegheny Mountains, showing the stone ties on which double tracks were laid

Courtesy of the Onondaga Historical Association

"Floral Hall" at the State Fair at Syracuse, 1849

From a photograph by Brady

The United States Sanitary Commission Lodge at a convalescent camp near Alexandria, Virginia, May, 1863

The work of the Sanitary Commission was carried on by funds raised at the Sanitary Fairs

From a sketch by Theodore R. Davis in Harper's Weekly for May 27, 1876

President Grant and Don Pedro, the Emperor of Brazil, starting the Corliss Engine at the opening of the Philadelphia Centennial as I can get water to turn my mill wheel." In 1817 and in 1831 Stevens bought out first one and then the other of his partners and took over the sole control. By energy and perseverance he soon mastered the business in all its details, and not only the business but progressively all its possibilities. The business improved steadily, often because of quick decisions. Details in Nathaniel Stevens's mills were no longer small, but he kept his eye on all of them. For over fifty years he conducted the industry masterfully and trained his successors. When he died in 1865, he left it going strong, steadily increasing in product and improving in quality. Three of his five sons continued the business there in Andover and vicinity. The other two carried the Stevens name and personality westward through the State, one with a linen mill in Webster, the other with a woolen mill in Ware. Such was the woolen textile industry of the mid-nineteenth century, as seen in the person of one of its creators.

Now we turn to the sudden rise of the young textile giant—cotton. Cotton was the indigenous fiber of the United States, by nature the material for an American industry. Cotton was a world material that, it proved, belonged centrally here and which, when the conditions and the methods of manufacture had been solved, occupied as if by right the main industrial field.

It would hardly seem possible now that what to us is ordinary cotton did not go back into those unluxurious times before the Revolution when everything was very simply done by hand. To assure us that this was the fact, we may quote Alice Morse Earle, who says of cotton:

> Our greatest, cheapest, most indispensable fibre is also our latest one. It never formed one of the homespun industries of the colonies; in fact it was never an article of extended domestic manufacture.

Eli Whitney's cotton gin

From a drawing by E. G. Lutz from a replica of Whitney's model in the New York Museum of Science and Industry

But when in 1793 Eli Whitney deftly produced his cotton gin, cotton responded, promptly acknowledged the call to power, and stepped forth in its native majesty. Cotton was King!

Eli Whitney's cotton gin consisted of a series of circular saws with fine teeth, which revolving tore the cotton lint from the teeth and sent it through a guide into a receptacle. Before it was ginned, about two thirds of the weight of the cotton consisted of seeds. Before the invention of the cotton gin, it would take one person two years to clean or deseed the cotton and turn out an average-size bale. The cotton gin could in a single day produce from three to fifteen bales. It will then be readily seen that the cotton industry soon after the invention of the gin appeared like a giant rising suddenly on the manufacturing horizon.

Eli Whitney opened opportunity to inventors of cotton manufacturing machinery. The carding of both wool and cotton was a highly important operation. Amos Whittemore (1759–1828) was one of the chief inventors during the transitional period from hand to factory manufacture. He invented in 1797 a machine for manufacturing the hand cards. It held the leather while it cut it for the backs and pierced it to hold the teeth; it also drew the wire from a reel, cut and bent it for the looped teeth, set them, bent them, fastened the leather on the back, and in fact turned out the complete cards. Whittemore, employing 60 men and 2000 children, produced 12,000 dozen cards a year. He furnished nearly all the hand cards used in those parts of the country. This was manufacturing, even though to further but one step of the entire process! John Randolph said that Amos Whittemore's machine had everything but an immortal soul.

The period of cotton manufacturing began with Samuel Slater, generally called the father of the cotton industry in America, who early in the 1790s started a cotton mill in Pawtucket, Rhode Island. Slater's mill was not, however, a mill that did everything by machinery. That achievement was something that had to be grown to. Francis Cabot Lowell (1775–1817) accomplished this. The almost complete cessation of ocean commerce resulting from the War of 1812 determined him to establish a cotton mill run completely by machinery. He was an inventor of human machinery—organization—as well as of physical. He interested his brother-in-law, Patrick Tracy Jackson, and a mechanical genius, Paul Moody, and during the winter of 1812–13 designed and constructed spinning machinery and a practical power loom. Nathan Appleton invested $5000 in the project. Lowell invited Appleton to come and see the power loom work—all by itself—Appleton left on record the impression it made:

> I well recollect the state of admiration and satisfaction with which we sat by the hour watching the beautiful movement of the new wonderful machine, destined as it evidently was to change the character of all textile industry.

Another year and all parts of Lowell's cotton factory had been invented or constructed, installed, synchronized and put in operation at Waltham, Massachusetts, the first mill in all the world which in itself combined all the operations of taking raw cotton and making of it finished cloth.

John Thorp (1784–1848) was one of the most important inventors to produce improvements after cotton manufacturing began to climb into the complete factory stage. In 1828 Thorp received three patents for improvements in spinning and twisting cotton. His process was entirely new both in the hand spinning and in the machine spinning with respect to the control and the twisting of the thread. It is now called "ring spinning" and is employed for more than 100,000,000 of the 160,000,000 spindles in the world (1935). The spinning is the most important operation in

Slater's Mill at Webster, Massachusetts

From John Warner Barber's "Historical Collections of Massachusetts," 1839

the manufacture of cotton and the Thorp patents are the basic patents.

But no such tremendous achievement as the 100,000,000 spindles was reached quickly, as may be noticed by the date (1935). "All things must work together" in manufacture as in everything, from religion down. Seen in the true perspective of the times and in the courage and originality that had to be exercised, with the development of Lowell's genius for organization, soon no longer exclusively Lowell's by any means, the comprehensive mastery of the market or a creative development of a market, the service of public affairs and what goes therewith, politics, the development of cotton manufacturing was indeed remarkable. New England dominated the industry, but the average number of spindles per mill in New England was in the year

1815	only about	500
1831	already over	1,500
1840	approaching	2,000
1860	nearly	5,000

Stated on another basis, during the period 1840–1860 the number of spindles in the country doubled to over 5,200,000, at a rate nearly twice as fast as the increase of the population. For a single mill the Merrimac Company operated 38,000 spindles before 1840, but the 100,000 spindle factory did not arrive until the Civil War brought its exceptional stimulus. To distinguish between cotton and woolen figures what is correct is not always intelligible to the layman. Another view of the result of machinery and the influence of manufacturing is seen in these figures of factory output:

1820	$ 4,413,068
1830	14,528,166
1840	20,696,999
1850	49,636,881

Another development in the manufacture of cotton came rather early. It added an operation to the process all its own, and it created an increased market for itself. Prints. To the eye of the customer prints multiplied the cotton material available for women's dresses. In appearance the simple material, whether of cotton or of wool, was also a single material. Its coolness for summer or its warmth for winter made little or no difference to the looks of a dress. The pattern printed on the material in ever varying design and in ever varying colors made each time to the eye a new material. By means of the cylinder press this new variety became available in quantity production. Prints became an important branch of cotton manufacture and of the cotton market along through the period 1820–1830, and they have been with us ever since, endowing dress with a grace, a lightness, an endless variety, and a good taste that was the more a boon as it was inexpensive, and so at the command, with little or no financial limitation, of all classes of people.

There was later another development coming out of the cotton industry, which however does not strictly belong in this period. It may be mentioned in anticipation however, for it does belong in cotton manufacture. The nineteenth century was quite characteristically a time when great things were in the seeding stage. Ideas, methods, industries that did not reach importance until later determined their future in the nineteenth century. A great book could be written on that aspect of the time, a fascinating book full of prophecy later come true, of great things while they were still little. The development referred to is the utilization of waste products in the use of that two thirds by weight of the raw product, in the turning to profit the cotton seed that Eli Whitney's cotton gin got rid of, and the elimination of which created the cotton industry. As late as 1880 the cotton planters of the United States were seriously distressed by the enormous quantity of cotton seed that accumulated every year. It was many times more than could be used for planting; and if disposed of by any but strictly limited methods it subjected them to legal fine and penalty.

The history of this industry has been concisely summarized by saying that

In 1860 cotton seed was garbage;
In 1870 cotton seed was fertilizer;
In 1880 cotton seed was cattle feed; and
In 1890 cotton seed was table food and many other things beside.

There were quite early scattered individuals who persistently experimented with the extracting of oil from cottonseed. Cottonseed oil sold at Providence in 1829 for 80 cents a gallon; and at New York and Philadelphia in 1833 for $1 a gallon. It is said that the first important undertaking in the United States to crush cottonseed for the oil was at Natchez, Mississippi, in 1834; and that New Orleans made a purchase of cottonseed oil for city lighting in the street lamps in or about 1835, but it proved to be an unprofitable venture. The greatest hope of those interested was in the use of cottonseed oil in lamps as a substitute for whale oil; but hope is proverbially genial and independent of hard facts. These were all curious facts, but hardly more than that. One sanguine dealer in the future declared before the middle of the century:

> The time will come when a man will just as soon think of throwing away his corn as his cottonseed.

And in 1859 another, who was no doubt called a dreamer or worse, asserted that

> Cotton seed oil and cake (the dried mush after the oil has been extracted) could add 50 per cent to the profit of the cotton industry.

By 1870 it was becoming realized that the cake had decided

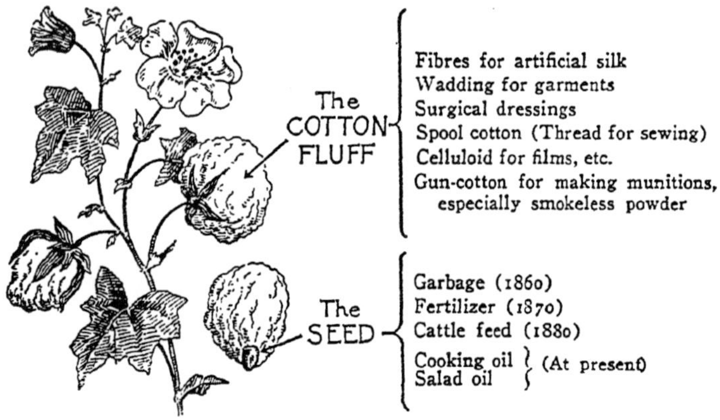

From a drawing by E. G. Lutz

The diversified uses of the cotton plant

value in fertilizer, as it replaced certain plant foods in the soil that had been removed by the previous cotton crop. Cottonseed was getting to have commercial value. In 1860 according to the census there were 7 cottonseed oil mills in the United States; in 1870, 26; in 1880, 40, with the cake selling for fertilizer at $20 a ton, used especially in the southeast, and as cattle feed in the southwest. By 1890 there were in America 119 cottonseed oil mills, crushing annually 1,000,000 tons of seed, and with products of a value of $19,700,000. Thereafter the story is one of rapidly expanding statistics and of new uses accompanied by higher prices resulting from the majestic sweep of the new science of industrial chemistry. Cottonseed has had an important share in the industrial revolution in the American cotton belt. Not only is this now the leading region of the world in the production of cotton but also in that new industry, the production of cottonseed oil.

In the everyday family life of the home the textile industries of America began. As the nineteenth century approached its end it certainly seemed that from the family life and the home the great textile industries had vanished. The connection of these industries with everyday life now consisted only in the people going downtown to the general store—or successively, to the retail store, the dry goods store, and the tailor's or the dressmaker's—selecting the material which pleased their individual tastes, buying it, and having it made up into a suit or dress—or buying the ready-made clothes. To revert to our initial figure of speech, the streams, the brooks and rivers had been lost in the ocean of the textile industries. The change was, however, but a transformation. What has become of the personal element? The personal element is multiplied. Instead of a seeming death in the Machine Age, the personal element in the textile manufacture has continued—in the masterful person of the industrial inventor, the industrial engineer, the organizer, the executive, the foreman, the worker controlling multiple machines—and so all the way to the purchaser and the retail consumer. In the persons of all these, the great textile

From "Harper's Weekly," September 3, 1859

A Cadet hop at West Point

industries have in fact returned back into the family, back into the home. As the father, mother, son, daughter, and the baby too, put on their new clothes, the new century has simply taken them out the front door to get their clothes made in association with a sufficient number of other people and they come back in again with their new clothes on, or ready to wear.

These clothes that the textile industries have produced during the nineteenth century—what were the styles, for men and for women, with the unlimited choice in materials that the development of the industries has given? There is a decided distinction between the material in the bolt and the dress or suit made from it. An art intervenes, and a skillful art at that. The making of clothes, whether men's or women's, began in the home. Dressmakers, women, in the earlier days made men's clothes as well as women's. A little later, when the makers of men's clothes took unto themselves the designation of tailors, and still later when really smart women's clothes were distinguished as tailor-made, an important fact was asserted which should not be overlooked. The word *tailor* comes from the French word *tailler,* meaning to cut. The tailor is the one who cuts the cloth to fit the measure of the wearer. Whether this cutting be simply a cutting of the cloth with scissors or shears for a single dress or suit; or whether it is the strong-arm slicing with a large sharp blade through many layers of cloth for the ready-made trade, it requires accurate skill. Recognition is

From "Peterson's Magazine," 1851

The exceptional bloomers

Recurring examples of the bell-shaped contour

From "The Recurring Cycles of Fashion." Agnes Young. Courtesy of Harper & Brothers

Recurring examples of the tubular contour

From "The Recurring Cycles of Fashion," Agnes Young. Courtesy of Harper & Brothers

due to the dressmakers who for years and years were the *tailleurs* as well as the seamstresses of men's and women's clothes alike—and recognition is due to the mothers who cut down the men's clothes for the small boys.

During the period of this volume of ours, 1776–1876, there have been three dominant types of women's dress,

Recurring examples of the back fullness contour

From "The Recurring Cycles of Fashion," Agnes Young. Courtesy of Harper & Brothers

changing from year to year. Each type lasted about a third of a century.[1]

SAFETY!

COMFORT!!

AND

ELEGANCE!!!

ARE INSURED BY WEARING

DOUGLAS & SHERWOOD'S

NEW

MATINEE SKIRT,

WITH THE

PATENT DETACHABLE

HOOP FASTENING

AND

ADJUSTABLE BUSTLE.

SAFETY!! since it effectually obviates the danger arising from entangling the feet, or foreign substances in the hoops!

COMFORT!! because the muslin skirt can be instantaneously removed from the springs by PATENT DETACHABLE FASTENINGS, washed, with other garments, and at no greater expense, and replaced on the hoops in a minute!

ELEGANCE!! because the scientific cut of the muslin skirt, and the fine material of which it is composed, give a graceful fall to the robe worn over it; and will, in hot weather, enable the wearer to dispense with any intermediate skirt.

The MATINEE SKIRT has eleven hoops, weighs but ten ounces, IS STAMPED WITH THE TRADE MARK of Messrs. DOUGLAS & SHERWOOD, *and is the best Skirt ever introduced to the Public*, and quite indispensable to every lady who desires to combine in her apparel SAFETY, COMFORT, and ELEGANCE! For sale at all the principal stores in the United States and Canada.

From "Harper's Weekly," January 22, 1859

Advertisement of the matinée skirt

One invention had a minor effect in dressmaking—the sewing machine. But this influence did not come when Elias Howe invented the lock-stitch sewing machine about 1846,

[1]Agnes Brooks Young: *Recurring Cycles of Fashion, 1760–1937.*

nor at the time it found a place in the home, but when it found itself permanently established in industry. Manual labor has always been remarkably skillful, especially in producing work of fine quality. Women's dresses have always, certainly within this period of ours, been individual creations, and the individual dressmaker, going from house to house and working in the home, was a familiar figure long after the home maker of men's suits disappeared before the mercantile tailor of the ready-made trade. The sewing machine made possible the wholesale manufacture of all clothing. It came into its own with the Civil War. The great demand at that time was for men's wear, for uniforms for the soldiers, for ready-to-wear-whether-they-fit-or-not. The distinction, the individuality, the "difference" in men's suits subsided, and the standardized suit forthwith was the rule. There was a great benefit to both men and women in the greater quantity of clothes they could have—in underwear, for instance—after the sewing machine started mass production, and made life more simply sanitary. But this is a matter of health and sanitation, not of fashion. A woman wore several or many of these ready-made, machine-produced dresses at home, during the day, but in no one of them did she glory. And men simply thereafter sought to be "genteel, well-dressed, and inconspicuous." Now, since the 1860s, their garments are, with very slight variations, standardized for life, even to the consecration of the clawhammer of the War of 1812 for evening dress.

Meantime, women continued on their way, following the

guidance of their likes and dislikes. Their dressmakers were quite capable of handling the many yards of the hoop-skirt and crinoline, and the intricacies of skirt, underskirt and overskirt set in place by the accurately arranged bustle. They turned out creations!

Finally, children's clothes! In the colonial days children's clothes were made exactly like the clothes of the grown-ups on a reduced scale. Just before the Civil War a tailor's wife in the village of Sterling, Massachusetts, was working over a gingham dress for her little one, but not with much satisfaction. She exclaimed to her husband how much easier it would be if there were patterns from which to make everyday clothes for themselves as there were for the fashionable clothes of the well-to-do. The husband took his wife's wish to heart and soon cut out a pattern for a man's shirt, then a pattern for a baby's dress, and then for a little boy's whole suit. The neighbors saw, demanded, and bought. By 1864 the sale of patterns for the making of clothes was a going business, with an office at 192 Broadway, New York. Thus did Ebenezer Butterick, on his wife Ellen's suggestion and with her help, supply the lack and enable even children to have their own clothes.

We now know some of the facts of dress in America during the last hundred or hundred and fifty years or so, and with those facts we shall doubtless be content. But we do not know why. Why did American women like the bell-shaped hoop-skirt and crinoline for thirty years or more, and why in the stern impartial eyes of men did they look so beautiful while they liked them? Why, before that, did they like dresses in the vertical and very different taste of Jane Austen? And why was the same thing true of every other type of fashion? Why did men so quickly discard all individuality in their garb and for a trace of variety in their sartorial life betake themselves to a subtlety that is not evident anywhere else in the vigorous interests of masculinity? Linen, woolen, cotton: reason prevails and may be followed as a guide in the fields of all three materials, but when it comes to making them up into clothes, then the art of the *tailleur* arbitrarily cuts in and we have one of the great mysteries of everyday life! Why?

Lock-stitch sewing machine

An early Wheeler & Wilson lock-stitch sewing machine

CHAPTER XIII

The Leading Metals

THE nineteenth century has commonly and correctly been reputed to have been a period during which, so far as America is concerned at least, the worst social evils man can devise were born and brought to a hideous perfection, with an even worse and more gruesome possibility for the future. It is useless to try to ignore these evils. Child labor; slavery, both black and white; forest devastation; flood and fire; political graft; the loan sharks infesting the land; industrial exploitation—to mention a few of them by their less vivid names—these are all plain facts, and would seem to be inseparable from the newer mechanical civilization.

But it is also a matter of general recognition that most of the great possibilities of the twentieth century were born or developed in this same nineteenth century. True democracy; popular education; religious intelligence; widespread transportation; free communication. That these have been greatly increased is simply a matter-of-fact truth. How can these blessings and those evils have generated and developed side by side at the same time and in the same national locale? There is no ready explanation. It is simply a fact, possibly fundamental in our very complex human nature.

But the student of the nineteenth century, seeking to understand the period, and the ordinary reader, stimulated by the period's incredible achievements for his more varied, less theoretical daily life, must not expect to avoid the frank recognition of that ugly mass of conglomerated evils, negative as those evils may be to any deep understanding or to any thrilling vision. Only through the realization of those evils can the vision, the understanding of the time be attained. So will the reader attain the vision of the nineteenth century and see, not a contemptible period, but a great century, one of the greatest, of which it may truly be said, "There were giants in those days!"

Where better can we get our glimpse of that time than in the mining industries? In this book a few of these industries supply all we can give, but enough to urge the reader to go on to the books of those industries, especially those that give abundant personal material. The mines confront us with evils that seem to bar the way; the devastation of the forests; the wrecking of the climate and the deluging with floods; burrowing down into mile-deep stopes; reproducing perfect hells (gorgeous though they be!) to melt stone and rock and earth in smoke and flame and molten glow, to produce a new world and to create untold possibilities! For this glimpse, we choose—copper and coal and iron. Gold and silver may be the precious metals. Platinum and other metals less familiar may be even more rare. But the incomparable miracles of the new civilization are worked by the transmitting copper, the self-obliterating coal, and the strong metal of power, iron.

Copper comes distinctively from the southern shore of Lake Superior. There copper is found pure, in nuggets, sheets and masses, rather than in veins of ore. The native copper is found in outcropping veins of conglomerate and amygdaloid. So was it when in the early days the Indians picked it up on the surface and hammered it to harden it into weapons and other implements. When the white men came it did not need to be smelted, but the transportation was depressingly expensive. What advantage was it that there were solid masses of practically pure copper weighing tons if there were hundreds of miles of roadless, impenetrable forest between the copper and any place where it could be sold, refined or manufactured and put into usable form? The smaller the lumps of copper the better, for then they could be carried on the back through the wilderness. Alexander Henry, a mining pioneer, writing in 1776, said:

> The copper ores of Lake Superior can never be profitably sought for but for local consumption. The country must be cultivated and peopled before they can deserve notice.

In 1766 he had gone up the Ontonagon River to see a copper boulder that the Indians had told him was lying on the surface. He found it, and estimated its weight to be something like five tons. So pure was the metal that he was able to cut off with an axe a piece weighing 100 pounds. Many stone hammers were to be found lying around it, and the mass itself bore many chisel marks. Both Indians and white men had chipped off what they could. This mass of copper is now in the Smithsonian Institution at Washington. Thither it was removed in 1843. It weighs 6500 pounds, about three and a quarter tons.

The development of the Lake Superior copper had to wait until other more humdrum works of faith had been accomplished: exploring in spite of hunger and thirst, clearing of forest on the chance that it was justified, the making of roads, and even of railroads, and, most difficult of all, the inspiring of confidence in the moneyed East, whereon a profitable market is built. And vision! It had to wait for Douglass Houghton, a scientist and all-round practical man, who went up into this region with General Lewis Cass in 1830. He was appointed Michigan State Geologist in 1837 and immediately started a topographical survey of the whole region with a well-trained competent staff. His first report in 1841 convinced the outside world that the necessary development was worth while. Active Federal interest was aroused. A settlement was made with the Chippewa Indians who ceded 30,000 square miles to the white men, and moved on west in 1843. The first mining permits were issued by the Government in 1844. Douglass Houghton was the great figure of the opening up of the southern shore of Lake Superior. But the next year he died, drowned when a sailboat in which he was crossing the lake capsized.

The surface copper was the mere scattering of weathered

fragments. The real resources of copper lay far beneath. On the assurances of Douglass Houghton underground mining began at about this time, and exposed larger masses of metal. In 1857 a mass weighing 420 tons was found in one mine at a depth of 150 feet; it was 46 feet long; its maximum width over 12 feet and its mean thickness 4 feet. With pick and powder and chisel it was removed. One shaft has since then been sunk vertically 2270 feet, or 3780 feet measured on the slant of the lode. Another shaft has been sunk to a vertical depth of 5720 feet (over a mile) or 9469 feet from the surface on the slant of the lode. The increasing output since the time of Douglass Houghton shows the development of the copper industry of Lake Superior. These figures may be shown beyond the assigned period of this volume in view of the forward-looking reach of the copper industries. In pounds per decade:

1845	24,880	1875	36,039,497
1855	5,809,334	1885	72,147,889
1865	14,358,592	1895	120,330,749

The everyday use of copper in the early period of America was in the form of kitchen utensils. For the moderate population of the time the supply of the metal, derived from surface mining, was sufficient, and it was easily the best metal for the purpose. It could be easily worked and easily hardened by hammering. It was durable, lasting from generation to generation; it was readily cleaned and remained free from oxidation. It could be rendered even harder by combining with zinc, which also was sufficiently obtainable, into brass. Later, in kitchen utensils, especially for the roasting of meat, copper gave way to a considerable extent to iron and later to aluminum.

While the Indians used copper in their own making of weapons before they benefited in this from their contact with the white men, the white men did not. They had brought a superior steel from Europe ready made into their swords, and they imported sufficient excellent steel or could manufacture sufficient good steel for arms, whether swords or rifles. This manufacturing of steel, whether practically personal, as at first, or in moderate quantity, as a little later, answered the purposes of the earlier period. The larger use of copper in armament came later with the breech-loading rifle, when it was an important material in every cartridge.

A new use of copper came with the hammering or the rolling of it into sheets and then the splitting of it into copper nails, making a much stronger and more durable article for building and for the making of furniture.

After the adoption of iron-clad ships in the Civil War, copper was also soon used in sheets for plating the hulls of the vessels. But the great use of the metal, in the form of copper wire, came with the full development of copper mining, supplying abundant quantity as never before, and with the development of the electrical industries. Its exceptional conductivity of electricity made it an especially efficient medium for telephone, telegraph, and electric-power transmission. With the coming of the electric era these industries have rapidly increased and have taken up a very large part of the output of the mines not only on the southern shore of Lake Superior but wherever else in the United States the metal is found. An additional value of copper is as a vehicle for silver and gold and other precious metals which are often found in association with it.

Coal is wood. It is wood that has been treated by heat under pressure for thousands, for millions of years. The result of this is a physical condition that is very much like the minerals, the ores from which the metals are obtained. And the way coal is obtained, out of mines, most of them undersurface, also is like the way the metal ores are obtained. So it is usual and correct to think of coal as a mineral itself. But it *is* wood. Sometimes one can see that it is wood and that it still consists of trees with bark and branches and leaves, and of ferns. The color is changed. Green no more; black. And it has become stony; some of it very stony, and therefore sometimes called stone-coal.

But there is one great difference between coal and the metals. When one has got through with the metals, he has a valuable commodity remaining, of which he can make articles of practical use or of beauty, railroad tracks, tin cans, jewelry. When one has got through with coal, he has nothing—ashes and clinkers. The valuable residue of the ores is a substantial contribution to property. There is no valuable residue of coal. The value of coal is a service, the making of heat. In this usefulness its character as wood has not been lost. For the making of heat, wood and coal are parts of one series: 1. wood; 2. wood treated by heat under conditions excluding air, called charcoal; 3. coal; 4. coal treated by a method similar to that in making charcoal, called coke. All are fuel—wood and charcoal, contemporary; coal, geological; coke, geological and then contemporary. Of coal there are many kinds. Four will be sufficient: peat, wood decomposed in water, just fairly started toward being coal, found in locations that formerly were swamps, and usually needing to be dried to be burned; lignite, drier than peat, a very soft coal; bituminous coal, containing much less of the volatile gases than lignite and much more carbon, a real coal; anthracite, the highest, most matured coal, with the least of volatile gases and the most carbon. Pennsylvania anthracite contains from 85 to 93 per cent of carbon, "stone-coal," the best of all. Wood is excellent fuel, but it is fast-burning and is too expensive, prohibitively expensive when the quantity requirements of the industries are considered. In its original form of forest trees wood is a most important article. It takes twenty years to replace a tree, to grow it to commerciable forest size. The forests are essential in the regulation of the water supply, in the prevention of floods, and in the control of climate. The use of wood as an industrial fuel is simply to squander it. Its use as fuel has therefore been shifted over to one or another kind of coal.

As Lake Superior copper was used as an illustration for the metals and for the mining of many of them, so anthracite will be used in illustration of the various kinds of coal, remembering always that whatever the kind of coal in particular use, its value is always essentially a service, not a commodity, and that that service depends largely on the coal's being available, and therefore depends on transportation. So it is the transportation of the coal, whether man-back, mule-back, by water, or by steam, that ties all up into a valuable and value-increasing unity. Of course the importance of transportation was not confined to coal. Transportation is an element in the value of all the metals—of everything, of agricultural crops, and under the name of commutation, of suburban real estate.

The distinctive location of anthracite coal, especially during the nineteenth century, was eastern Pennsylvania. This might be called its historic location. Anthracite was known and used in various parts of Europe and of Asia for centuries; and bituminous coal too, probably even earlier. It is interesting that the building of chimneys in England at about 1368 was caused by the introduction of coal, very likely the bituminous, as getting rid of the objectionable smoke was naturally a large part of the purpose.

In 1796 George Owen wrote a vivid account of the coal situation, in *The Cambrian Register,* differentiating clearly between the anthracite and the bituminous.

For the most part, those that dwell neere the cole, or that may have it caried by water with ease, use most cole fiers in theire kitchings, and some in their halles, because it is a ready fiere, and very good and sweete to rost and boyle meate, and voyd of smoake, where yll chymnies are, and doth not require a man's labour to cleve wood and feed the fiere continually. Next unto the wood, or rather to be preferred before it for fuell, is cole fiere, for the generalitie of it, as that which serveth most people and especially the cheeffe townes. This cole may be nombred as one of the cheeffe commodities of this countrey, and is so necessarie, as without it the countrey would be in great distress. It is called stone cole, for the hardness thereof, and is burned in chimnies and grates of iron; and being once kindled, giveth a greater heat than light, and deliteth to burne in dark places; it serveth alsoe for smithes to worke with, thoe not soe well as the other kinde of cole, called the running coal, for that when it first kindleth, it melteth and runneth as wax and groweth into one clodd; whereas this stone cole burneth aparte, and never clyngeth together. This kind of cole is not noysome for the smoke, nor nothing so loathsome for the smell, as the ring coal is, whose smoake annoyeth all thinges neere it, as fine lynen, mens hands that warm themselves by it; but this stone cole yieldeth in a manner noe smoke after it is kindled, and is soe pure, that fine cambrick or lawne is usually dried by it, without any staine or blemishe, and is a most proved good dryer of mault, therein passing wood, fern, or strawe. This cole, for the rare properties thereof, was carried out of the country, to the cities of London, to the late lord treasurer, Burley, by a gentleman of experience to shewe how farre the same excelled that of Newcastel, wherewith the citie of London is served; and I think, if the passage were not so tedious, there would be greate use made of it.

Owen was championing the anthracite coal of Pembroke, Wales, against the bituminous coal of Newcastle on Tyne. The importance of transportation in the competition is not forgotten.

But the people of the American colonies, many of whom came from England, Scotland, Ireland, and Wales, while they doubtless remembered both stone and running coal in the home country, or had at least heard about them, did not find any of either available here, and they pretty much did without until about 1820. Probably the chief reason for this was the competition of the abundant wood easily and quickly available on every hand in the forests. Another was the lack of transportation for either fuel or ore. True, John Winthrop, Jr., as early as 1644 started and managed iron works at Saugus for the extraction of iron from bog ore, but the fuel he used was wood. The Colonists had come to a new and unexplored region, and it took a long time to settle it and develop it to a parity with the home country in every-day living conditions.

It is quite correct to say that anthracite coal was discovered anew, here and there, by accident. But more than discovery was necessary, even though the coal in many places lay near the surface. As early as 1788 Judge Jesse Fell, a pioneer in introducing coal to the public, used anthracite that he found on or near the surface in the manufacture of nails at Wilkes-Barre, Pennsylvania. In 1791 Philip Ginter, a hunter, returning to his cabin on Mauch Chunk Mountain, stumbled over a black shiny stone. He picked it up and guessed right that it was "stone coal," the new fuel he had heard about. He showed it to some men he knew, who formed a Lehigh Coal Mine Company in 1792. But they did nothing about it except to take up something like 10,000 acres of land, including the mountain. About the same time another hunter, Nicholas or Neccho Allen, found coal up the Schuylkill River, near Pottsville. One night, after spending all day on the mountain, he made a fire under a ledge of rocks, wrapped himself up in his blanket, and went

TO THE

Blacksmiths

OF THE CITY OF

PHILADELPHIA.

The Subscriber having succeeded in overcoming the prejudice of his Workmen against the LEHIGH COAL, after two years solicitation and repeated trials, attended with disappointment, has had them used for 13 months past, to great advantage for himself and satisfactory to his journeymen (one of them that was the most adverse is now using them at Boyertown, Berks County, at $ 75 per hundred bushels, in a neighborhood where Charcoal can be purchased for one-tenth of the sum)—now offers his advice and assistance *gratis*, to such Smiths as shall call on him, between the 13th and 19th of March inst. in altering their FIRE-PLACES to fit them for using said Coal. He will be found at the Bethlehem Stage Office, Sign of the Swan, Race Street, or the Seven Stars Tavern, New Fourth Street, above the Hay Market. The address of any person, desirous of obtaining information, left at either place, will be attended to. Gentlemen of the above business are informed that he is not concerned in the Coal speculation, but offers his assistance in aid of the profession, to fulfil a promise made the Coal Company last fall, which he could not heretofore attend to, owing to indisposition.

JOSEPH SMITH.

Philadelphia, March **13, 1815.**

Courtesy of The Lehigh Coal & Navigation Co.

An effort to widen the market for coal

to sleep. Later he was awakened by a strong light in his eyes, "The mountain was on fire." He had built his fire on an outcrop of anthracite coal!

The use of the coal grew, but slowly. It would not kindle easily, especially as compared with wood. Many said that it simply would not burn. Some of it was shipped down the Schuylkill to Philadelphia. Oliver Evans, the inventor, burned some in a grate; and so did a Quaker by the name of Frederick Groff, but it was a curiosity, not a commercial success. In 1812 Colonel George Shoemaker took nine wagonloads of coal to Philadelphia to sell, but he had to give seven of them away; in fact he narrowly escaped arrest as an impostor. Of the two he did sell, one load was bought at one dollar a bushel by Josiah White and Erskine Hazard, who ran an iron-wire mill by water power on the Schuylkill. They tried it in their furnace on two occasions, but poke it as they would they could not make it burn, and at last went home cured of any thought of buying more. One of the workmen left his jacket there, however, and came back to get it. He found a hot fire going and the furnace door white hot. Realizing that anthracite needed a strong draft and that it should not be poked, Josiah White and Erskine Hazard became convinced of the merit of anthracite, and later, in 1817, turned their interest and activities to the Lehigh Valley. Josiah White spent six days in looking over the region, and then leased with some friends 10,000 acres from the Lehigh Coal Mine Company, which had failed in 1808, and took hold of the possibilities energetically.

They had acquired an abundant body of anthracite coal. The coal quarries started by the Lehigh Coal Mine Company showed this to be a positive fact. Their problem was how to get the coal from the top of the mountain to market.

They planned a road $8\frac{1}{2}$ miles long, all down grade, from the mine to the river, with an extra half-mile to carry the cars into the mine. Then they went to Harrisburg and secured an Act of Legislature permitting them to improve the navigation of the Lehigh River, approved March 20, 1818. Thereupon they formed two companies, the Lehigh Navigation Company, in August, and the Lehigh Coal Company, in October. Two years later, in 1820, these were merged into the Lehigh Coal & Navigation Company, incorporated February 13, 1822. These different organizations were adaptations to meet the various responsiveness of the public in raising money and to meet the challenge of practical considerations. There is an interesting human story in them. Sweepingly summarized, the Lehigh Coal Company attended to mining the coal, and getting it down to the river; and the Lehigh Navigation Company took charge of transporting it to market down the Lehigh River, to the Delaware, and to Philadelphia or other cities where it could be sold. But in a short time the fact impressed itself on all concerned that these were all one problem and that one organization was the right way to deal with the opportunity. Therefore the merger and the Lehigh Coal & Navigation Company.

It will be evident that the development of the several parts of the business went along together, though it is more convenient to treat them separately here. The vein of coal was found by an outcrop on the mountain, near the summit. It was possible therefore that the mining should at first be by quarrying, as during the holding of the Lehigh Coal Mine Company it was. When the mining went underground, the shaft or, technically speaking, the drift naturally followed the slope of the vein of coal into the mountain. There was nothing unique or specially significant for us in the method of the coal mining. The first crucial matter to be solved was not getting the coal down to the river but the transportation thereafter to market. Accordingly, first of all application was made to the legislature for permission to improve the navigation of the river. This was granted and the act of the legislature approved by Governor William Lindlay on March 20, 1818. At first it seemed that the market for their anthracite consisted only of the blacksmiths and the barrooms along the way. Wood was the general fuel in Philadelphia, while New York and other accessible cities used bituminous coal for their fireplaces. Accordingly the transportation of other commodities besides coal was considered in the plans for improving the navigation.

A road down the mountain to bring the coal from the mine required simply hard work of a not unfamiliar kind, clearing forest, levelling ground, and calling it a road. White and Hazard planned their road so that it went all its distance of 8½ miles on a descending grade, at the steepest 4½ feet in a distance of 100 feet, near the summit, and only 1 foot in a 100 at the gentlest. It was claimed that this road was the first laid out with a surveying instrument by dividing the whole descent by the distance and locating the road and building it as regularly as the lay of the ground would

From a drawing by Harry Fenn in "Picturesque America," edited by William Cullen Bryant, 1874

The Mauch Chunk Railroad

permit. The road was operated by gravity and mule return. Brakes were an essential part of the construction of the coal cars. The mules that dragged the empty cars back to the mine rode down in a car and were fed on the way. The descending speed of these coal cars was about 15 miles an hour, but this was too much for the mules; "they got and kept sick." Nonetheless, having become accustomed to going down in this way, in style, with refreshments provided, it was only with difficulty that they could be persuaded to go down in any other way, as, for example, on their own feet. So the brakes had to be called into requisition to delay the speed of progress. Possibly this was the first coal strike!

The output of coal increased during the next ten years, however, so that continual repairs to the road were necessary, coating the surface here and there with stone. By 1827 it was decided to turn the road into a railroad. That did not mean a road with cars propelled by steam power, a meaning with which the word has been gratuitously endowed more recently. In 1827 a railroad was simply a road with two rails laid on it lengthwise, on which the cart wheels could run far more smoothly and with much less propelling effort than on the ordinary road. The rails were of wood, as the sleepers on a railroad track still are of wood, and were covered with strips of iron 1½ inch wide and ¼ inch thick. The operation of the railroad was by "gravity and mule return" as before. But it was a great improvement. Begun in January, it was in operation in May, 1827, an achievement of the Lehigh Coal and Navigation Company.

Domestic architecture on the Mauch Chunk Mountain

From drawings by Harry Fenn in "Picturesque America," edited by William Cullen Bryant

The river was much more rough above Mauch Chunk than below, though all the way to the Delaware it had a swift current. But Josiah White and Erskine Hazard were masterful men, and did not hesitate to start out at once to master the river. For immediate purposes it was the navigation below Mauch Chunk that must have the first attention, to take care of the coal coming down from the mountain. But there was more coal in the hills and mountains upstream. The mouth of Nesquehoning Creek practically at Mauch Chunk was made the dividing point between two sections of the river. Here they started, in the days of the Lehigh Navigation Company, to construct a system of channels with contracting of these channels funnel-fashion. This was wild country and scarce were the places where they could put up a camp on the banks. So they took care of their construction gangs in the river itself, on a chain of four scows, which took to itself the name of Whitestown on the Lehigh. Two scows, 35 x 14 feet, supplied lodging and eating room for the 70 hands. One scow, 30 feet long, afforded space for the management. And one scow, 25 feet long, served as kitchen and bakehouse. All were of one story, 6 feet high. The gang could build a small wing dam and the channel wall in from one to six days. Then they pulled up anchor and floated on downstream to the next job. The men wore strong shoes with holes in the toes, as their work was in water a good part of the year. The bunks had either straw or just plain board for all alike, managers and men. They were paid in private checks on the Allentown Bank.

All seemed to be going well, when late in 1818 a severe drought came and put to naught the alluring predictions of local origin to the effect that the river never went low. Artificial freshets were the solution for this trouble. For this purpose Josiah White invented a sluice-gate that filled the need and restored regular transportation down river to the coal. They were novel-looking indeed in the eyes of some of the local geniuses. One of these, whose inquisitiveness was his most hard-working quality, asked what on earth they were, and what for. An Irishman, who had never felt that he was confined to the literal truth in such circumstances, told the man that they were bear-traps. The name stuck. Bear-traps became their regular name, though no one knows whether a bear ever was caught in one. There is still a narrow street in Mauch Chunk called Trap Alley. Twelve bear-traps were built in 1819. They were effective, but in the spring of 1820 reverse fortune came. The winter ice and freshets destroyed some of the dams and sluice gates. So a great raft was put together for some sixty men and floated down the river repairing the bear-traps as it went. Probably it was a suburb of the original Whitestown on the Lehigh. At any rate, regular transportation of coal was restored.

Wisdom and energy, a strong combination, had by this time set Josiah White and his associates free to realize that all these problems—of mining, of transportation, and of marketing—were in fact one closely jointed system of problems and that in unity is strength. Accordingly, as has already been noted, the two separate organizations were united in the single Lehigh Coal and Navigation Company, on April 21, 1820, with formal incorporation on February 13, 1822. In 1820, the first regular shipment of anthracite coal was sent to Philadelphia by the new company; it consisted of 365 tons, to be soid at $8.40 a ton. In 1821, 1073 tons were sent to Philadelphia. The boats on which this coal was shipped were arks, described earlier in this book. They were much like the scows of which Whitestown was composed but usually shorter and wider, being about 25 x 16 feet. At first two and later four of these arks were hinged together, as the rivermen became more expert in handling them, thus rendering them more responsive in steering past the dams and sluices and less subject to the capricious current. They were steered by long oars or sweeps, like the rafts. When the end of the voyage was reached at Allentown, or wherever the coal was unloaded, the hardware was taken off to be sent back to Mauch Chunk, and the dismembered arks were sold for lumber. The men walked back the 80 miles. But within a few years the tavern keepers along the road put on a wagon service to carry the men back, with regular stops at the taverns. The wood was cut for the planks to make these arks in definite dimensions, a sort of crude standardizing. Five men when they had become expert could throw an ark together and launch it in forty-five minutes. It will be realized that such facile structures could with equal or greater ease be broken up at the other end of the trip. Yet they were quite strong enough to serve their purpose—and coal is a heavy cargo.

At this point in the story another figure comes into the Lehigh Valley, a young Connecticut Yankee by the name of Asa Packer, passing through in 1822 on his way to apprentice himself to his uncle, Edward Packer, a carpenter in the village of Brooklyn, over the mountains in Susquehanna County. Asa saw what was going on along the Lehigh River under the direction and impelled by the motive power of the Quaker, Josiah White, and his friends, and he was impressed. But he went on. Having started to go to his uncle's he went. He was apt to carry out anything he really determined to do. But he did not forget. Eleven years later, in 1833, at the age of 28, he came back to the Lehigh.

Meantime Josiah White continued his fight to discipline the river, with some success. Finally he and Erskine Hazard decided upon building a canal alongside the river. When the canal along the Delaware River was completed it would be possible to ship coal straight through from Mauch Chunk to Philadelphia. The market for anthracite coal was only for domestic uses, but the public was rapidly becoming convinced of its practical value, so there was a period of prosperity for the Lehigh Coal and Navigation Company during the later 1820s. Under the direction of Canvass White, who had rendered eminent service in the building of the Erie Canal, the Lehigh Canal was finished in 1829. But until the Delaware Canal was finished in 1832 the outlet for coal and all traffic of the Lehigh Canal was seriously restricted at Easton. Coal was booming as an industry, but at this time a new coal field came into activity and developed the upper

Schuylkill Valley and the town of Pottsville at the expense of the Lehigh Valley and Mauch Chunk.

About this time Asa Packer came back to the Lehigh, at first as a carpenter, building a canal boat, of which he kept the ownership, and which he operated between Mauch Chunk and Philadelphia. Then he built a second canal boat. He was beginning at the bottom, where he was laying a foundation for his future. He took contracts for building dams in the improvement of the Lehigh River above Mauch Chunk. He and his brother had a store. With his savings he bought coal lands near Hazleton in the new coal fields on the upper Susquehanna where coal lands were still cheap. For a while he went over to Pottsville, as the commercial outlet of these mines. Then he divided their interests with his brother; his brother took over the Schuylkill Valley and Asa returned to the Lehigh Valley, to concentrate on its development from Mauch Chunk. He was not worrying about the coal; there was plenty of that. He was thinking about the best means for its transportation, and about its market.

Josiah White, Erskine Hazard, and the Lehigh Coal and Navigation Company, under stress of the competition from Pottsville and the decreasing demand for their product, realized that, despite the many superior qualities of their anthracite, it was not beyond competition as a fuel for smelting iron. Iron ore was abundant in the Lehigh Valley, and near an equally abundant coal. But the anthracite was slow kindling and slow burning, and except occasionally not supreme for furnace use. They saw great opportunities ahead if they could produce cheap iron. A great demand for iron was on its way; it would become a great industry.

James Branmont Neilson (1792–1865) of the Glasgow Gas Works in 1834 discovered the essential hot blast for smelting. In 1836 George Crane of the Yniscedwin Iron Works in Brecknockshire, Wales, and David Thomas (1794–1882) successfully applied the principle to the use of anthracite as their fuel. Josiah White had a nephew in Wales. He sent him to see George Crane. Subsequently Erskine Hazard went over to see Crane in 1838, and on December 31, 1838, made a contract with David Thomas to come over to Pennsylvania to build furnaces for the hot-blast method of smelting iron ore with anthracite coal. The Lehigh Crane Iron Company was formed, and the Lehigh Valley once more rose into extraordinary advantage of industrial position. David Thomas arrived in New York on the clipper ship *Roscius,* on June 5, 1839, after a run of twenty-three days. It was an event in the industrial history of America. In August ground was broken for the first furnace of the kind at Craneville, now called Catasauqua, and the first run of iron was made on July 4, 1840, and proved a great success. The ore used was two-thirds hematite and one-third magnetic iron ore. The blast heat, blown with two-and-a-half-inch nozzles by canal water power, was 600°. The furnace remained in blast until January, 1841, when its fires were quenched by a revengeful flood in the Lehigh River. In the six months it had produced 1080 tons of pig iron. This same furnace continued in operation over eighty years. Anthracite took its place in the lead as a fuel, not only for domestic purposes, but also for smelting, and the leading figure in this development was David Thomas.

Asa Packer believed in steam. He believed also as a matter of course in the economical way of building a road, of making the road consist essentially of the two parallel tracks over which the wheels ran, whatever the means of propulsion. These tracks, while at first of wood, were soon covered with a strip of iron, or rail. These roads were naturally called rail-roads. Asa Packer believed in using steam to propel the cars on these rail-roads. Steam power and rail-roads made a good combination, as he was sure they would. Indeed the name rail-roads has long since meant only steam railroads.

Conservative and profitable business developed canals for the transportation of coal to market. For such heavy traffic as coal, iron, and lumber water carriage with its lower freight rates was generally considered to be better. For years Asa Packer urged the construction of such a steam railroad upon the Lehigh Coal and Navigation Company, but without avail. The Lehigh Canal was carrying 1,000,000 tons of freight a year, and that was convincingly good business. In 1846 a company was organized called the Delaware, Lehigh, Schuylkill, & Susquehanna Railroad, but no activity followed. In 1851 Asa Packer took a financial interest in the railroad. In order to preserve its charter, which would have expired in seventeen days, he graded a mile of the railroad's right of way on his own responsibility. Acquiring control and putting all he had of fortune and of energy into the work, he made a success of the steam railroad, and on September 12, 1855, under the name of The Lehigh Valley Railroad, its first train ran by steam power from Easton to Mauch Chunk.

Meantime the railroads were developing rapidly, extending over the entire United States and incorporating new regions by very practical ties into American unity. The railroads needed a greater and greater annual mileage of iron rails, and of rails that were heavier to bear the increasing weight of the new locomotives and trains. This made a demand for more and more iron, and for more and more fuel to smelt the iron ore. Anthracite had a much higher percentage of carbon in its native state than bituminous coal, but comparatively the available supply was limited. Under the stimulus of this fact, it was found that by cooking the bituminous coal, heating it without allowing it to burn freely, driving out the volatile and combustible impurities, a fuel was obtained even better than anthracite. This fuel came to be called coke. Generally speaking, to produce one ton of metallic iron there is required two tons of iron ore and four tons of fuel. Therefore, in the industrial management of iron manufacture the iron ore always goes to the fuel. In the years following 1859 it was found that there were veins of a specially cokable bituminous coal in the neighborhood of Connellsville, Pennsylvania, on the Youghiogheny River, a tributary of the Monongahela, on the western slopes of the Allegheny Mountains. So it came about that iron ore was brought to this region for smelting, not only from the Pennsylvania and West Virginia mines but even from the Lake Superior region of Michigan and Wisconsin and Minnesota, and Pittsburgh became the manufacturing center of the iron and steel industry of the United States and of the world.

There also arose steadily a demand for a stronger and stronger metal. This was supplied by the invention and business development of a process that came to dominate the entire industry. In 1856, in England Henry Bessemer (1813–1898) discovered that by an extra hot blast he could make good steel with use only of the carbon in the pig iron, and so "without fuel." It was so inexpensive as to make quantity production of first-class steel entirely practicable. In America the Bessemer process and rights were handled by Alexander Lyman Holley (1832–1882) who by his ability as an engineer and by his improvements became recognized as the foremost steel-plant engineer in America. In 1857 the United States Patent Office declared that William Kelly (1811–1888), who had made a similar invention independently, was the original inventor, but the development of the process was not as able and effective, so his claim was at a decided disadvantage. In 1866 the Bessemer and Kelly claims were compromised and the industry was saved the hindrance of controversy and litigation. So the Bessemer process has magnified the output and value of the iron and steel industry that centers at Pittsburgh.

Railroads were by no means the only industry that made a demand for more and better iron and steel, and therefore coal and coke. One of these was the cast iron pipe industry, which became insistent in behalf of water supply and sanitary drainage in about 1876. None of these produced

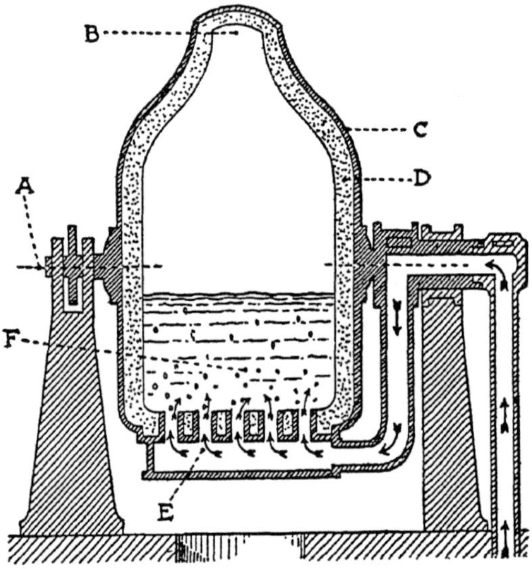

From a drawing by E. G. Lutz

The Bessemer converter

A. Axis upon which the converter turns when it is tilted to pour out the molten metal. *B.* Spout. It is from this spout that we see issuing the burst of flame and the outpouring of sparks when the converter is in operation. *C.* Outer steel casing. *D.* Lining of siliceous rock or other material. *E.* Air entering through the holes of the false bottom. *F.* Molten iron.

its greatest demand and market during the period of this volume. But the beginning of this tremendous development was in that part of the nineteenth century during which the United States of America were knitting close their entity into a national unity, between 1775 and 1875. Railroad building and coordination, bridge building, iron-clad ships and steel ocean liners, steel construction of skyscraper office, factory, and residential buildings, all these and many more began the realization of their possibilities in the nineteenth century and extended their development into the twentieth century and into the future giving to America its extraordinarily creative value in the life of the world.

Shoeing an ox

From a drawing by R. J. Tuckler in "Ye Old Log House. [illegible]ymes and Pioneer Sketches" by Jno. S. Minard

CHAPTER XIV

Horse-Power in Agriculture

"MORE power to your elbow!" is an old expression of good will. In other words, may you have abundant power close at hand. America has progressively had more and greater power at hand from the colonial days to the present days of electricity. Jared Van Wagenen, Jr., a good authority in regard to agricultural development, whose concise monograph, *The Golden Age of Homespun,* is full of personally acquired and affectionately remembered information, says:

Students of this phase of our history have declared that the halcyon day of the homespun age was not, as might be supposed, prior to the Revolution, but rather following that struggle and reaching its highest development in the first quarter of the century behind us. There was good reason for this. England had an old industrial life going back for very many years and trade with her colonies was carefully fostered, while any industrial development in America was not only discouraged but in some ways actively hampered. The Revolution cut us off from European supplies and after peace came again it was urged as a patriotic duty, reinforced by poverty and the smoldering enmities of the war, that we ought to be independent of overseas wares. . . .

I feel sure that in 1825 we had a largely self-supported and self-contained rural social organization, but a new era was ready to be ushered in. I think it would be possible to demonstrate with something like mathematical exactness that the fruitful decade

1840–1850 was the most revolutionary of any ten years in our long agricultural history. During that very short period we largely passed from the age of the hand tool to the use of animal power.

The animals were of course horses, mules, and for special strength when speed was not essential, oxen.

To trace this development in the everyday life of agriculture it may be well to select as our illustrative line the implements for the harvesting of the wheat and other grain crops in New York State. At first on all farms these implements were simple tools and were used by hand. As animal power came into use, it was first on the larger farms, the use of animals gradually extending to the moderate-size farms, while partly as a result of practicability and partly of the greater crops raised for market on the larger farms the small farms turned to truck gardening or raised only enough grain—maize, for instance—for home or at most local consumption.

Going back into the tenuous records of oral tradition, in the early years of the nineteenth century there was the sith with its accompanying tool, the mathook. The sith was decidedly superior to the sickle as a tool for reaping. It was shorter in all its members than the scythe and, compared with that graceful and imperious affair, a rather stunted, awkward-looking device. The sith required special skill in handling. It was held in the strong right hand (and the right hand had to be strong), while the left hand managed the mathook. With the mathook a cut of standing grain was caught and drawn in within reach of the sith, which instantly flashed forward and cut the selected grain, every straw of it, evenly, at the right height and quickly, from the remaining stubble. So the reaper strode swiftly, without a pause, down the field, leaving a windrow of grain on its straw behind him.

Next came the scythe, to this day a familiar instrument to all farmers and to all who have a country place of some extent and like to cut the hay themselves. The scythe has lasted not as the chief harvesting instrument, which it once was, but as a perennial resource for cutting out the corners and the edges of the grain and hay fields, and of course for the smaller fields. Naturally much heavier than the sith, requiring the use of both hands, of both arms, it did its own selecting of the cut to be taken and forthwith (if properly handled) severed the cut and laid it smoothly on the ground. A day's work with the scythe was hard work.

Early in the nineteenth century, if not before, the grain cradle began to come into use. In part it was like a scythe, or it would be better to say that a scythe blade was the cutting element of it. It was equipped with an arrangement of long tines or fingers to catch the grain as it was cut and enable the reaper deftly to lay it to one side in an even windrow. The cradle was naturally much heavier than the scythe. As Van Wagenen says, it took a mighty biceps and an unbreakable back to make a good cradleman. And it took exceptional skill to make a good cradle. Quoting our authority again,

Long ago in Schoharie County, one Erskine Bouck made cradles by going into the woods where ash trees had been felled and digging out the entire stumps, from the buttressing roots of which he could split out pieces having the natural crook for the "fingers." Finally from his wonderfully skilled and patient hands came a cradle which for slenderness and toughness and lightness and elasticity and "hang" was in its way as much of a triumph as a Stradivarius violin. Bouck cradles were known far and near and sold for $5.00 in the day when this was deemed a large sum of money. . . . Today when we buy a cradle it was made in a factory with snath and fingers sawed from the log and steamed and bent into shape like a wagon felloe—a heavy, awkward, ill-balanced, misbegotten tool compared with those that came from the workbench of the master craftsman. Nor does it greatly matter, because the last of the mighty race of old-time cradlers is about to depart and in future we shall not use the implement even to cut the swath around the field to make way for the binder.

In 1820 or thereabouts the cradle was the almost universal harvesting instrument, and its prevalence lasted quite until the Civil War or maybe until after when the incoming agricultural machinery drove it from its dominant position. An average cradler could cut four acres of standing grain in a day, some even an acre or possibly two acres more if the conditions were favorable. But at its best and at the height of its period the cradle was not an individual tool. The cradle was used in finely organized teamwork, though many of the cradlers were very particular about their instruments, and wanted them made exactly right, as good musicians and expert riflemen are particular about theirs. Quoting further from Van Wagenen:

Many men declared that they enjoyed cradling, but mowing

was by common consent a gruelling task. Cradling was hard, exhausting labor but performed by a good man it was a beautiful exhibition. A band of well-matched cradlers going down a field of golden grain had all the rhythmical measured swing of a college eight-oared crew, and—save in memory—we can never see that spectacle again.[1]

We might now forge ahead into the development of harvesting implements during the whole middle half of the nineteenth century. But agricultural life did not consist even mainly in the harvesting of the crops. More than half of the population of the United States were farmers through most or all of this period. Any and all of their duties, occupations, and interests were of everyday importance in American life in the maintenance and the expansion of the ideals and the power of that life over the continent. During these decades the increase and spread of the American population was unprecedented in the history of the world. In this period the aspirations of the world became focussed on America. It is possibilities, especially as yet unrealized possibilities, that inspire progress and continued advance. America offered greater possibilities and offered them more freely to all than had ever been known. This increase and spread may be seen by a glance at the following figures taken from the United States Censuses from 1790 to 1880. The location of the center of population is here only approximately stated. In 1780, before the Colonies had achieved their independence, or the States had been united by the Constitution, the

[1]Van Wagenen knew about college eight-oared crews; he was at Cornell in the days of old Charlie Courtney.

total population was about 2,781,000. In the next ten years the population jumped by 1,148,214, more than 40 per cent.

Year	*Population*	*Center of Population*
1790	3,929,214	23 miles east of Baltimore, Maryland
1800	5,308,483	18 miles west of Baltimore, Maryland
1810	7,239,881	40 miles northwest of Washington, D. C. (in Va.)
1820	9,638,453	16 miles east of Moorefield, West Va.
1830	12,866,020	19 miles west of Moorefield, West Va.
1840	17,069,453	16 miles south of Clarksburg, West Va.
1850	23,191,876	23 miles southeast of Parkersburg, W. Va.
1860	31,443,321	20 miles south of Chillicothe, Ohio
1870	38,558,371	48 miles east of Cincinnati, Ohio
1880	50,155,783	8 miles west of Cincinnati, Ohio (in Ky.)

By the end of the hundred years of our period there were as many people living west of Cincinnati as east. In all this mighty wide-flung migration at least half of the people were raising food of one kind or another to feed all of them, but it is a mistake to think of all farm life as the same. What farm life was like was as varied as the local conditions and the kind and degree of agricultural development might dictate. It may be that from this fact—whatever the national or racial origin—the generally versatile quality of the American character has come.

To preserve in this account at least a suggestion of the variety in farming, we will follow the grain a little farther during the manual or hand-tool period, through the binding and the threshing, before we follow the harvesting implements in the strict line of our survey. Fortunately we can still benefit from the vivid personal testimony of our former authority. The use of machines was coming into many lines of work but the binding of the sheaves continued for many years to be a manual operation, for the simple reason that no machine had appeared that could equal or approach the speed and skill of the men and the women themselves. It was a common feat for the binder to tie a sheaf, toss it high into the air, and bind another sheaf before the first sheaf touched the ground. One of the earliest discoveries or inventions in the history of mankind, going back to the early agricultural age, was "the binder's knot, that deft twist and tuck which the expert accomplishes so rapidly that the eye can scarcely follow the hand."

In the early days there was in Schoharie County a woman, Mrs. Stahl, the mother of a family, who could bind sheaves behind a cradler all day long, keeping close behind him, and who then at the end of the day as a climax would catch the last cut off the cradle in her arms and bind it without letting a straw of it touch the ground. Then the sheaves had to be piled together into shocks, until they were carted off to the barn. This too was no work for novices. It required speed and skill so that the sheaves would stand upright and stay in place and protect the grain from the rain. A neighbor, Asa Abbott, all his life, bound his grain by hand and shocked the sheaves of several acres of oats beautifully all in a single day, every shock being properly protected by a cap-sheaf. The farms of these neighbors were not far from the farm that Jared Van Wagenen has tilled all his life, and his father and grandfather and great-grandfather before him.

But the machine age was approaching. As far back as the 1840s there was offered to progressive-minded farmers a grain-binder's wheel-rake which would take care of the longest straw and which weighed only 15 pounds. It was pushed along the cradle-swath, and when ready stepping on a pedal would tilt the bundle up into convenient position for binding without bending the back. There was a picture of one of these implements in *The Cultivator* for August, 1850. Van Wagenen's comment on it was that he had no doubt it could be worked, but that there was no evidence it ever attained any general use. Its significance was that agricultural inventors and farmers were getting to think mechanically. Many efforts and failures always go before success.

To get the grain out of the heads and free from the husks or chaff the operation was the threshing. In the earlier days of the hand-tool period this was done on the barn floor with the flail. The sheaves were unbound and the gavel or unbound sheaves were laid evenly on the floor in two rows with the heads overlapping. Then two men beat the grain-heads with flails in alternate rhythmic blows. The agricultural flail was a strong wooden handle, two or three feet long with a shorter, thicker stick called the swingle or swiple attached to the end by a tough thong of eelskin. The flail was a peace-time descendant, centuries old, of a mediæval war-time weapon called a swingel, which had an iron ball, often heavily spiked, attached to the handle by an iron chain.

When thoroughly threshed, the grain and chaff were scooped up into the large shallow winnowing basket or tray and tossed into the air so that the breeze would blow the chaff away while the grain would fall back into the basket or tray. This winnowing basket or tray has for centuries been called a fan, and the operation fanning. This use has been familiar at least since 1611 in the English translation of the New Testament where John the Baptist says (St. Matthew 3:12), "Whose fan is in his hand, and he will thoroughly clean up his threshing-floor."

At an early time animal power was introduced into harvesting through the threshing. Horses and mules had of course always been used to drag the plow and the harrow. But now a post was erected in the middle of the threshing floor with a sweep attached, to which to hitch the team, and unshod horses or oxen were driven round and round, trampling out the grain, while with pitchforks men turned and shifted the gavel on the floor so that the threshing should be thorough. During most of this time oats, barley, and buckwheat were threshed in this way, but wheat, rye and peas were still flailed, the rye longest of all.

Then came machinery, at just the right time in every phase of work to which it applied, endowing farming with the possibility of one man's doing as much work as previously it had required six men to do. Take work away from men who needed it? Yes and no. Literally, yes. But rather releasing them to do work which otherwise would not be done. The vast fertile prairies of the Middle West were clamoring for men to come and settle and work the rich soil, promising them manifold greater returns than they could make in the smaller-scale agriculture of the East.

But machinery came gradually, by grace of the more prosperous and venturesome-minded farmers, not by any disruptive invasion. As far back as 1830 one T. D. Burrall of Geneva, New York, began to manufacture threshing machines, probably developing the idea of a man who in 1822 moved from New Hampshire out into New York. The motive power was animal, the horses pulling a circular sweep. Then, probably by 1845, came the advance of having the horses contribute their power on a treadmill. In the old illustrations the artist seems to have reduced the flailsman and the cradler to their just proportions as compared with the magnificent and efficient animal power of the horses.

The development of American agriculture through machinery was in part an expansion westward with the migrations, but it was not only that. It was also intensive in what and how much could be accomplished. The line we have chosen to illustrate this development is the harvesting machinery. This developed in response to the opening up of the vast prairies of the Middle West, and indeed found its full opportunity there, though reaching everywhere in time and to the degree that was practicable. The scythe and the cradle were able to harvest the grain crops of New York and other Eastern States very satisfactorily. It was natural, therefore, that the harvesting machines did not become generally prevalent in New York and the East until the 1860s or even until the 1870s. What the farmers and their families and the neighbors in the near-by villages saw in the fields every day during the harvest season were scythesmen and cradlers, singly or in lines going down the grain fields in good time and doing a beautiful complete job.

But the scythe and the cradle were quite inadequate for the fields of Ohio, Indiana, Illinois, and the trans-Mississippi States. There what every one saw in the fields, before the agricultural machines came, were acres and acres untouched, often even unsown, because there was no adequate means for harvesting so great an area. Entering a claim for such large farms was an act of pure optimism and speculation, based on hope and the low prices. It is then in accord with the facts of the situation and indeed significant that the two chief inventors of harvesting machines in the early days soon took their machines west to demonstrate them to the public and to build up their markets.

There was another condition, both east and west, which emphasized the importance of speed in harvesting. When the grain was ripe or when the hay was ready for cutting, if it was not cut soon, the weather might ruin the whole crop. Harvesting machinery therefore that would cut more and cut faster, while an advantage in the East, was a necessity for the expansion of American civilization throughout the entire Ohio-Mississippi-Missouri River Valley.

The first attempt to invent machinery to cut the grain crops was made certainly as far back as 1803, when a United States patent was granted for such a device. There were not a few of these attempts during the first quarter of the nineteenth century. But if it be not disrespectful to these courageous-minded pioneers to say so, these attempts may be characterized as a recognition of the fact that such machines would be desirable if they could be invented. Two inventors heralded the arrival of machine harvesting in practical form by the success of their machines in the field—Obed Hussey (1792–1860) and Cyrus Hall McCormick (1809–1884). Horses were the motive power in the harvesting machines and in all the agricultural inventions of both these men. All agricultural machines, by whomsoever invented, were propelled by animal motive power until the oil industry and automobiles ushered in a new era. Great advances, extraordinary advances were made in the development of the machinery—in the working out of mechanical principles and in the achievements of manufacture, but during all the last century the power was supplied by that reliable old friend of the settler and of the farmer, the horse, hauling in single or double harness of strong leather. Animal power kept something of the personal quality in all farm labor for many, many years, and in some regions does so still.

Obed Hussey was what fifty or seventy-five years ago was often colloquially called a "genius." When he was pursuing an idea he worked brilliantly; at other times he inclined to laziness. To carry out a mechanical idea was for the time being his whole intent. At those times he was determined

From a drawing in "Mechanic's Magazine," April, 1834

Obed Hussey's reaper, 1833

and intolerant of opposition. Who could know his idea better than himself or better judge whether each step carried it through practical details toward realization? Yet at the same time he was extremely modest and sensitive.

Obed Hussey was known for having invented mechanical devices of various kinds, a corn-grinder, a sugar-cane crusher, a machine for making hooks and eyes, before he turned his ingenuity to a reaper. In 1830, when he was thirty-eight years old, some one, probably a practical farmer of his acquaintance, suggested to him that he work on a machine to cut grain. The suggestion appealed to him. He went ahead and worked on it, making successive models, but without first trying to find out what others might have done already, not even caring to find out if such a machine was really needed. His idea was a good one; it was his; all he asked was to be let alone. In the winter of 1832–33 he went to Cincinnati and there began to build a full-size reaper. It was completed in time for the harvest of 1833. It was exhibited and given a public trial under the auspices of the Hamilton County Agricultural Society, near Carthage, Ohio, on July 2, 1833. He applied for a patent and was granted a United States patent for it on December 31, 1833. The machine was drawn by a horse or a team, hitched in front of it, and walking along one side of the standing grain. It had a cutting apparatus set off to one side, and a platform to receive the cut grain. Hussey set up his factory at Baltimore and from 1834 to 1838 manufactured his reapers and sold them in Illinois, New York, Maryland, and Pennsylvania.

Six months after Obed Hussey was granted his patent, Cyrus Hall McCormick was granted a United States patent for a reaper, on June 21, 1834, and began to manufacture. A bitter rivalry naturally arose between them. Each obtained another patent. At the time of the expiration of the original patents, in 1848, McCormick applied for an extension of his patent. So did Hussey, but he neglected to do so until after the time required for such applications had elapsed. However, neither was granted an extension. With the expiration of those patents, the patented devices were placed at the disposal of any and all to use freely in their inventing. The result was active and numerous competition. Hussey was not a business man. He was not able to stand up against it. He sold out his business in 1858, and went into another line of invention, a steam plow. Two years later on his way to Portland, Maine, by train, he kindly got off at a way station to get a child a drink of water. The train started. He tried to get on; he slipped and fell under the wheels of the cars and was instantly killed.

Cyrus Hall McCormick was primarily a business man. He was one of the virile family of the McCormicks, the eldest of the sons of Robert McCormick (1780–1846). As the name suggests, they came of one of those Presbyterian Scotch-Irish breeds, hard-working, hard-fighting, who came across the Atlantic from Ulster, went through into the mountains of Pennsylvania, and then drifted south along the mountain ranges into the Valley of Virginia.[2] There they settled in a place they called Walnut Grove, partly in Rockbridge County and partly in Augusta County, not far from the Natural Bridge.

[2] *Everyday Things in American Life,* Volume I, Chapter VIII, "Scotch-Irish in the Mountains," pages 110–124; also see the Index.

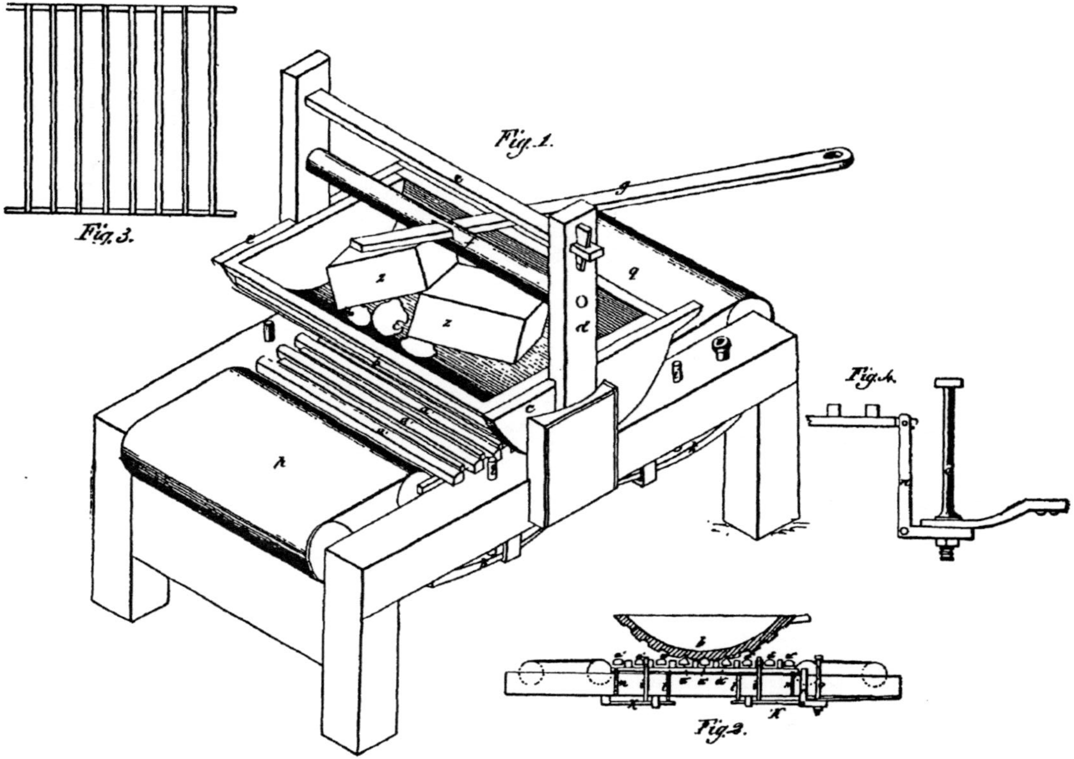

The hemp brake, a side interest of Robert McCormick

From the patent drawing by courtesy McCormick Historical Association

Robert McCormick had an inventive streak in him. He invented several agricultural implements and got patents for them—a hempbrake, a blacksmith's bellows, and a grist-mill, for instance. For twenty-two years, persistent in spite of continual failures, he kept at his efforts to invent a machine to cut grain, trying out one idea after another. At last, in 1831, he got something. In this a number of sickles projected horizontally from a wooden bar. It cut straight grain fairly well, but only when the grain stood up; if the grain leaned over or had fallen flat, as was frequent after bad weather, the machine was useless. So finally he gave it up and turned his attention to an iron furnace, which was called after the lava-streaming volcano, Cotopaxi.

When in 1831 Robert McCormick gave up his attempts to invent a reaper, Cyrus H. McCormick, at that time twenty-two years old, took up his father's idea. What was more natural? Cyrus had been helping his father in that work as much as he could for years. He had already done some minor inventing himself. That reaper idea was a family affair. Robert McCormick had begun his work on it about the time that Cyrus was born, in 1809. Cyrus had always been familiar with "the McCormick reaper" as an elusive family bonanza which, if realized, would lead them on to success and fortune. Cyrus had inherited that Scotch-Irish quality of persistence. He had also learned from his father the practical principle—when something has been thoroughly tried, but has nonetheless failed, do not be a die-hard; try something new!

Accordingly in 1831 Cyrus at once started out on the track of a new principle. He constructed a reaper almost forthwith. It was crude but it worked. He tried it out on the home fields there at Walnut Grove. He made some improvements on it and some additions to it, and then, on July 25, 1831, gave a public exhibition of it on a crop of late oats on the farm of John Steele of Steele's Tavern, Virginia. He did not apply for a patent for two years or more. A United States patent was granted to him on June 21, 1834, six months after the date of Hussey's patent. Whatever be the legal merits of that fact, and though he was granted two more patents for improvements, Cyrus McCormick relied for success rather on business competition in the market.

By 1843 McCormick and Hussey were in the full rivalry of sales competition in the farm markets of the grain-growing States. There were other manufacturers of reapers and related machines, as there still are, but not comparable to these two. At first McCormick constructed his reapers at Walnut Grove, where he could give the work personal attention. But in 1843 he began to sell rights to build McCormick reapers to licensees in various parts of Virginia. In 1844 he arranged for their manufacture at Brockport, New York, at Cincinnati, and at other points outside his own State. The results of this business policy, however, were not satisfactory. The licensees were not as careful as he regarding the material and assembly of the reapers they made. Accordingly, in 1847, he decided to concentrate all his manufacturing at one point, central to the future market of his output, where he could supervise it all himself. He fixed upon Chicago, the small but promising port on Lake Michigan. (In the same year the first railroad reached Chicago.)

After a painting by N. C. Wyeth

Testing Cyrus Hall McCormick's first reaper

The new policy was at once successful. By 1850 Cyrus H. McCormick had built up a business that was practically national.

In 1848, as has been already said, the basic patents of both Hussey and McCormick expired. The result was an increasing flood of competition, of inventors who devised improvements on reapers and got patents for them. McCormick's policy was to buy these up as fast as he could when

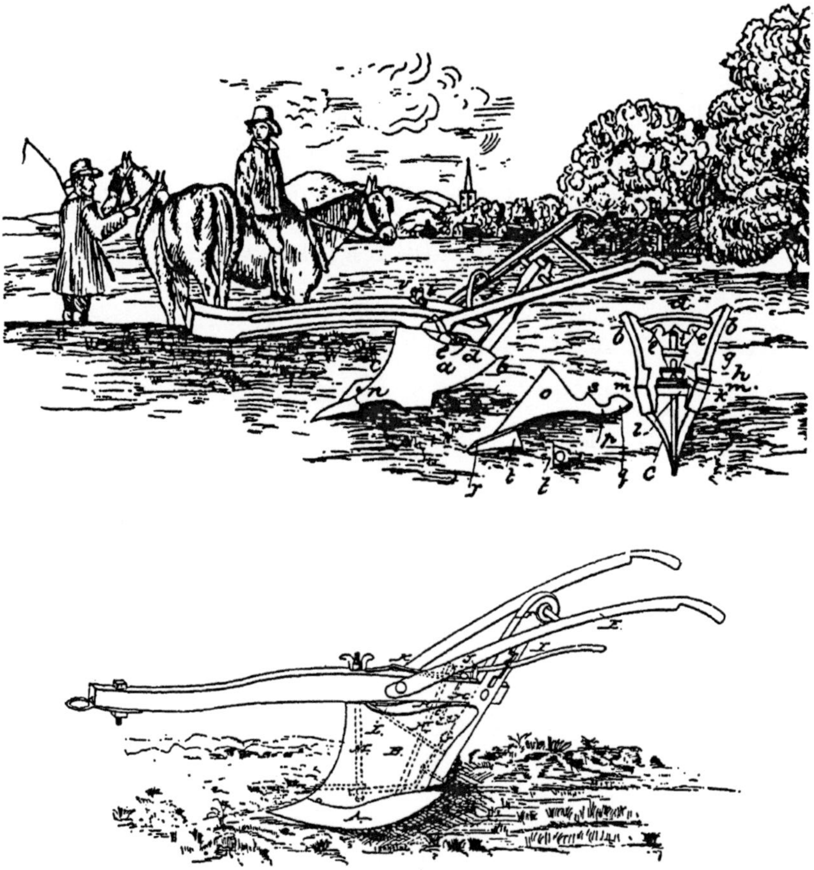

Self-sharpening horizontal plow (*top*) and side hill plow invented by Cyrus Hall McCormick

From patent drawings by courtesy McCormick Historical Association

they had any practical merit. Hussey stood on his dignity as the first inventor even if his patent had expired and he had failed to get an extension. He obstinately refused to recognize the changed business circumstances and by purchase transform troubles into advantages. Consequently during the next ten years Hussey's business declined steadily, and in 1858 he gave it up and sold out. McCormick was left in the lead in the reaper competition, although in 1850 he and Hussey had thirty active competitors, and in 1860 McCormick had over one hundred. The McCormick reaper and the corporation that Cyrus developed from a nucleus of members of his family and friends soon dominated the industry.

In the face of this fact it must be recognized that McCormick was one of the great pioneers in modern business management. He was one of the first to introduce guarantees into advertising, to give reduced prices for cash payments and to accept deferred payments as a regular policy. He also introduced labor-saving machinery into his factories for the specific purpose of ensuring quantity production. All these directly tended to increase his sales and to spread the use of machinery throughout the agricultural States.

To the everyday people of America the reaper and similar horse-powered machines became steadily more and more a familiar everyday thing. In New York the cradle was an adequate implement for the comparatively small crops for a long time and the reaper had not come into common use until about 1875, but in the Middle West its prevalence began not long after 1850 or 1860. So it was that the McCormick reaper and the corporation that Cyrus developed from a nucleus of members of his family and friends soon dominated the industry.

The bitter rivalry between Hussey and McCormick was by no means limited to those two. It was a free-for-all. Nor did it end with Hussey's death in 1860, nor with McCormick's death in 1884. The ultimate award of those who are competent to judge is that Hussey's machine was better for mowing, where the crop was grass for hay; and that McCormick's was better for reaping where the crop was wheat, oats, or rye, for the grain.

But there was a phase of the service rendered by the reaper other than its direct work at harvest time, a phase that exercised very great influence for the benefit of the country. These harvesting machines, godsends as they were, could not be operated to advantage in fields that were still strewn with rocks and stumps of trees and such reminiscences of the pioneer days. Accordingly the farmers soon began to clear their lands. This very greatly improved the value of the lands for cultivation in the agricultural areas of the Middle West and of all parts of the United States. The influence was also felt in the opening and rapid settlement of vacant and of new lands. In this way the reaper and its kindred agricultural implements contributed directly to the development of new States and of new industries, building up the American civilization on a national scale. And the motive power in all these agricultural machines during all of this period, during all of the nineteenth century, was the horse, with the mule in reserve, and for grubbing out rocks and stumps, the strength of the ox.

If, as is the fact, Obed Hussey was granted a United States

patent six months before a United States patent was granted to Cyrus McCormick, why should McCormick rather than Hussey be generally acclaimed as the inventor of the reaper? It reminds us of the similar ascription in the case of the steamboat. John Fitch and Robert Fulton; Obed Hussey and Cyrus H. McCormick! There is a fact in the patent law that is not always clearly remembered. The United States patent system was planned for the benefit of the people as a whole, not, except incidentally, as a reward for any individual, however clever and original an inventor he may be. The United States Government in its patent system considers that it would be to the advantage of the people as a whole that a valid inventor should be allowed a monopoly of manufacture for fourteen years and possibly longer to develop his invention further and to recover expenditures. Accordingly one requirement is the priority of the idea; and another that the idea shall have been reduced to practice. Thereafter the people, before they award their acclaim, by common consent seem to require a third proof of the value of the invention to the people—a convincing degree of commercial success. Robert Fulton, partly by grace of Chancellor Livingston, brought to the steamboat this proof of commercial success; John Fitch did not. So, too, Cyrus McCormick, not Obed Hussey, brought the proof of commercial success to the reaper. Is it not true that on the whole the voice of the people is probably just?

CHAPTER XV

Steam in Transportation

WESTWARD expansion—how could it be accomplished swiftly, widely, adequately? The triumphant solution of that problem was embodied in the steam locomotive. But an earlier problem, now almost forgotten by the general public, and its triumphant solution, are nonetheless commemorated in the single all-inclusive word for the whole system, the railroad.

The entire nineteenth century was characterized by transportation, as the colonial period was by settlement. As we take a glimpse of the chief means for developing transportation, we may well revert for a moment to two features considered in previous chapters of this volume—the bridges and the corduroy roads.[1]

Just as travellers in the early days wanted to reach across a stream, however wide it might be, and get on their way without delay for detours up or down stream to a ford, or without waiting for the sluggish convenience of a ferry, so they wanted to get on also over the land, toward their destination, through the forest, or wherever it might be; and they wanted to make progress safely, speedily, and

[1]Chapter IV, "Covered Bridges," especially pages 50–52; and Chapter III, "Early Roads and Turnpikes," especially pages 19–21.

comfortably. The insistence on such conditions increased as intercommunication developed and trade between communities grew. This meant not merely that the forest trees must be cut down and the stumps grubbed out, making what was then boldly called a "road." It meant that the surface of the road should be even, smooth, hard, and as level as practicable—and not just temporarily so, until the next rain-storm washed everything out. As years and decades passed, improvements increased, but the need and the demand increased still more.

Swampy land was the worst. A regular swamp was not a serious difficulty. It was its own excuse for going around. But swampy land was at certain seasons fairly dry. Accordingly the corduroy surface was devised for these swampy stretches. The corduroy consisted, as has been told, of logs laid parallel lengthwise in the roadway, with smaller logs of the length of the width of the road laid on top crosswise, close together. Thereon was shovelled and tamped down a layer of earth, to fill the chinks between the cross pieces and make a smooth surface. It was not, comparatively, a bad road. The stages and other vehicles could go over it quite as well, sometimes, as over other sections of the road; that is, until the next hard rain came and washed the earth out from between the cross pieces. Then it was that the corduroy road got its bad reputation. Every traveller of any mileage experienced some corduroy sooner or later. Repairmen could not come and restore it after every rain. Between construction and reconstruction there were sometimes periods when travellers expressed their feelings about the corduroy in the coarse lingo of the time. Nonetheless the corduroy road should be appreciatively remembered by the comfortable traveller of the present in his streamlined Pullman as one of the pioneer ancestors of his safe, time-saving, favorite railroad.

This special pleading is justified by the testimony (almost a testimonial) of a traveller of that time. Aaron Hamton, a New Jersey Quaker, in the summer of 1813 travelled on horseback across the State of New York to the neighborhood of Buffalo, to buy land. He kept a diary, which showed him to be matter-of-fact in temperament and reasonable at least in intention.

> We came at length to the Genesee river & crossed on a bridge & passed through an Indian Reservation called Cannewagus which is a small tract but very rich Bottom land. . . . After leaving the Indian Reservation we passed through several miles extent of Barren land which was not settled. However I think there was not more than 5 miles without a house. . . . The road very bad in places. The mud holes very deep & some log road which makes traveling very tedious and unpleasant. It is made by laying logs across the road where the mud is too deep to travel through, and being joined together they form a kind of rough bridge & some of these are perhaps nearly 3 miles in length. In some places these logs are well covered with earth & the road over them is very good and smooth. We have now got through the Barren & crossed the line but we find some deep mud holes and some log road still. However there is some good dry road & fine improvements with elegant buildings as we draw nigh to Batavia.

In the history of unsettled country the horse was still the

motive power for travel, and continued to be until the need for greater speed and for increased weight of transportation carried the demand for horsepower beyond the powers of the horses. When steam came as the motive power, a smoother road was essential, and a permanently smooth and albeit a strong road.

In America the first task requiring so special a road surface was the carting of the granite blocks for the building of the Bunker Hill Monument, three miles from the quarries in Quincy, Massachusetts, to the Neponset River, whence they could be moved to Charlestown by the reliable old water transportation of lighterage. To bear up under this extraordinary haulage weight it was proposed that the route be covered with a "rail-road." This gave occasion for a beginning which, though realized by few, if any, was truly of major importance, the inception of the American railroad system.

As the fiftieth anniversary of the Battle of Bunker Hill approached there was a general impulse to celebrate it by some specially notable event. It should indeed be a celebration of all that had followed that bravely fought little battle, a celebration of the national existence and progress thus far. This was a time of prosperity, the Era of Good Feeling. There was no need to put restraint on any plans that would be adequate to the occasion. There are always three men who are essential to the success of such an undertaking. There is the dreamer: in this case it was the architect, Solomon Willard; there is the practical business man, in this case,

Gridley Bryant; and there is the financier, who "finds" the money, in this case Thomas Handasyd Perkins. Solomon Willard proposed and designed an Egyptian obelisk on a huge American scale. Egypt was familiar to every one through the Old Testament; further, Napoleon had gone down into Egypt and the Pyramids had looked down on his soldiers. Such a monument, 221 feet high, could be seen everywhere! It would be in accord with the popular instinct of the time. Every one would want to climb to the top (294 steps) and view the City of Boston and the country round about. The suggestion was accepted. The Bunker Hill Monument Association was formed and work was begun on the foundation. On June 17, 1825, the fiftieth anniversary itself, the cornerstone was laid with full Masonic rites by the Grand Master of the Order, John Abbott, in the presence of forty of the soldiers who had fought in the battle, 200 other Revolutionary soldiers, and thousands of citizens, who gathered not only on the hill itself but also on the roofs of the houses of the town of Charlestown below. The Marquis de Lafayette was present and assisted the Grand Master by spreading the mortar for the stone, and Daniel Webster delivered the principal address. It was a notable occasion indeed. Certainly at first and for a long time afterward "everybody" watched, anticipatorily. To climb a height was in those days one of the regular forms of recreation. For example, a young lady of twenty-one, from Boston, a niece of George Ticknor, was awarded a special certificate testifying that on Tuesday, September 6, 1825,

The Centenary of Bunker Hill

From a drawing by Edwin A. Abbey for the "Celebration of Centennial Anniversary of the Battle of Bunker Hill." Printed by order of the City Council, 1875 she "ascended to the peakymost point of Mt. Washington." How many monuments in which height is the distinctive feature have been erected during the fifty or sixty years following that on Bunker Hill, among them Baltimore, Indianapolis, and highest, most beautiful of all, the Washington Monument! A public demand gathered around the Bunker Hill Monument as it rose from the summit of the hill. Had there been any suggestion to abandon the project there would have been a general protest.

But to the group of men who were responsible for the project it soon became evident that the difficulties of the work were truly great. In particular the hauling of the stone was slow and uncertain. The dirt road would not answer. So it was that Gridley Bryant suggested that they build a rail-road, literally a road of rails along the three miles from the Quincy quarries to the bridge on the Neponset River. The idea was too novel for most of the members of the Association to see anything in it. Thomas H. Perkins, however, did, and he was willing to put money into it. He joined Gridley Bryant and together they put the rail-road through. A company to build the road was incorporated on March 4, 1826, and the unique rail-road was opened on October 7, 1826.

The foundation of the road was of crushed granite, of which there was of course plenty available. Over this stone sleepers were laid eight feet apart, and on these wooden rails. These wooden rails were of pine timber, 12 inches high and 6 inches thick; along the top iron plates were spiked 3 inches wide and ¼ inch thick. The wooden rails were 5 feet apart; in other words, anticipating later technical terms, the gauge was 5 feet. This first American rail-road probably cost Mr. Perkins $50,000. Mr. Bryant also designed the cars for hauling the granite—four of them. The wheels, as well as the body, were of wood and were 6½ feet in diameter; the body hung below the axle.

The Boston Daily Advertiser for October 9, 1826, had an account of the opening of the road.

> This rail-road, the first we believe in this country, was opened on Saturday in the presence of a number of gentlemen who take an interest in the experiment. A quantity of stone weighing sixteen tons, taken from the ledge belonging to the Bunker Hill Association, and loaded on three wagons, which together weighed five tons, making a load of twenty-one tons, was moved with ease, by a single horse, from the quarry to the landing above Neponset Bridge, a distance of more than three miles.
>
> This road declines gradually the whole way, from the quarry to the landing, but so slightly that the horse conveyed back the empty wagons, making a load of five tons. After the starting of the load, which required some exertion, the horse moved with ease in a fast walk. It may therefore be easily conceived how greatly transportation of heavy loads is facilitated by means of this road. . . .
>
> The carriages run upon the iron bars and are kept in place by a projection on the inner edge of the tire of the wheels. The wheels are of a size considerably larger than the common cartwheel. We learn from a gentleman who has visited the principal rail-roads of England, that in point of solidarity and skill in construction, this road is not exceeded by any one there.

This Granite Railway of Massachusetts was a special-purpose rail-road, to haul granite from the Quincy quarries for the Bunker Hill Monument. It was a freight railroad. When that Monument was finished, in 1842, after sixteen years abuilding, its function became only incidental, if it did not go out of existence altogether. Through these sixteen years, however, it was closely allied in its service to the loftiest national sentiment and to the broadest and most vigorous popular interest, that of seeing the world and of seeing it as a whole. Further, itself an engineering novelty, it directly nurtured special interest in the problems of the future. But it never carried passengers, and it was never run by steam, until as an historical road it was purchased by the Old Colony Railroad in 1871. During its own proper life its trains were always horse-drawn. It belonged from first to last to the period of animal power in transportation.

At first, to those who had transportation problems to deal with, a rail-road was not radically different from any other road. It was popularly considered more special, "fancier"; whether better, remained to be seen. Nor was it in fact radically different as long as the motive power continued to be animal power. Other instances may be noted. The rail-road of the Lehigh Valley Company, as we have seen, used mules satisfactorily for seventeen years, until 1844. The Baltimore & Ohio used horses at first, until 1832. The Boston & Albany used animal power until 1834. In the inception of the Delaware & Hudson this fact was stated clearly. This rail-road was to carry the coal of the Delaware & Hudson Canal Company from their newly acquired mines in the Carbondale district of Pennsylvania to market. The question came up to the consulting engineer of the Company, Benjamin Wright (1779–1842), who had rendered notable service in the building of the Erie Canal. As he said it would be impracticable to construct a canal through the mountains, he reported, "There remains then only a good road, or a railway. The latter, I think, will be preferred." The Granite Railway may well serve as an example of transportation during the time when animal power prevailed.

Simple objections steered the development of motive power into its best course. One idea—absurd to us with our splendidly clear after-sight, but by no means absurd to people who were accustomed to water transportation, on the rivers as well as on the lakes and the sea—was to propel the cars by sails. It was tried and proved to be good power —when there was a fine breeze and in the right direction. But sometimes there was no breeze. So of course the idea did not last very long.

What was practicable? What could by ingenuity be made practicable? It was a long process of trial and error, in which open-mindedness, faith, courage, and good sportsmanship in failure, as well as technical knowledge and business ability had their part to play. It was a great period, a generation of heroic achievements and failures, of which the story is inevitably in large measure lost.

When the country was mountainous, greater power was necessary. When heavier loads had to be transported, animal power was out of all proportion too expensive. When the distance to be covered was longer, greater speed was needed to satisfy the marketing requirements. Then steam came, and solved all these difficulties. But steam did not simply blow in at the window. Steam came by the mental sweat and nervous wear of many, by the restraint and sacrifice of industrial inventors. Steam was made practicable by restraint. The steam engine was the consummation of restraint. It came from England.

To the notable group of English pioneers we may add the name of an American, Oliver Evans of Philadelphia (1755–1819). He was a versatile inventor, making a number of improvements in flour-mill machinery and in "steam carriages." He is best known by his steam dredge, to which he gave the name of the Orukter Amphibolos or Amphibious Digger—whether because of a streak of irrepressible humor or because of a vein of extra-classical seriousness (as was not impossible at that time) who can say! As the first steam-engine builder in America, Oliver Evans and his Orukter Amphibolos had a curious significance. With steam, water transportation was just taking land transportation into partnership. A description of the machine and of its introduction to the public is given in Oliver Evans's own words:

> In 1804 I constructed at my works, a mile and a half from the water, by order of the Board of Health of the City of Philadelphia, a machine for cleaning docks. It consisted of a large flat or lighter with steam engine of the power of five horses on board to work machinery to raise the mud into lighters. This was a fine opportunity to show the public that my engine could propel both land

From "The Mechanic," Boston, 1834

Oliver Evans's dredger "Orukter Amphibolos," 1804

and water carriages, and I resolved to do it. When the work was finished I put wheels under it, and though it was equal in weight to two hundred barrels of flour, and the wheels were fixed on wooden axle-trees for the temporary purpose in a very rough manner, and attended with great friction of course, yet with this small engine I transported my great burden on the Schuylkill with ease; and when it was launched into the water I fixed a paddle wheel at the stern, and drove it down the Schuylkill to the Delaware, and up the Delaware to the city; leaving all the vessels going up at least half way, the wind being ahead.

This exhibition occurred on or about July 13, 1805. Oliver Evans also put an advertisement in the newspapers, providing for the defraying of the expenses of the exhibition; it read in part as follows:

The above machine is now to be seen moving around the Centre Square at the expense of the workmen, who expect 25 cents from every generous person who may come to see its operation; but all are invited to come and view it, as well those who cannot as those who can conveniently spare the money.

At first the persistent though desultory efforts to find ways to put the power of steam to practical use were not well differentiated. This was natural, indeed inevitable. But by 1810 or 1815 steam engineering had clarified into three distinct lines, aimed at three distinct purposes:

1. The operation of manufacturing machinery;
2. The propulsion of water traffic, whether passenger or cargo, in boats;
3. The operation of land traffic, both passenger and freight, in trains on rail-roads.

These purposes defined three different types of engine as necessary for the work to be done—stationary engines, naval engines, and locomotives. Rail-roads of good surface continued as a matter of course to be of prime importance; indeed they have been of ever increasing importance. But the development of the steam locomotive has swept to the lead in land transportation; and so true is this that the very word railroad now brings up the picture of a steam locomotive sweeping swiftly ahead rather than of the rails or the road on which it runs.

John Stevens of Hoboken (1749–1838), grandson of John Stevens, who came to America from England in 1699, was a true aristocrat. He conducted his own affairs, which were large, in accordance with high standards. He took a direct interest in travel and transportation with far vision and with practical wisdom. Difficulties were not discouraging to him; they were challenges. In the application of steam his service to manufacturing may be represented by his steam bellows, for which he received one of his three patents in 1791. His service to navigation by his vertical steam boilers and his steamboats has been stated.[2] His service to land transportation will be referred to here. It was said of him that he was far ahead of his time. He was in himself the dreamer, the practical businessman, and the financier.

John Fitch opened Stevens's eyes to the importance of steam. John Stevens saw Fitch's steamboat on the Delaware River in 1788. Thereafter he concentrated his interest and attention on that field of development. One result of the competition that sprang up was the institution of the Patent Law in 1790 by Congress. In 1791 John Stevens was granted three patents, one of which was for a multitubular steam boiler for propelling boats. Then came the years in which he gave his chief attention to steamboats. But in the midst of this he directed attention to land travel. In 1802 he became President of the Bergen Turnpike Company, and as such had occasion to study land travel and transportation both as a means and as a problem.

In 1810 the New York State Legislature responded to the agitation led by Christopher Colles and Gouverneur Morris by appointing the first commission for considering the con-

[2]See Chapter VI, "Great Water Highways into the West," especially pages 111–114.

struction of the Erie Canal. In 1812 John Stevens in opposition advocated building a railroad across the State from the Hudson River to Lake Erie instead. In a pamphlet on the "Superior Advantages of Rail-ways and Steam Carriages over Canal Navigation," he said:

> Concede that there are now no Steam Rail-ways anywhere in the world. This is not to say that they will not come—and that soon. As civilization progresses, water-carriage will prove too slow and cumbersome to satisfy the demands of humanity. And this, too, though it remain relatively cheap. What has been accomplished in comparatively few years with Steam Boats points, as I conceive, directly at the Steam Carriage. Merely by developing a method of correctly applying the same principles on land, a great saving in time and cost will be effected.

As James K. Finch has said, "This was surely a prophetic vision of the railroad era, and of its total eclipse of inland canals in America." But DeWitt Clinton with his brilliant leadership prevailed and the Erie Canal was built and rendered its extraordinary service to the State and to the Nation from 1825 until in 1905 the New York State Barge Canal was put in its place.

John Stevens, following his convictions, urged the legislatures of five States to grant charters creating railroad companies. These States were New York, New Jersey, Virginia, North Carolina, and Pennsylvania. In 1815 the New Jersey Legislature passed the first American Rail-road Act, for a railway from the Delaware River near Trenton to the Raritan River near New Brunswick. But those who had money to invest thought that Stevens's ideas were ingenious but visionary. So the plan fell through. In 1823 the Pennsylvania Legislature passed an act declaring that "on a memorial and representation of John Stevens an iron rail-road was authorized from Philadelphia to Columbia," a distance of eighty miles. On Stevens's part this was to be the beginning of a railroad reaching from Philadelphia to Pittsburgh, and in the other direction from Philadelphia to New York. This company was called in the charter as it was in John Stevens's memorial, The Pennsylvania Railroad. But again the company so created failed to raise the necessary funds and in 1826 the act was repealed.

The public was in truth, and always is, an essential element in the solution of such a situation. Colonel Stevens's home estate on the Hudson River, Stevens's Castle, was a show place, visible to all who went up and down the river. He used it as such to win the interest and belief of the public to the practicability of steam railroads for land travel and transportation. On the lower lawn of his estate he built a circular railroad track a half-mile long, and in his shops he constructed a steam locomotive, using his own multitubular boiler. He also built a railroad carriage of a size sufficient to accommodate six passengers. This little train he frequently had run around the grounds, so that people could see for themselves that it was entirely practicable to haul carriages by steam engines over an iron railroad track, and furthermore to run trains by steam around a *curved* track. Many people had an opportunity also to have a ride on the steam railroad themselves. This engine, though never used on a commercial railroad, was the first American-built steam locomotive. It served its purpose. An accurate model of it is in the National Museum at Washington.

Public opinion steadily changed and was reflected in the votes of the legislative representatives. By 1828 a new law provided that the Pennsylvania Railroad should be built by State funds, and by 1834 the Philadelphia-Columbia section was in full operation. In 1830 the New Jersey Legislature passed a bill chartering the Camden & Amboy Railroad & Transportation Company, realizing the hopes of the charter of 1815, and in 1832 this was successfully opened for business. Within the lifetime of John Stevens his dream of the steam railroad was becoming fulfilled. He has justly been called the founder of the Pennsylvania Railroad. But steamboats and railroads were not the sum total of his contributions to American civilization in the nineteenth century. Other contributions were his plan for a water system for New York City, for bridging the Hudson River; for a vehicular tunnel, for elevated railways in New York, and for an armored navy. But the greatest of all was what he did for the railroads.

No one man can build a railroad, not even a John Stevens. The public interest, serving large and noble purposes and measuring what it does by high ideals, is always essential. Finally, necessary to continuous success is a series of leaders of character and ability. The Pennsylvania Railroad had such leaders in J. Edgar Thomson (1808–1874), Thomas

A. Scott (1823–1881), and later, George B. Roberts (1833–1897), and Alexander J. Cassatt (1839–1906).

But it required a long complicated development in the building up of a great human, scientific and industrial organization finally to produce what we now know as the Pennsylvania Railroad. It was not until July 18, 1858, that the first through train went without any transfer of passengers from Philadelphia to Pittsburgh and the Pennsylvania Railroad had begun to be a complete railroad. The Pennsylvania was not the only railroad of its time. It was one of many. It is cited here, briefly, to emphasize the importance of leadership and of character in leadership, as two other railroads will be cited to call attention, even more briefly, to other elements in the business development of the nation in the solution of the problem of its transportation. The story of railroads is told in a voluminous literature. The more the reader dips into the biographies of the men who wrought out that great system, the more clearly he will understand and appreciate that story. The railroads do not consist primarily of steam locomotives and iron or steel railroad tracks, but of men, taking up the component problems in succession, carrying on their solution, and in turn handing them on to a succeeding generation.

The Baltimore & Ohio Railroad was distinctively an illustration in its beginning of group cooperation. A number of the business men of Baltimore got together to look out for their mutual interests. That great round valley in the center of the North American continent, as it was settled and developed, how should its products go to market? South, by the Mississippi River to New Orleans? Northeast, by the Great Lakes and the St. Lawrence River through Montreal? East, by the National Road or the Ohio River and the Chesapeake & Ohio Canal through Baltimore? East, again, through Pittsburgh and over the mountains by inclined planes and canals through Philadelphia? Now a third time, east, by this new Erie Canal and the Hudson River through New York? Special competition between Baltimore, Philadelphia, and New York was growing keen.

One of these Baltimore men, Philip E. Thomas, received from his brother in England a letter telling of the success of a new freight railroad, the Stockton & Darlington, soon to be followed by another, for passengers. Thomas read this letter to his friends, and they all forthwith approved the suggestion that such a line be built here for the benefit of Baltimore. Soon thereafter, on February 12, 1827, a preliminary meeting of twenty-five business men was held at the home of George Brown, a banker. They appointed a committee to consider the question of building a railroad and to report one week later. The committee reported in favor of starting to construct at once a "double Rail-road" between the city of Baltimore and some point on the Ohio River, thus by no means limiting the extent or destination of the line. One of their number, an attorney, John VanLaer McMahon (1806–1871), meantime drafted a charter to be submitted to the Maryland Legislature for enactment. There was an amusing interruption to this meeting which showed with what determination as well as how swiftly matters were progressing. One man thought such important matters should be discussed more deliberately; it may have been George Brown.

"Stop, man!" he said. "You are asking for more than the Lord's Prayer!"

"All this is necessary," replied McMahon. "The more we ask for, the more we'll get."

"Right, man; go on!" the objector agreed, withdrawing his criticism.

On February 28, 1827, the Maryland Legislature granted the charter declaring the name to be The Baltimore & Ohio Railroad Company. By March 20, 41,781 shares of stock had been subscribed for, though there were only 15,000 shares to be distributed; and on April 24, 1827, the company was formally organized with Philip E. Thomas (1776–1861) as President, and George Brown (1787–1859) as Treasurer. Twelve men were chosen for the board of directors, one of whom was Charles Carroll of Carrollton, one of the signers of the Declaration of Independence, now ninety-one years old. Despite his age, he was active in his interest.

Construction began forthwith on a first section, twelve miles, to Ellicott's Mills. By July 4, 1828, the Baltimore & Ohio was ready to lay its cornerstone, and therewith to get the public enthusiastically interested. The public response was all that could be desired. The ceremony took place on the farm of James Carroll on Gwynn's Run, and Charles

Carroll himself laid the cornerstone. The ceremonies then continued in charge of the Free & Accepted Order of Masons. The laying of the cornerstone was preceded by a great industrial parade, in which 5000 marched and at least 75,000 looked on and cheered. The population of Baltimore according to the census of 1830 was 80,625, so it will be seen that the public did indeed take part in the great occasion. As exemplifying the real unity of the public on this occasion, including people of all classes, occupations and religions, what Charles Carroll said had special significance:

> I consider this among the most important acts of my life, second only to my signing the Declaration of Independence, if even it be second to that.

It was found that the cost of construction averaged about $17,000 a mile, including the building of bridges. But as progress was made westward into hilly and into mountainous country, the cost rose, and the charter's capitalization of $5,000,000 began to look inadequate. Private money would clearly be necessary. This was natural. And private money did come to the support of the project. On one such occasion Alexander Brown (1764–1834), the father of George Brown, stepped in with help in an emergency, raising the sum of $200,000. He had started life in Ireland, where he had a small linen business. In 1800 he came to America. He expanded his business, exporting cotton as well as importing linen. One by one, as his business increased and spread, he took his sons into partnership with him. The family business became more and more the general management of large projects and the strengthening of sound business—the regular occupation of banking. He was the progenitor of a group of banking companies—Alexander Brown & Sons of Baltimore (still existing), Brown, Shipley & Company of New York and London, and Brown Brothers & Company of Philadelphia. Accordingly, when the Baltimore & Ohio found itself in a financial stringency, George Brown, the treasurer and the Baltimore son, went to his father, and he "found the money," a beautiful instance of the simple and natural operation of practical finance in the early days.

The charter of the Baltimore & Ohio did not determine the question of motive power. It was rather generally taken for granted that horses would be used. A railroad was a railroad, a particularly practical improvement of the road bed. But there were some who believed in going the whole way into original transportation. One Peter Cooper (1791–1883) strenuously urged steam. It might be that a prominent English engineer had said that the route, as shown by maps, was entirely too twisty and too hilly for the use of a steam engine. Cooper, a man in the prime of a life of varied manual labor and mechanical ingenuity, owned a large part of the Canton Iron Works in Baltimore. His scornful retort to discouragement was:

> I will knock an engine together in six weeks that will pull carriages ten miles an hour.

He proceeded to knock such a steam engine together, and

did so within the time he said he would, and it stood the test, hauling a load of forty persons over the rails at more than ten miles an hour. It was not an impressive-looking affair. It was pretty small, and got the nicknames of "Tom Thumb" and "The Teakettle." But it fulfilled its builder's promise.

The stagecoach companies did not like the prospects at all. Accordingly on September 18, 1830, they brought up one of their best horses with a carriage of passengers to show how easily a good horse could beat anything like that on suitable rails. It was an impromptu race, but a real one. At first the horse drew ahead. Then Peter Cooper put on more steam and "Tom Thumb" came along, passed the horse-drawn carriage, and steam outdistanced animal power most of the way. But "Tom Thumb" sprang a leak in its boiler, and so the horse won the race. However, everybody who had watched the race saw, and approved the decision of the board of directors that leaks could be repaired and could be prevented, and that steam was the right power for the Baltimore & Ohio in establishing commercial and passenger transportation between their city and some point on the Ohio River to be decided upon in due time in the future.

A third principle of development should be noticed in our introduction of the railroads as everyday things in popular interest. Great achievements, especially if they are universal, start as small affairs. That is where the triple leadership comes in, to make a great thing out of a small. It is the part of a leader to say "No" firmly and "Yes" creatively. In

Top: Exciting trial of speed between Mr. Peter Cooper's locomotive, "Tom Thumb," and one of Stockton & Stoges's horse-cars

Bottom: The "Best Friend," the first locomotive built in the United States for actual service on a railroad

From "The History of the First Locomotives in America," by William H. Brown, 1874. Courtesy of the New York Historical Society

American railroads a good instance may be found in what has become the New York Central Lines.

The great leader in this development was the imperial-minded Cornelius Vanderbilt (1794–1877). He started his career with a little sailboat wherewith he ferried truck-garden produce from Staten Island to New York. He worked his way up by 1846 to prominence in the water-transport business around New York, and up the Hudson River to Albany. In this way he got the sobriquet of Commodore Vanderbilt. But he was at least as truly a financier as he was a trader and business man. He made everything serve his purposes. He saw before most others that the future of the steam railroads promised greater returns than did that of steamboats. He therefore sold out his water interests and in 1862 began systematically to buy into the small local one-track railroads through the central part of New York State, thus gaining influence in their direction. As fast as he gained a controlling interest in them he merged them, thus unifying their interests and steadily increasing the profit and the mileage possibilities of every one of them.

The first of these little roads was the Mohawk & Hudson, between Albany and Schenectady, only fourteen miles long. It was chartered in 1826 and finished by 1831 with recourse to inclined planes of one foot grade in eighteen, and worked by stationary engines. In August of that year the *DeWitt Clinton,* the third American-built locomotive, passed a test successfully on its tracks. By 1853 Vanderbilt had accumulated the local lines necessary to make a through railroad between

Albany and Troy at the eastern end and Buffalo on the western. A list of the little companies that Vanderbilt merged will give a vivid idea of what he did. To appreciate the genius of his achievement it must be remembered that in gaining the support of public interest the local is far stronger and more virile than the grandiose. To every one along the line

The first steam railroad passenger train in America

the new railroad, great and far-reaching as it was, had been developed from their own little line! Those local railroads were:

Mohawk & Hudson
Schenectady & Troy
Utica & Schenectady
Syracuse & Utica
Auburn & Syracuse
Auburn & Rochester
Rochester & Syracuse
The Tonawanda
Rochester, Lockport & Niagara Falls
Attica & Buffalo
Buffalo & Lockport

By 1853 these railroads were merged into one through system, and on May 17, 1853, a new corporation was created, named the New York Central Railroad. Vanderbilt then started out to gain a railroad approach to New York City and its great port for travel and transportation from the West in competition with the water course of the Erie Canal and the Hudson River. In 1863 he began to buy an interest in the Harlem Railroad, which had now been extended from a little one-mile affair in downtown New York to a railroad with inland connection to Albany; it is now the Harlem Division. By the winter of 1866–67 he had also gained control of the Hudson River Railroad, and in 1869 his system was completed, temporarily, with the incorporation under his control of the New York Central & Hudson River Railroad. It is evident why the New York Central had the leading place in the name; it is historically correct. In 1872 this company leased the Harlem Railroad, thus disposing of any possible rail competition to New York City.

One of the New England railroad systems also began in a multitude of short local lines. It has been said that 165 incorporations were merged into the ultimate Boston & Maine, and that building was actually done in the case of two thirds of them. The first or one of the first of these was the Boston & Lowell, twenty-six miles long, incorporated in 1829 for the benefit of the textile factories in the northeast part of Massachusetts, and in operation by 1833. What these railroads were in the everyday life of the public, of everybody, may be gleaned from the description written by a noted traveller of a trip on this Boston & Lowell Railroad. The traveller was Charles Dickens, and he made the trip to America, and to Lowell, in 1842.[3]

Before leaving Boston, I devoted one day to an excursion to Lowell. I made acquaintance with an American railroad, on this occasion, for the first time. As these works are pretty much alike

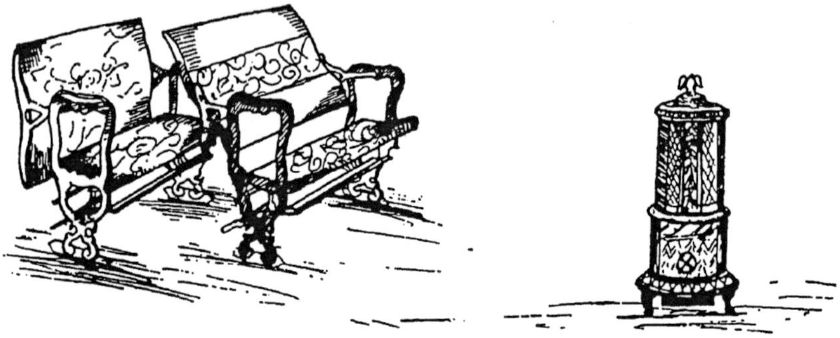

The comforts of travel in 1837

From "The Development of Transportation Systems in the United States," by J. L. Ringwalt, 1888. Courtesy of the New York Historical Society

all through the States, their general characteristics are easily described.

There are no first and second class carriages as with us (in England); but there is a gentlemen's car and a ladies' car: the main distinction between which is that in the first everybody smokes; and in the second nobody does. There is a great deal of jolting, a great deal of noise, a great deal of wall, not much window, a locomotive engine, a shriek, and a bell.

The cars are like shabby omnibuses, but larger: holding thirty, forty, fifty people. The seats are placed crosswise, a narrow passage up the middle, and a door at both ends. In the centre of the carriage there is usually a stove, fed with charcoal or anthracite coal; which is for the most part red-hot. It is insufferably close.

In the ladies' car there are a great many gentlemen who have

[3]See Charles Dickens: *American Notes,* Chapter IV, "An American Railroad." The text is freely abbreviated, passages being selected and combined.

ladies with them. There are also a great many ladies who have nobody with them: for any lady may travel alone from one end of the United States to the other and be certain of the most courteous and considerate treatment everywhere. If a lady take a fancy to any male passenger's seat, the gentleman who accom-

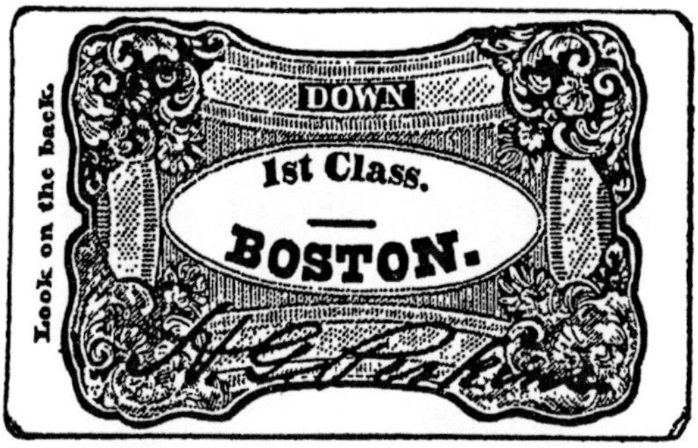

From "Scribner's Magazine," September, 1888

Boston & Worcester Railroad ticket of about 1837

panies her gives him notice of the fact, and he immediately vacates it with great politeness.

The conductor or check-taker or guard, or whatever he may be, wears no uniform. He walks up and down the car, and in and out of it, as his fancy dictates; leans against the door with his hands in his pockets and stares at you, if you chance to be a stranger; or enters into conversation with the passengers about him. A great many newspapers are pulled out, and a few of them are read. Everybody talks to you, or to anybody else who hits his fancy. Politics are much discussed, so are banks, so is cotton. Quiet people avoid the question of the Presidency, for there will be a new election in three years and a half, and party feeling runs very high: the great constitutional feature of this institution being that directly the acrimony of the last election is over the acrimony of the next one begins.

Except when a branch road joins the main one, there is seldom more than one track of rails; so that the road is very narrow. The character of the scenery is always the same. Mile after mile of stunted trees: some hewn down by the axe, some blown down by the wind, some half fallen and resting on their neighbors. Now you emerge for a few brief minutes on an open country, glittering with some bright lake or pool; now catch hasty glimpses of a distant town with its clean white houses and their cool piazzas, its prim New England church and schoolhouse; when whir-r-r-r! almost before you have seen them comes the same dark screen: the stunted trees, the stumps, the logs. It rushes across the turnpike road, where there is no gate, no policeman, no signal, nothing but a rough wooden arch, on which is painted WHEN THE BELL RINGS, LOOK OUT FOR THE LOCOMOTIVE. On it whirls headlong, dives through the woods again, emerges in the light, clatters over frail arches, rumbles upon the heavy ground, shoots beneath a wooden bridge which intercepts the light for a second like a wink, suddenly awakens all the slumbering echoes in the main street of a large town, and dashes on haphazard, pell-mell, neck-or-nothing, down the middle of the road.

I was met at the station at Lowell by a gentleman intimately connected with the management of the factories there. There are several factories in Lowell, each of which belongs to what we should term (in England) a Company of Proprietors, but what they call in America a Corporation. I went over several of these, such as a woollen factory, a carpet factory, and a cotton factory. . . . I returned at night by the same railroad and in the same kind of car. Glancing all the way out at window, I found abundance of entertainment watching the effects of the wood fire, which had been invisible in the morning but were now brought out in full relief by the darkness, for we were travelling in a whirlwind of bright sparks, which showered about us like a storm of fiery snow.

So it was that year by year, all over the country, the railroads came to be everyday things in American life. The same human principle of local development first, naturally, was no less working out new railroad systems in the Middle West, as in the East. For instance, the Chicago, Burlington & Quincy began in the 1840s and 1850s with a number of

Railroad poster of 1843

From an old timetable (furnished by the "A B C Pathfinder Railway Guide")

little railroads in Illinois and as by way of an extreme achievement just across the Mississippi. These small railroads threaded together a number of incipient communities that believed in getting together and that considered Chicago a good meeting place. The present name of the Burlington Railroad is simply made of the names of three of these small towns. It may emphatically be objected that Chicago is by no vagary of the imagination a small town. But in literal fact, in the 1840s Chicago was a small town. Chicago's imperial size and power is the free gift of the railroads and of their associated industries. The name of the Burlington Railroad is an historical epigram.

It may be convenient to call this the first half of the railroad development, but there is no end to this or to any such development, call it "half" or whatsoever. It is nonetheless evident that in this first "half" the railroads reached over and through the mountains to the great productive valley of the Mississippi Basin.

By the 1850s every one "in the East" was getting familiar with railroads; they were becoming quite everyday things. By the end of the 1850s this was true somewhat also in the region between the Alleghenies and the Mississippi River. But not west of the Mississippi, for in that region there was none. A transcontinental railroad was only an idea. The idea was spoken of, written of in the newspapers, urged before Congress. People heard about such a thing as a railroad to California, but only as an idea, and usually not as a very sensible idea at that. There were five routes proposed. In 1853 Jefferson Davis, Secretary of War under President Franklin Pierce, was authorized to have these five routes explored and surveyed. They were. Being a Southerner Davis naturally favored the southern route with some justification in view of the great accession of territory following the Mexican War (1846–1848) and the Gadsden Purchase

(1853–1854). But none was built before the Civil War. One, the Union Pacific Railroad, was built through within the period of this volume.

The story of the Union Pacific, built with unprecedented speed, westward from Council Bluffs, Iowa, by the Union Pacific Railroad Company, with Irish labor, and eastward from Sacramento, California, by the Central Pacific Railroad Company with Chinese labor, until they met with jubilant ceremony and the driving of the last spike, of California gold, at Promontory Point, Utah, just north of the Great Salt Lake, on May 10, 1869, was a dramatic story indeed but only a story. Not for years was that railroad to any appreciable number of the American people anything like an everyday experience. It was something heard about, like the herds of bison and the fighting with hostile Indians.

A single excerpt from a contemporary description, telling how the rails were laid, will show the appeal to the imagination of this great constructive work:

> On they came. A light car, drawn by a single horse, gallops up to the front with its load of rails. Two men seize the end of a rail and start forward, the rest of the gang taking hold by twos, until it is clear of the car. They come forward at a run. At the word of command the rail is dropped in its place, right side up with care, while the same process goes on at the other side of the car. Less than thirty seconds to a rail for each gang, so four rails go down to the minute. Quick work, you say, but the fellows on the Union Pacific are tremendously in earnest. The moment the car is empty it is tipped over on the side of the track to let the next loaded car pass it, and then it is tipped back again; and it is a sight to see it go flying back for another load, propelled by a

The Age of Speed

The title printed under these pictures in 1861 was: *Top:* Emigrating from Connecticut to Eastern Ohio in 1805, distance 600 miles, time 90 days, number of passengers 10. *Bottom:* Migrating in 1861 from Connecticut to Iowa, distance 1300 miles, time 3 days, number of passengers 360!

From "Eighty Years' Progress in the United States," by Eminent Literary Men, 1861 horse at full gallop at the end of 60 or 80 feet of rope, ridden by a young Jehu, who drives furiously. Close behind the first gang come the gaugers, spikers, and bolters, and a lively time they make of it. It is a grand anvil chorus that those sturdy sledges are playing across the plains; it is in triple time, three strokes to the spike. There are 10 spikes to a rail, 400 rails to a mile, 1800 miles to San Francisco—21,000,000 times are those sledges to be slung; 21,000,000 times are they to come down with their sharp punctuation![4]

The railroads to the Pacific Coast have since 1869 come into the everyday experience of practically all Americans; certainly they wait at their service, great legacies from the nineteenth century. But the appeal to the imagination is one of the greatest of all powers, if not the very greatest. Many great services, many great men can be appreciated only through the imagination. Among these is that towering figure, the greatest man of the nineteenth century.

During the 1850s Abraham Lincoln was best known in Illinois as a railroad attorney. Continually he acted as attorney for the Illinois Central and for the Chicago & Rock Island railroads. At second hand we have his own account of his first experience with the Illinois Central. The son of Robert Rantoul, Jr. (Robert S. Rantoul), says he first met Lincoln at the White House in 1863.

When he got my card from the officer in attendance, he repeated the name to himself several times and then said, "I wonder if you are connected with a lawyer of that name who came to

[4]From General Grenville M. Dodge: "How We Built the Union Pacific Railway," quoted in John W. Starr, Jr.: *One Hundred Years of American Railroading.*

Building the Union Pacific Railroad in Nebraska

From "Beyond the Mississippi," by Albert T. Richardson, 1867

Illinois about 1850 to secure from our legislature the charter of the Illinois Central Railroad?" I told him that was my father. Upon which he burst forth with a great roar of laughter and much gesticulation, and said that he did all he could to stop it, but was not successful. He said he was retained by local capitalists who, although they could not then build the road as they had already been intending, were very unwilling that eastern capitalists should step in and secure a grant which would make it forever impossible for them to build a road. But they were defeated. He favored me with some minutes of interesting conversation on this theme, and spoke with much amused good humor of the incident.

The facts are few and the connection slight that associate Lincoln with the putting through of the transcontinental railroads. But these few facts are sufficient to assure us that Lincoln's interest was sincere, intelligent and strong. In 1856 the Chicago & Rock Island Railroad Company sought him out to be their leading counsel in the important Rock Island Bridge Case, which settled the legal right of railroads to build a bridge across the Mississippi River and other navigated streams.[5]

In August, 1859, Lincoln went to Council Bluffs, Iowa, to make a speech. At the same time a young engineer named Grenville M. Dodge arrived and encamped with his party in a ravine north of the 1500 town. He had been making a survey for the promoters of a proposed Pacific Railroad. To

[5]One of the most charming and characteristic incidents told of Abraham Lincoln is how, when he was preparing for the trial of this Rock Island Bridge Case, he sat out on the stringers of the bridge and talked with a fifteen-year-old boy to learn about the currents of the river flowing beneath them. See John W. Starr, Jr.'s *Lincoln and the Railroads,* pages 95–96.

Lincoln this was an opportunity to get some first-hand information. So he hunted Dodge up.

> Mr. Lincoln sought me out and engaged me in conversation about what I knew of the country west of the Missouri River. He greatly impressed me by the marked interest he displayed in the work in which I was engaged, and he expressed himself as believing there was nothing more important before the nation at that time than the building of a railroad to the Pacific Coast. He ingeniously extracted a great deal of information from me about the country beyond the river, the climate, the character of the soil, the resources, the rivers, and the route. When the long conversation (two hours) was ended, I realized that most of the things I had been holding as secrets for my employers in the East, had been given to him without reserve.[6]

When the Republican National Convention at Chicago nominated Lincoln for President in May, 1860, the platform contained a plank reading:

> That a railroad to the Pacific Ocean is imperatively demanded by the interests of the whole country; that the Federal Government ought to render immediate and efficient aid in its construction; and that as preliminary thereto, a daily overland mail should be promptly established.

May it be that this plank was inserted at Lincoln's own suggestion? Certainly it had his sincere approval.

President Lincoln called an extra session of Congress in July, 1861, at which a bill was introduced for a railroad to be named the Union Pacific Railroad Company. This was entitled "An Act to aid in the construction of a railroad and telegraph line from the Missouri River to the Pacific Ocean,

[6] *Ibid.*, page 196.

and to secure to the government the use of the same for postal, military, and other purposes." It was signed by President Lincoln on July 1, 1862.

It is pertinent to notice that at this time President Lincoln signed also the Morrill Act, creating with Federal aid the Agricultural Colleges and Experiment Stations. This was probably the most discouraging time of the whole war. This man was the one who said:

> If I could save the Union by freeing all the slaves, I would do it; if I could save the Union without freeing any of the slaves, I would do it; if I could save the Union by freeing some of the slaves and not freeing some, I would do it.

The main purpose of these two bills, in Lincoln's mind, was to help save the Union. The name of the Union Pacific Railroad was most appropriate.

One of the questions specifically committed to the President for decision was the question of the width of the track-gauge. At the time when railroads were first being built in the East, by local independent companies, there was the utmost confusion in regard to gauge. In consequence the locomotives and cars of one company could not often run over the rails of the next company. During the past thirty years, by dint of experience, the gauge had been standardized for practically all the railroads east of the Mississippi. Naturally all those who were concerned in the operating or the using of these Eastern railroads wanted the gauge of the Union Pacific to be determined at the same width, 4 feet, 8½ inches. The officials of the Central Pacific Railroad, however, were insistent that their gauge (and that of the Union Pacific) should be 5 feet. It seems certain that Lincoln in his own opinion approved of the narrower, standard gauge. But he was also anxious not to repel and antagonize the Pacific Coast people who still were very far distant. He was most of all concerned to bind California and the Coast to the Union and its cause. He was not afraid to seem to wobble in his decision; neither was he afraid to reverse himself. At one time he signed a ruling that the gauge should be 5 feet. He was one of the most tactful men that ever lived, and one with the keenest sense of proportion in his judgments. What influence he quietly exerted—indeed if any—we do not know. On March 2, 1863, in regular course Congress passed a bill in favor of the standard gauge of 4 feet, 8½ inches, which the Senate had passed by a vote of 26 to 9; and on March 3 President Lincoln approved it.

In the spring of 1863 General Grenville M. Dodge was ordered by General Grant to report to President Lincoln at the White House. Unable to think of any reason for this order, Dodge supposed it must be that he was to be reprimanded for some "offense." The fact was that President Lincoln was considering the question of the starting point of the Union Pacific, another question the law had assigned to him for determination, and he remembered his talk with the young engineer on the hotel porch in Council Bluffs in 1859. So he sent for him. General Dodge summed up concisely the result of this second talk with Lincoln:

President Lincoln, after going over all the facts that could be presented to him, and from his own knowledge, finally fixed the eastern terminus of the Union Pacific Railroad where our surveys determined the proper locality—at Council Bluffs.

After this discussion of the location, he took up with me the question of building the road. The law of 1862 had failed to bring any capital or men to undertake the work, and I said to him that in my opinion private enterprise could not build the road.

Mr. Lincoln said that the Government had its hands full, and could not assume the task, but was ready to support any company to the fullest legal extent, and amend the law so as to enable such a company to issue securities that would furnish the necessary funds.

Leaving Washington, General Dodge went to New York and told the chief officials of the Union Pacific Company, among them John A. Dix, Henry Farnam, T. S. Durant, and George Francis Train, what the President had said. Taking courage, they prepared a new bill which was presented to Congress at the next session. President Lincoln signed this amendatory bill on July 2, 1864. In the platform of the Republican National Party for Lincoln's re-election one plank read:

That we are in favor of the speedy construction of the railroad to the Pacific Coast.

As late as December 6, 1864, Lincoln said of this great undertaking:

The great enterprise of connecting the Atlantic with the Pacific States by railways and telegraph lines has been entered upon with a vigor that gives assurance of success, notwithstanding the embarrassments arising from the prevailing high prices of material and labor. The route of the main line of the road has been definitely located for one hundred miles westward from the initial point at Omaha City, Nebraska, and a preliminary location of the Pacific Railroad of California has been made from Sacramento, eastward, to the great bend of Truckee River, in Nevada.

Who can doubt that Lincoln deliberately and on purpose used the Union Pacific, with consummate skill, to draw the people of the East and of the West closer together. The tall figure of this true representative of the people rises majestically over the building of the first transcontinental railroad, even though it was not finished until four years after he had passed from the scene of these responsibilities. It rises over all the transcontinental railroads, as it rises over everything in which everyday people are interested or are concerned. He said that God must love the common people, He made so many of them. May we not say as a self-evident truth that God must have loved the common people, because He made Abraham Lincoln to represent and to stimulate the best that was in them!

The Saratoga Special 1872

CHAPTER XVI

Celebrating a Hundred Years

THE American people of the 1870s recognized the great fact that their multifarious population had preserved a creative unity for a hundred years. In the memory of every one living the Constitution of the United States had always been the binding force of the nation, giving freedom and permanency of conditions to all. They rejoiced in this great fact, and the sentiment that surrounds the number 100 afforded a good excuse for celebrating. An important feature in the situation was that the opportunity to work was general and depended only upon each man finding a specific job or on his making one for himself. Accordingly the American people celebrated the Declaration of their Independence by an exhibition of what they could do in the way of work, and they invited all other peoples of the world to show what they could do in a splendid friendly competition. They celebrated their successful nationality with an Industrial Exhibition. The place naturally Philadelphia! The year—1776 plus 100—1876!

The idea of industrial exhibitions was not new. Such occasions had grown up through the life of the people. The first was possibly the Berkshire Cattle Show of Elkanah Watson's Berkshire Agricultural Society in western Massachusetts in 1810. It was the first of a numerous type. County agricultural fairs spread all over the country. The limitation was that it was practicable to include as exhibitors only those who could bring their live-stock to the fair on their feet. The first State fairs were held in 1841 at Syracuse, New York, and at New Brunswick, New Jersey. As these State fairs developed, the small farmer naturally could not so generally take part as an exhibitor. The distance from his own fields made it too expensive a proposition. But he attended, learned much from the big farmers, had a good time, he and his family, and was greatly stimulated in his individual efforts and in the spirit of cooperation and of the large point of view. From the standpoint of entertainment there was no question: the central feature was the horse races, whether the horse-trots or the running races. After these probably the contests in catching the greased pig were the most popular—at least for the spectators.

The first exposition that might be thought of as national in appeal was the Crystal Palace Exhibition at New York in 1853. Its official name was The Exhibition of the Industry of All Nations. It followed the example and borrowed the name of Prince Albert's Crystal Palace in London in 1851. It was a fruitful idea to borrow. Sir Joseph Paxton's extraordinary structure had taught the world what could be done in building with steel and glass, but the New York Crystal Palace was not a success. Sir Joseph sent over plans for the structure but they were too large for the ground available, which is now known as Bryant Park. Those who undertook to reduce the building plans to the necessary size were not experts in the new kind of construction. The roof leaked whenever it rained and ruined the exhibits. Nonetheless America got an idea from England's splendid example.

There were other exhibits. During the Civil War, the sanitary fairs—what nowadays we should say were for the Red Cross—accomplished much. In 1855 the United States was represented at the Paris International Exposition, and again in 1867 at the much larger and finer Paris International Exposition at which the exhibit of American machinery was distinctly notable. American appreciation of such international exhibitions had full opportunity to have results and a number of suggestions were made for some such celebration of the approaching national centenary.

Meantime industrial exhibitions on a regional scale were carried out, as at Buffalo in 1869 and at Louisville, Kentucky, in 1870, appealing to the interest of the valley at the old-time transportation meeting point, the Falls of the Ohio. In 1870, 1871, and 1872 Cincinnati had a series of expositions which was increasingly popular and had strikingly splendid civic and cultural results. The attendance reached 300,000 in only six weeks in 1870; 400,000 in 1871; and 540,000 in 1872. Alfred T. Goshorn (1833–1902), a business man of Cincinnati, was notably influential in the management of these exhibitions.

On March 3, 1871, Congress passed an act creating a United States Centennial Commission to have charge of holding "an International Exhibition of Arts, Manufactures and Products of the Soil and Mine in the City of Philadelphia in the year 1876." Also in 1871 the Franklin Institute of Philadelphia concentrated the general interest by a petition to the municipal authorities to grant the use of Fairmount Park for such a purpose. There were to be ninety-two members of the Commission created by Congress, to be appointed by the President on nomination of the Governors of the States and Territories. They were well chosen as representatives of the people in the various regions to insure a confident interest in the success of the Exhibition and of the celebration. Among them were the Union General, Joseph R. Hawley of Connecticut, the Confederate General, Robert Lowry of Mississippi, Richard C. McCormick of Arizona, George B. Loring of Massachusetts, Orestes Cleveland of New Jersey, Stephen B. Elkins then of New Mexico, Alfred T. Goshorn of Ohio, Asa Packer of Pennsylvania, and George H. Corliss of Rhode Island. When the Commission was organized General Joseph R. Hawley (1826–1905) was chosen President and Alfred T. Goshorn (1833–1902) Vice-President and Director-General. Mr. Goshorn's experience in his own State undoubtedly rendered him the best choice that could have been made for the active management.

On June 1, 1872, Congress passed an act providing for the financial conduct of the Exhibition by a Centennial Board of Finance. John Welsh (1805–1886) of Philadelphia was chosen to be President of this Board. Among the twenty-eight Directors were former Governor William Bigler and Samuel L. Felton of Pennsylvania, George Bain of Missouri, Abram S. Hewitt and William L. Strong of New York, John S. Barbour of Virginia, and William Sellers and

John Wanamaker of Philadelphia. A representative Women's Centennial Executive Committee with Mrs. E. D. Gillespie as President was also appointed to cooperate with the Centennial Commission and the Centennial Board of Finance. The control of the Exhibition was thus thoroughly representative of the people of the United States.

On July 3, 1875, President Ulysses S. Grant issued a proclamation formally announcing the Centennial Exhibition. In this he said:

> In the interests of peace, civilization, and domestic and international friendship and intercourse, I commend the Celebration and Exhibition to the people of the United States; and in behalf of this Government and people, I cordially commend them to all nations who may be pleased to take part therein.

In response to this proclamation and invitation 39 States and territories and 38 foreign nations were represented by exhibits. The dates of opening and closing were finally set for May 10 and November 10, 1876.

Under the direction of the Centennial Board of Finance there were erected in the 450 acres assigned to the Exhibition in Fairmount Park five buildings for the purposes of the main exhibition:—the Main Exhibition Building, the Art Gallery and Memorial Hall (to be permanent), Machinery Hall, Horticultural Hall (permanent), and the Agricultural Building. These altogether covered 236 acres. There were besides many buildings erected by States, foreign nations, and private exhibitors as well as by the United States Government for the exhibition of the work of its various departments. The admission charge was uniformly fifty cents.

The opening ceremonies were held in the space out of doors between the Main Building and the Art Gallery. There on May 10 an estimated 200,000 people gathered in

From "Harper's Weekly," June 17, 1876

Centennial restaurants—indoors and out

addition to the 4000 specially invited guests. These included the high officials of the United States Government, the United States Supreme Court, the Congress, and the Army and Navy. Loud cheers greeted the entrance of General William Tecumseh Sherman, General Winfield Scott Hancock, and General Philip H. Sheridan. The welcome was also specially cordial when Dom Pedro II, Emperor of Brazil, appeared.

Music inevitably had a large part in the ceremonies. One of the advantages of such occasions is that they necessarily bring out the best in an art. Music in America as known and loved by the people generally was in an elementary stage. Instrumentally it was strong in the brass and the percussion. The band was the generally known musical organization. There were, however, certainly, cultural minorities, as at Bethlehem, Pennsylvania, Boston, Philadelphia, New York, and Cincinnati, that appreciated and supported good music. Vocal music grew from songs of sentiment with piano accompaniment, or through church music, and progressed into the choral singing of cantatas and oratorios with organ or a limited orchestral accompaniment. Stephen Collins Foster (1826–1864) was the first American composer to sing the life of the American people and to be universally and lastingly accepted by them.

The Philadelphia Centennial Exhibition rendered noble service to American music and to American life by recognizing those who were striving to introduce the best music of Europe to American hearing and to do creative work in American composing. This recognition was particularly given to Theodore Thomas, John Knowles Paine, and Dudley Buck. Theodore Thomas (1835–1905) was the outstanding conductor of his time. To him was given the main direction of the music at the Exhibition, with an orchestra of 200 instruments and a chorus of 1000 voices. But popular appreciation could hardly be said to be eagerly waiting. Music as planned and promised would be one of the new features. Theodore Thomas's concerts in New York had failed to pay expenses so seriously that in 1869 he took his orchestra of 54 instruments on tour to recoup its deficits. These concerts on tour, which he continued for a number of years, did much to apprise the American people of the glorious beauty of good music.

John Knowles Paine (1839–1906) was born at Portland. His grandfather, John K. H. Paine, built the first organ in Maine. He began his study of music with Hermann Kotschmar, a noted organist and able musician in Portland. In 1872 President Charles W. Eliot made him Assistant Professor of Music at Harvard College, and in 1873, despite strong opposition, promoted him to be a full professor. It has been said of him that he produced and established a high standard in the teaching of music, and that he was the first in this country to teach music as an art rather than as a trade. Yet strangely enough, in that center of education and culture, Francis Parkman (1823–1893), who was a member of the College Corporation, was persistently hostile to the musical course and regularly attacked it with the adapted phrase, "Musica delenda est."

Dudley Buck (1839–1909) was born in Hartford. After earnest and thorough study both in America and in Europe, he attained the highest musical positions Boston had to give at that time: organist of St. Paul's Church, and organist of Music Hall. The great Walcker organ in Music Hall had been acquired through Dudley Buck's own fine services while he was in Germany.

The opening ceremonies began with the playing by the orchestra under Theodore Thomas of a special march entitled "The Washington March," followed by twelve national airs. The airs were those of the Argentine Republic, Austria, Belgium, Brazil, Denmark, France, Germany, Great Britain, Italy, the Netherlands, Norway, and Russia. Richard Wagner's Inauguration March, composed on invitation specially for the occasion, was then rendered for the first time anywhere. At its close Bishop Matthew Simpson (1811–1884) of the Methodist Church offered a prayer. Bishop Simpson was associated in the public mind with the memory of Abraham Lincoln, for he was a personal friend. The day after Lincoln's second inauguration he preached a sermon in the House of Representatives, and it was he who pronounced the eulogy at the grave at Springfield, Illinois. In the prayer at the opening ceremonies Bishop Simpson said:

> Grant that this association in effort may bind more closely together every part of our great Republic, so that our Union may be perpetual and indissoluble. Let its influence draw the nations of the earth into a happier unity. Hereafter, we pray Thee, may all disputed questions be settled by arbitration, and not by the sword, and may wars forever cease among the sons of men.

The Centennial Hymn, a chorus, of which the words were written by John Greenleaf Whittier (1807–1892), the gentle Quaker and stern abolitionist, and the music composed for organ and orchestra by John Knowles Paine, conducted by Theodore Thomas, appropriately followed the prayer. Two of the stanzas of Whittier's poem are:

Our fathers' God! from out whose hand
The centuries fall like grains of sand,
We meet today, united, free,
And loyal to our land and Thee,
To thank Thee for the era done,
And trust Thee for the opening one.

Be with us while the New World greets
The Old World thronging all its streets,
Unveiling all the triumphs won
By art or toil beneath the sun;
And unto common good ordain
This rivalship of hand and brain.

Mr. John Welsh, as president of the Centennial Board of Finance, then presented the buildings that had been erected under the direction of the board, and the other equipment, to the United States Centennial Commission, and General Joseph R. Hawley, as president of the Commission, accepted them.

A cantata, *The Centennial Meditation of Columbia,* was then performed under the baton of Theodore Thomas, by the chorus of 1000 with full orchestra and organ accompaniment. The words were written by Sidney Lanier of Georgia (1842–1881), Confederate soldier, poet and musician. The music was by Dudley Buck. The words of both the Whittier and the Lanier poems were technically adaptable for musical composition. In Lanier's poem, from the soul of Columbia come the words:

Now Praise to God's oft-granted grace,
Now Praise to Man's undaunted face,
Despite the land, despite the sea,
I was: I am: and I shall be!—
How long, Good Angel, O how long?
Sing me from Heaven a man's own song!

To which the Angel replies:

Long as thine Art shall love true love,
Long as thy Science truth shall know,
Long as thine Eagle harms no Dove,
Long as thy Law by law shall grow,
Long as thy God is God above,
Thy brother every man below,
So long, dear Land of all my love,
Thy name shall shine, thy fame shall glow!

General Hawley, as president of the Centennial Commission, forthwith presented the Exhibition to the President of the United States, Ulysses S. Grant. President Grant, rising amid vociferous applause, the Emperor of Brazil also rising and joining in the demonstration, responded in part:

My Countrymen: It has been thought appropriate, upon this Centennial occasion, to bring together in Philadelphia, for popular inspection, specimens of our attainments in the industrial and fine arts, and in literature, science and philosophy, as well as in the great business of agriculture and of commerce.

That we may the more thoroughly appreciate the excellencies and deficiencies of our achievements, and also give emphatic expression to our earnest desire to cultivate the friendship of our fellow-members of this great family of nations, the enlightened agricultural, commercial, and manufacturing peoples of the world have been invited to send hither corresponding specimens of their skill to exhibit on equal terms in friendly competition with our own. To this invitation they have generously responded; for so doing we tender them our hearty thanks.

While proud of what we have done, we regret that we have not done more. Our achievements have been great enough, however, to make it easy for our people to acknowledge superior merit wherever found.

I declare the International Exhibition now open.

Thus on this great occasion spoke the great soldier whose most characteristic words were "Let us have Peace!"

At 12 o'clock noon precisely, at a signal from General Hawley, the American flag was unfurled from the Main Building and the great chorus, under Theodore Thomas's direction, with orchestra and organ accompaniment, brought the ceremonies to a climax by singing the *Hallelujah Chorus.* From a hill in the exhibition grounds a salute of 100 guns was fired and chimes were rung from many parts of Fairmount Park. The President of the United States accompanied by the director-general, Alfred T. Goshorn passed through the Main Building, greeting the foreign commissioners, each in front of his nation's exhibit. Thence in procession to the Machinery Building. There President Grant, with the Emperor of Brazil at his side, started the great Corliss engine, which through 23 miles of shafting and more than 40 miles of belting ran all the machinery assembled in the building.

This engine was the product of the inventive and manufacturing genius of George H. Corliss (1817–1888) of Providence, Rhode Island. It was of the beam type, had two cylinders 40 inches in diameter and of 10 foot stroke. Its flywheel was 30 feet in diameter with a speed of 360 revolutions per minute. At that time it was the greatest achievement of American steam power, and to all who gazed at its ceaseless, almost silent operation during the 159 days of the Exhibition it represented the tremendous possibilities of America's future.

For us, sixty-five years and more afterward, to gain a true idea of the exhibits of this Centennial Exhibition we probably must avail ourselves of the illustrated volumes published at the time, forgetting all comfortable comparisons with our own subsequent achievements. President Grant correctly spoke of American philosophy as the culmination of what America had to exhibit. By philosophy he meant not whatever metaphysics might be prevalent among the abstract-minded of the time but the general attitude of the American people toward life—something much more practical. In the light of that understanding it is necessary to regard the industrial and fine arts there exhibited from the standpoint of the living conditions of that time. The exhibits of American painting and sculpture would probably nowadays be regarded with little or no favor as expressing our tastes, much less our ideals; many of them would be thought sentimental and crude. Yet the American exhibits compared favorably with the painting and sculpture exhibited by foreign nations. Taking the historical standpoint—that is, putting ourselves as far as we can in their places and seeing all as the interpretation of their lives and of their ideals, there will emerge a thrilling realization of the wide expanse and the great achievements of American civilization during that period. To this reward there may be added an honest recognition of the fact that seventy-five years hence our efforts may seem equally naïve and quaint, and that without the aspiration and toil of the nineteenth century our twentieth-century civilization could never have been. The generation that can instinctively appreciate an earlier generation's work and art is fortunate; it is receiving a legacy.

It may well be that the greatest thing accomplished by the Centennial Exhibition was that Americans from all over the country became acquainted with each other in the light of the best that they could do. Special individualities, even eccentricities, of people from different sections were brought rather to the friendly appreciation than to the critical prejudice of people from other sections; and also of people from other nations, from which so many of our own people had come during the past hundred years.

The Centennial Exhibition was closed by the President of the United States, on November 10, 1876, with appropriate ceremonies similar to those at the opening. It was a rainy day. By the time the hour for the exercises came the rain had become a downpour. Nonetheless, an enormous crowd had assembled at the expected location. It was of course necessary to move everything indoors. The Judges Hall was the place chosen. A special incident was the unfurling from the balcony of the hall of a century-old flag, "the flag of the *Bonhomme Richard,*" by Miss Sarah S. Stafford, an elderly lady of Trenton, New Jersey. This flag had been given by the Marine Committee of Congress to Lieutenant James Bayard Stafford as a token of appreciation for notable service.[1] Certainly the incident of the unfurling vividly marked the passing of time in the hundred years which had now been gloriously celebrated.

As President Grant declared the Exhibition closed, he signalled to the telegraph operator, who transmitted the numbers "7–6." This rang the gong beside the Corliss Engine in Machinery Hall, stopped the engine and all machinery, and electrically released the notice to the principal capitals of the world:

"The President has this moment closed the International Exhibition; 3.37 P.M."

The total number of admissions was 9,857,625. The total cash gate receipts amounted to $3,819,497. The International Centennial Exhibition had summed up and truly represented to the verily international people of the United States the America that had grown up and spread over much of the continent in the one hundred years since the Declaration of Independence in 1776.

[1]Stafford served as a regularly enlisted midshipman and as an acting lieutenant during the Revolutionary War under Captain John Barry, but not under John Paul Jones, though it may be that *as a volunteer* he was present for a time on the *Bonhomme Richard*. Jones specifically stated that the flag of the *Bonhomme Richard* went down with the ship, but possibly the flag in question was an extra flag and actually was on the *Bonhomme Richard* during the fight with the *Serapis*.

Bibliography

The following books of interest and value are suggested for further reading. Those marked with * are of special interest for their illustrations.

Dictionary of American Biography.

John Fiske, *The Critical Period of American History.**

Ralph H. Gabriel, Editor: *The Pageant of America.**

Seymour Dunbar, *History of Travel in America.**

M. W. Brewington, *Chesapeake Bay Log Canoes, Mariners Museum.**

Adelbert M. Jakeman, *Old Covered Bridges.**

Clara E. Wagemann, *Covered Bridges in New England.**

Rosalie Wells, *Covered Bridges in America.**

Thomas B. Searight, *The Old Pike, A History of the National Road.**

Noble E. Whitford, *The Canal System and Its Influences.* (History of the State of New York, Volume V, Chapter IX.)

George W. Ward, *The Early Development of the Chesapeake and Ohio Canal Project.* (Johns Hopkins University Studies.)

Newcomen Society Addresses. (Princeton University Press.)

William O. Hotchkiss, *Early Days of the Erie Canal.*

H. C. Stanford, *The Historic Potomac.*

Charles Penrose, *1838 April Fourth 1938, The Sirius and the Great Western.*

Laird Bell, *The Midwest Lumber Cycle.*

George H. Payne, *History of Journalism in the United States.*

Willard G. Bleyer, *Main Currents in the History of American Journalism.**

Royal Cortissoz, *The New York Tribune.*

Frank Luther Mott, *A History of American Magazines.**

Fiske Kimball, *American Architecture.**

Fiske Kimball, *Domestic Architecture of the American Colonies and of the Early Republic.**

Howard Major, *The Domestic Architecture of the Early American Republic; The Greek Revival.**

Marie Kimball, *The Martha Washington Cook Book.*

BIBLIOGRAPHY

Baynard Rush Hall, *The New Purchase,* James Albert Woodburn, Editor.

Constance Rourke, *Audubon.**

Donald C. Peattie, *Singing in the Wilderness.**

Nancy McClelland, *Historic Wall Papers.**

Agnes Brooks Young, *Recurring Cycles of Fashion.**

T. A. Rickard, *History of American Mining.**

E. J. Hartman, *Josiah White.* (Thesis at Lehigh University.)

Newcomen Society Addresses. (Princeton University Press.)

Leonard Peckitt, *Iron in Industry.*

Quincy Bent, *75 Years of Steel.*

Milton C. Stuart, *Asa Packer.*

Howard N. Eavenson, *The Pittsburgh Coal Bed.*

Paul H. de Kruif, *Seven Iron Men.**

Jared Van Wagenen, Jr., *The Golden Age of Homespun.* (N. Y. S. Agric. Bulletin 203.)*

Victor S. Clark, *History of Manufacturing in the United States.*

Arthur H. Cole, *The American Wool Manufacture.*

Percy H. Bidwell, *History of Agriculture in the Northern United States.*

Logan Esarey, *History of Indiana,* Volume I, Chapter XVI, "Systematic Internal Improvements."

H. W. Dickinson, *A Short History of the Steam Engine.**

Wilbur F. Decker, *The Story of the Engine.**

John Moody, *The Railroad Builders.* (*Chronicles of America.*)

John W. Starr, Jr., *One Hundred Years of American Railroading.**

H. W. Dickinson, *Robert Fulton.**

John W. Starr, Jr., *Lincoln and the Railroads.*

Edward Hungerford, *Men and Iron, The History of New York Central.**

Richard C. Overton, *Burlington West, A Colonization History of the Burlington Railroad.**

Frank Leslie's *Illustrated Historical Register of the Centennial Exposition, 1876.**

James D. McCabe, *The Illustrated History of the Centennial Exhibition, 1876.**

Index

Index

INDEX

INDEX

INDEX

INDEX

INDEX

CPSIA information can be obtained at www.ICGtesting.com
Printed in the USA
BVOW03s1213180114

342316BV00001B/39/A

9 781406 704228